DELILAH S. **DAWSON** • MATIAS **BASLA** • REBECCA **NALTY**

SPARROWHAWK™

BOOM! STUDIOS

BOOM!
S T U D I O S

SPARROWHAWK, February 2020. Published by BOOM! Studios, a division of Boom Entertainment, Inc. Sparrowhawk is ™ & © 2020 Delilah Dawson. ™ & © 2018, 2019 Delilah Dawson. All rights reserved. BOOM! Studios™ and the BOOM! Studios logo are trademarks of Boom Entertainment, Inc., registered in various countries and categories. All characters, events, and institutions depicted herein are fictional. Any similarity between any of the names, characters, persons, events, and/or institutions in this publication to actual names, characters, and persons, whether living or dead, events, and/or institutions is unintended and purely coincidental. BOOM! Studios does not read or accept unsolicited submissions of ideas, stories, or artwork.

BOOM! Studios, 5670 Wilshire Boulevard, Suite 400, Los Angeles, CA, 90036-5679. Printed in China. Second Printing.

ISBN: 978-1-68415-395-4, eISBN: 978-1-64144-378-4

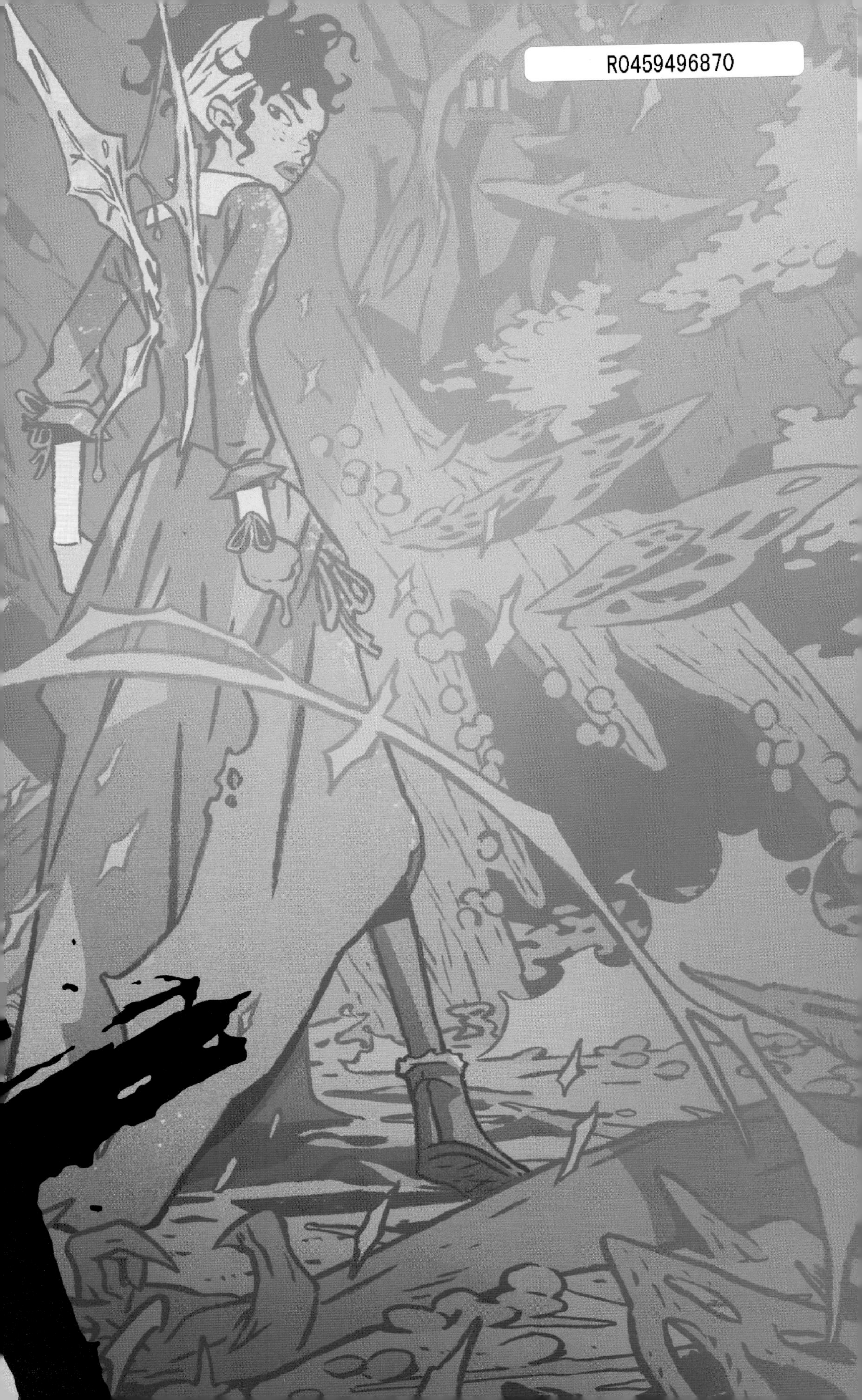

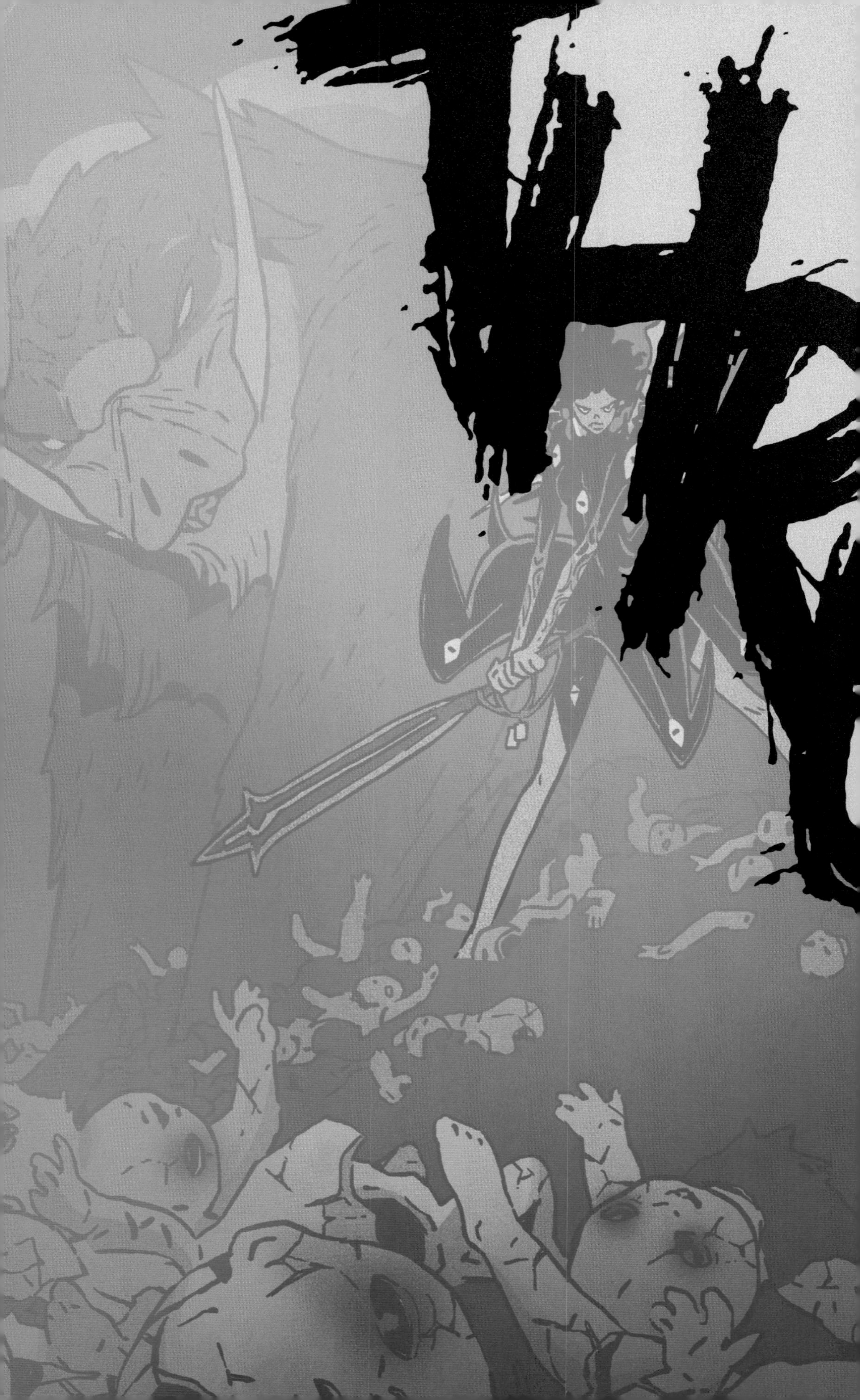

SPARROWHAWK ™

WRITTEN & CREATED BY
DELILAH S. DAWSON

ILLUSTRATED BY
MATIAS BASLA

COLORED BY
REBECCA NALTY
(CHAPTERS 2-5)

LETTERED BY
JIM CAMPBELL

COVER BY
MIGUEL MERCADO

SERIES DESIGNER
MICHELLE ANKLEY

COLLECTION DESIGNER
SCOTT NEWMAN

EDITOR
CHRIS ROSA

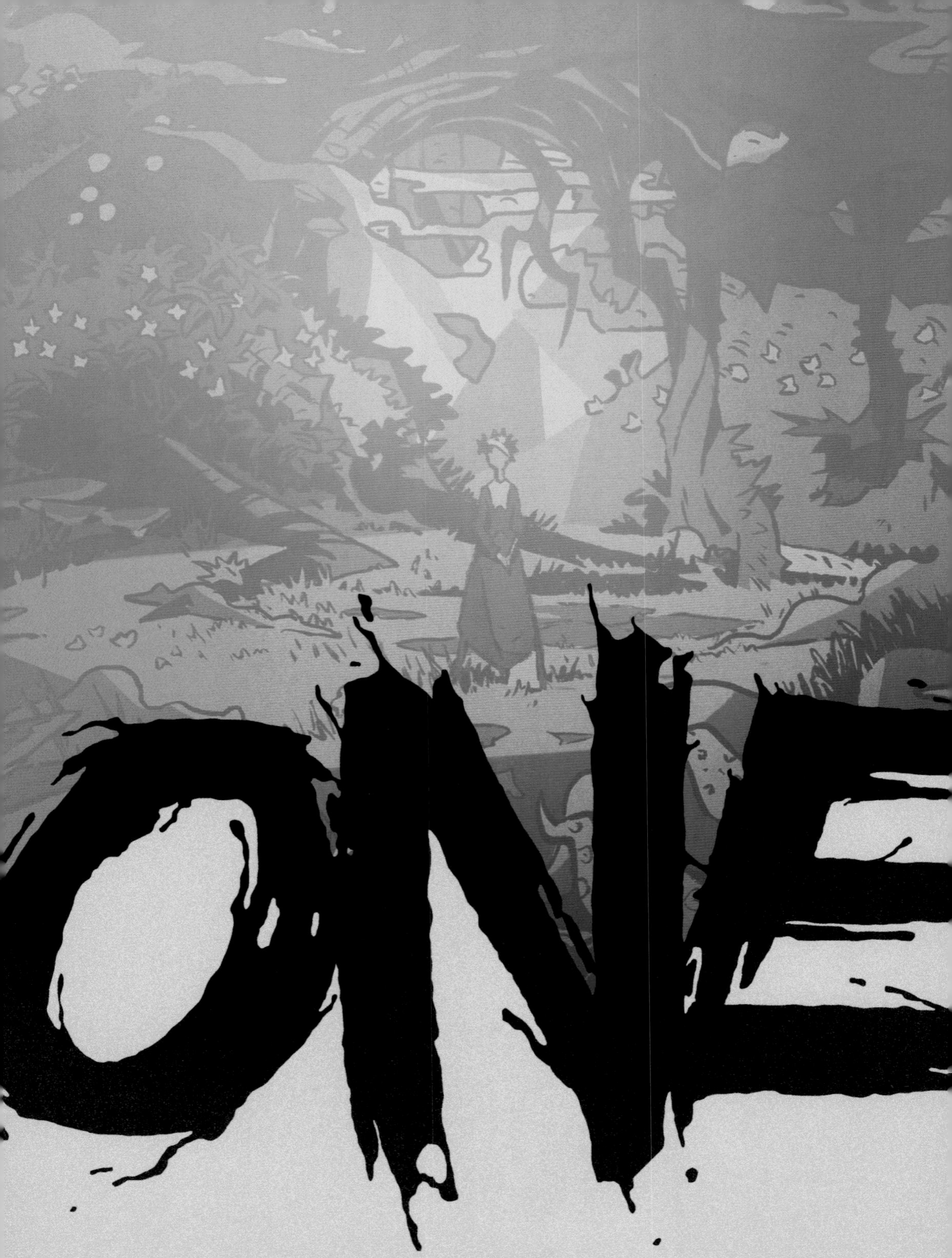

ONE

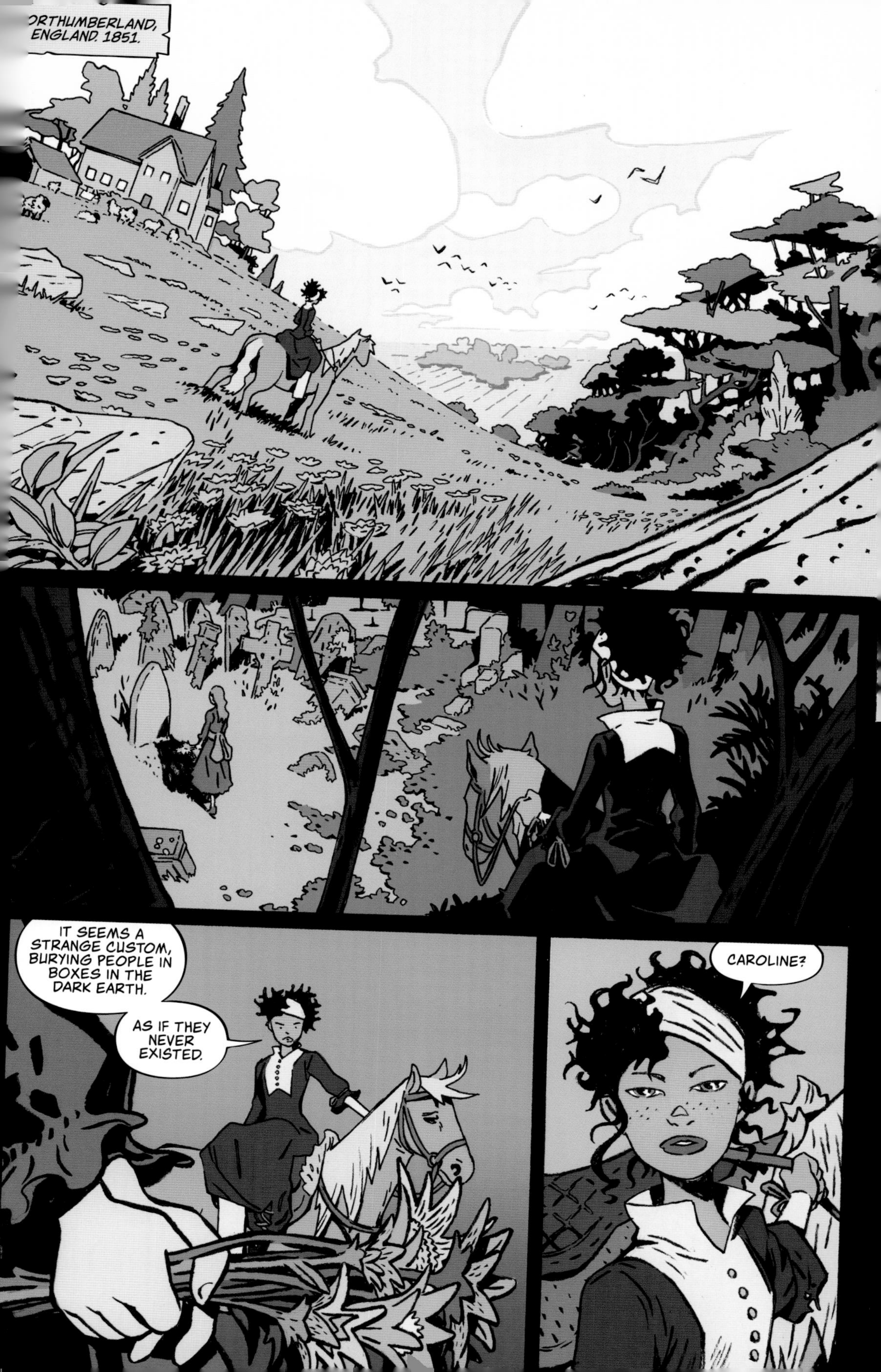
NORTHUMBERLAND, ENGLAND. 1851.
IT SEEMS A STRANGE CUSTOM, BURYING PEOPLE IN BOXES IN THE DARK EARTH.
AS IF THEY NEVER EXISTED.
CAROLINE?

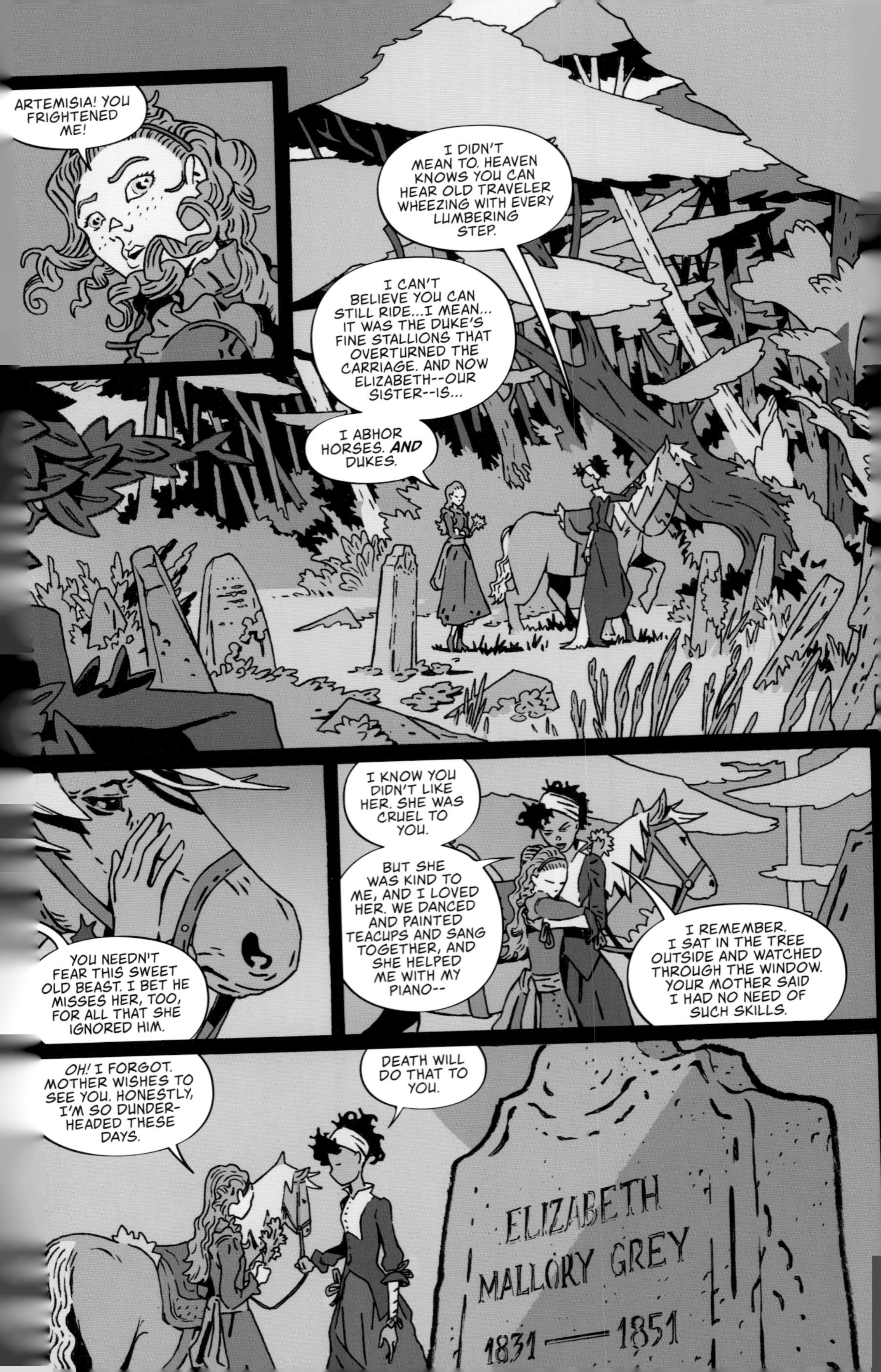
ARTEMISIA! YOU FRIGHTENED ME!
I DIDN'T MEAN TO. HEAVEN KNOWS YOU CAN HEAR OLD TRAVELER WHEEZING WITH EVERY LUMBERING STEP.
I CAN'T BELIEVE YOU CAN STILL RIDE...I MEAN... IT WAS THE DUKE'S FINE STALLIONS THAT OVERTURNED THE CARRIAGE. AND NOW ELIZABETH--OUR SISTER--IS...
I ABHOR HORSES. AND DUKES.
YOU NEEDN'T FEAR THIS SWEET OLD BEAST. I BET HE MISSES HER, TOO, FOR ALL THAT SHE IGNORED HIM.
I KNOW YOU DIDN'T LIKE HER. SHE WAS CRUEL TO YOU.
BUT SHE WAS KIND TO ME, AND I LOVED HER. WE DANCED AND PAINTED TEACUPS AND SANG TOGETHER, AND SHE HELPED ME WITH MY PIANO--
I REMEMBER. I SAT IN THE TREE OUTSIDE AND WATCHED THROUGH THE WINDOW. YOUR MOTHER SAID I HAD NO NEED OF SUCH SKILLS.
OH! I FORGOT. MOTHER WISHES TO SEE YOU. HONESTLY, I'M SO DUNDER-HEADED THESE DAYS.
DEATH WILL DO THAT TO YOU.
ELIZABETH MALLORY GREY
1831 —— 1851

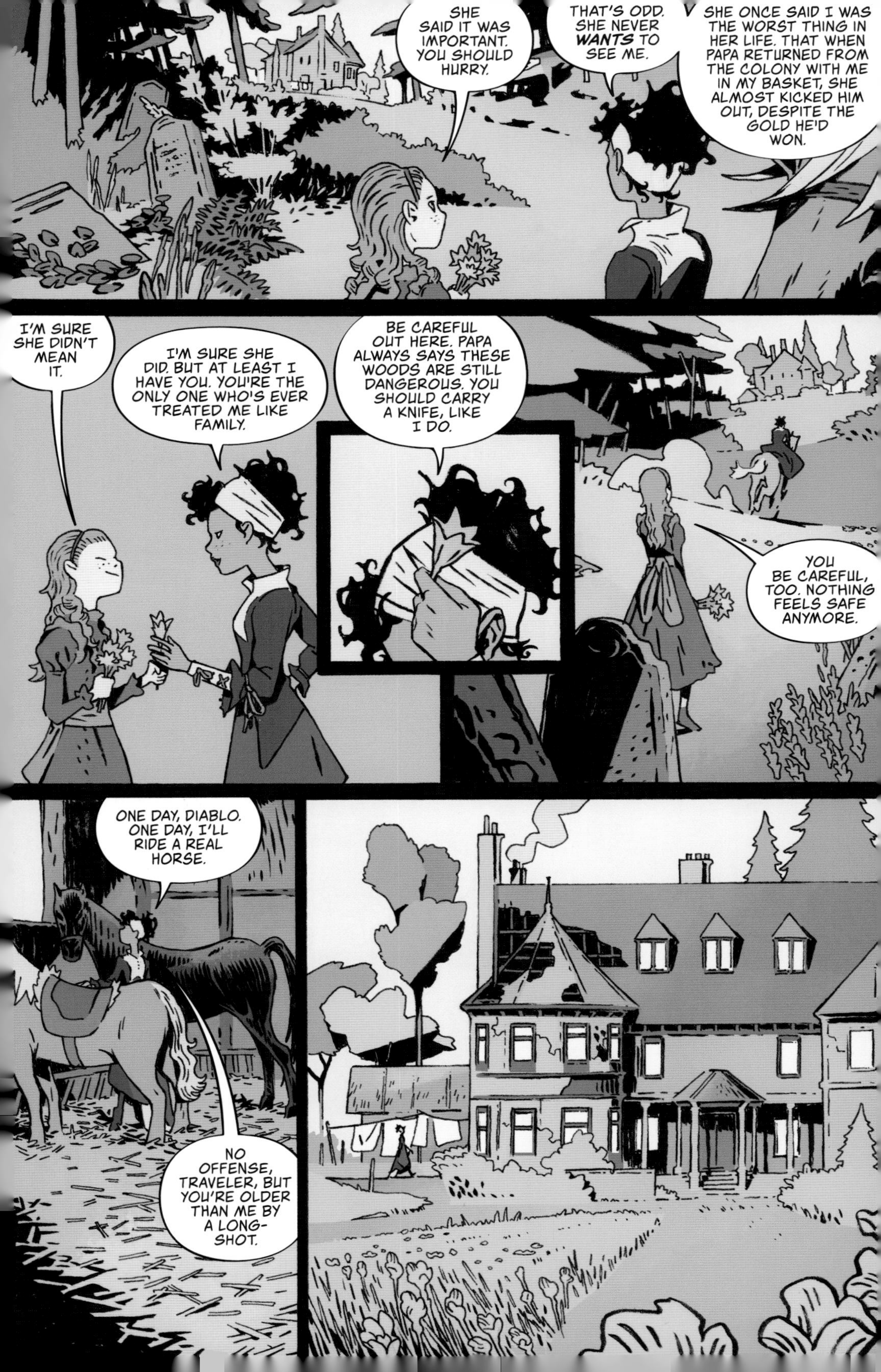
SHE SAID IT WAS IMPORTANT. YOU SHOULD HURRY.
THAT'S ODD. SHE NEVER WANTS TO SEE ME.
SHE ONCE SAID I WAS THE WORST THING IN HER LIFE. THAT WHEN PAPA RETURNED FROM THE COLONY WITH ME IN MY BASKET, SHE ALMOST KICKED HIM OUT, DESPITE THE GOLD HE'D WON.
I'M SURE SHE DIDN'T MEAN IT.
I'M SURE SHE DID. BUT AT LEAST I HAVE YOU. YOU'RE THE ONLY ONE WHO'S EVER TREATED ME LIKE FAMILY.
BE CAREFUL OUT HERE. PAPA ALWAYS SAYS THESE WOODS ARE STILL DANGEROUS. YOU SHOULD CARRY A KNIFE, LIKE I DO.
YOU BE CAREFUL, TOO. NOTHING FEELS SAFE ANYMORE.
ONE DAY, DIABLO. ONE DAY, I'LL RIDE A REAL HORSE.
NO OFFENSE, TRAVELER, BUT YOU'RE OLDER THAN ME BY A LONG-SHOT.

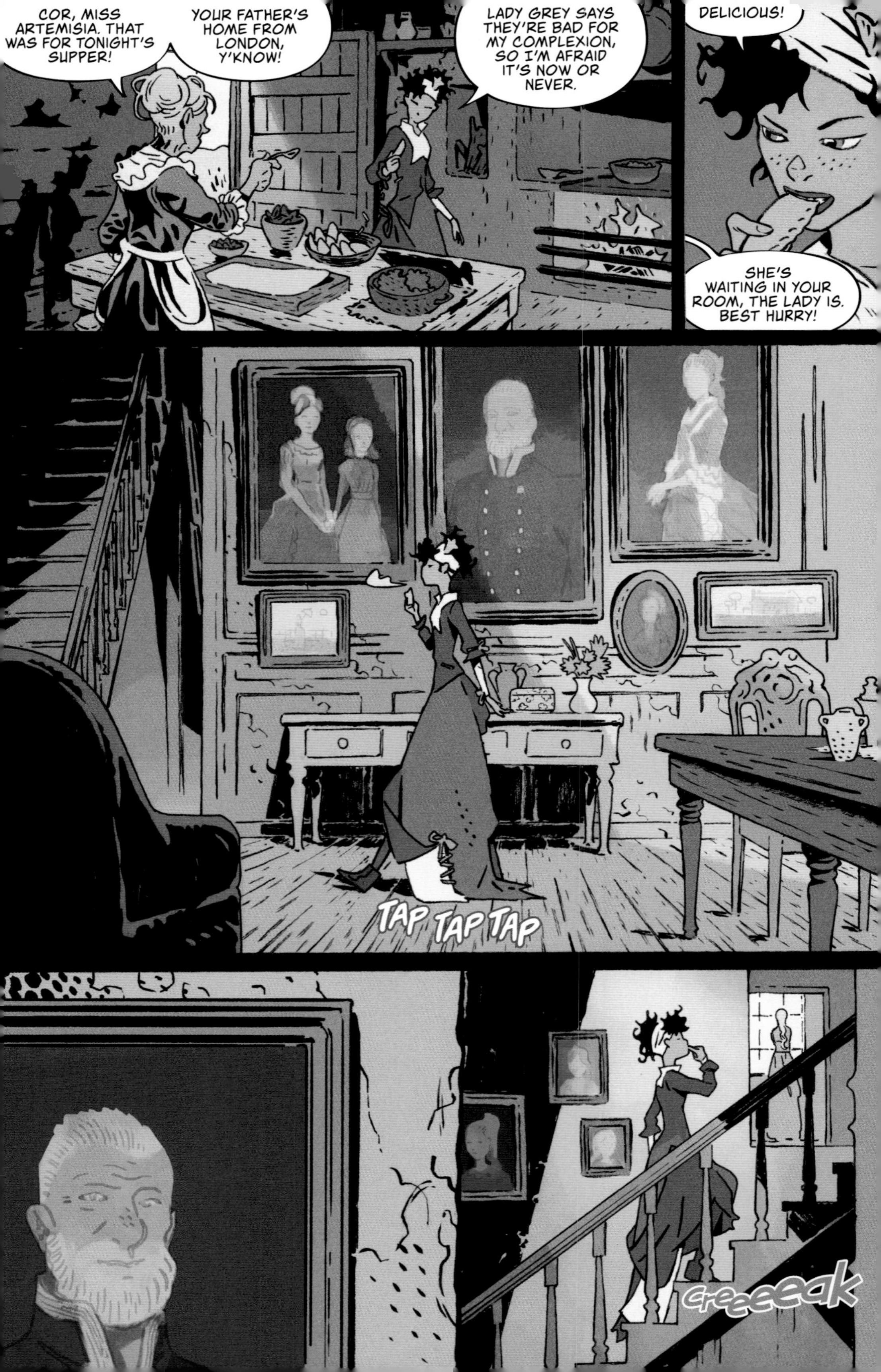
COR, MISS ARTEMISIA. THAT WAS FOR TONIGHT'S SUPPER!
YOUR FATHER'S HOME FROM LONDON, Y'KNOW!
LADY GREY SAYS THEY'RE BAD FOR MY COMPLEXION, SO I'M AFRAID IT'S NOW OR NEVER.
DELICIOUS!
SHE'S WAITING IN YOUR ROOM, THE LADY IS. BEST HURRY!
TAP TAP TAP
creeeeeak

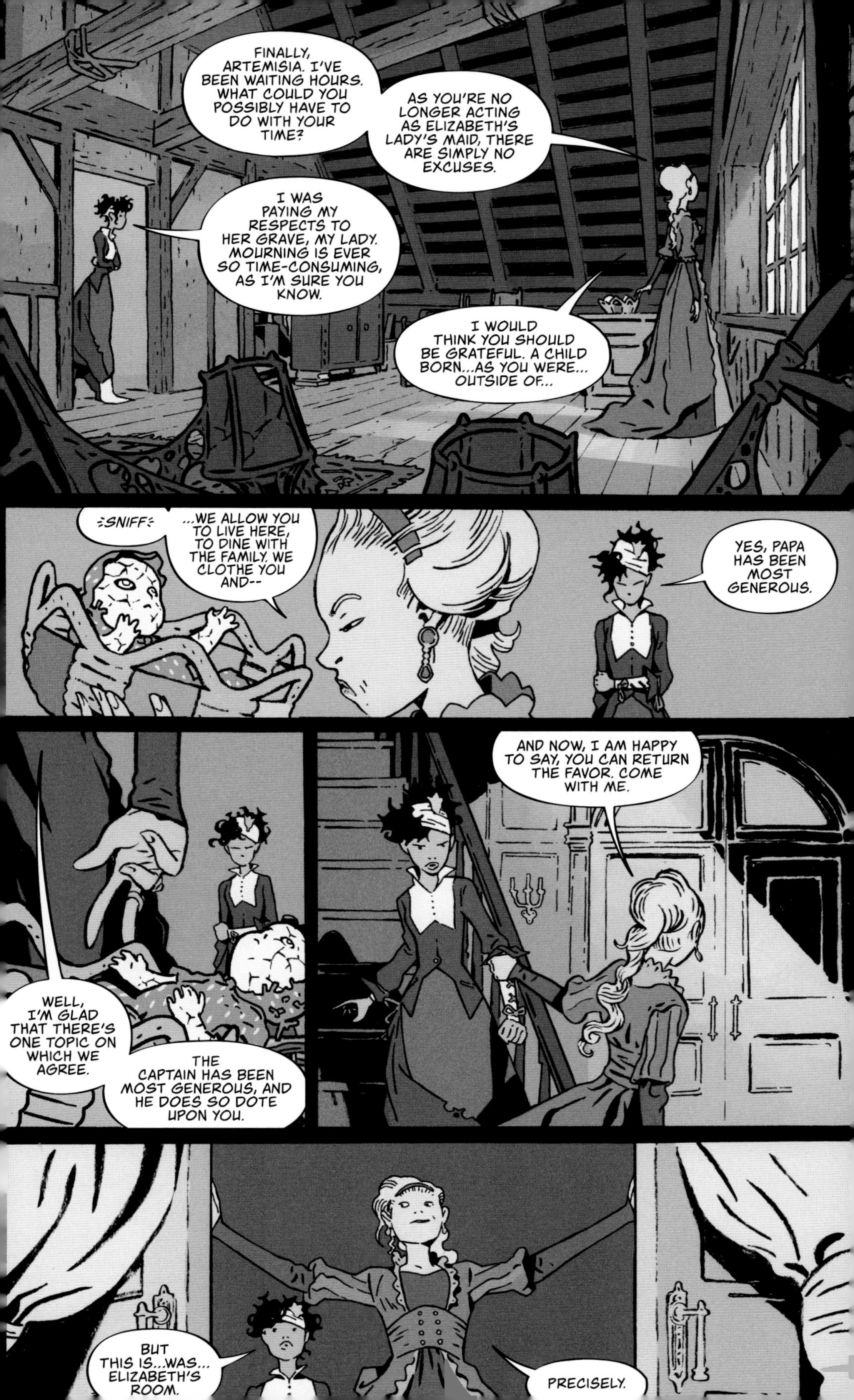
FINALLY, ARTEMISIA. I'VE BEEN WAITING HOURS. WHAT COULD YOU POSSIBLY HAVE TO DO WITH YOUR TIME?
AS YOU'RE NO LONGER ACTING AS ELIZABETH'S LADY'S MAID, THERE ARE SIMPLY NO EXCUSES.
I WAS PAYING MY RESPECTS TO HER GRAVE, MY LADY. MOURNING IS EVER SO TIME-CONSUMING, AS I'M SURE YOU KNOW.
I WOULD THINK YOU SHOULD BE GRATEFUL. A CHILD BORN...AS YOU WERE... OUTSIDE OF...
SNIFF
...WE ALLOW YOU TO LIVE HERE, TO DINE WITH THE FAMILY. WE CLOTHE YOU AND--
YES, PAPA HAS BEEN MOST GENEROUS.
WELL, I'M GLAD THAT THERE'S ONE TOPIC ON WHICH WE AGREE.
THE CAPTAIN HAS BEEN MOST GENEROUS, AND HE DOES SO DOTE UPON YOU.
AND NOW, I AM HAPPY TO SAY, YOU CAN RETURN THE FAVOR. COME WITH ME.
BUT THIS IS...WAS... ELIZABETH'S ROOM.
PRECISELY.

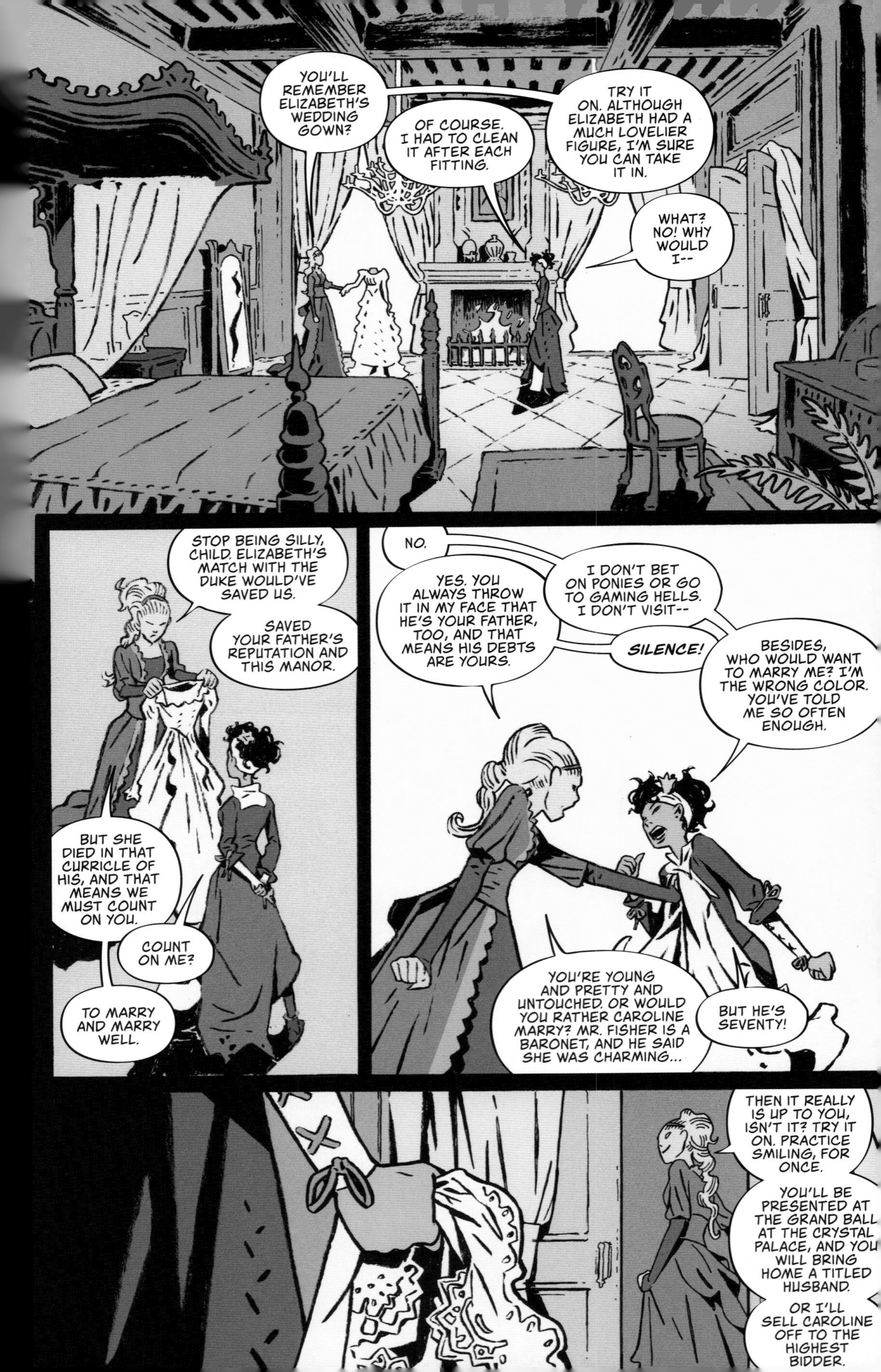

YOU'LL REMEMBER ELIZABETH'S WEDDING GOWN?
OF COURSE. I HAD TO CLEAN IT AFTER EACH FITTING.
TRY IT ON. ALTHOUGH ELIZABETH HAD A MUCH LOVELIER FIGURE, I'M SURE YOU CAN TAKE IT IN.
WHAT? NO! WHY WOULD I--
STOP BEING SILLY, CHILD. ELIZABETH'S MATCH WITH THE DUKE WOULD'VE SAVED US.
SAVED YOUR FATHER'S REPUTATION AND THIS MANOR.
BUT SHE DIED IN THAT CURRICLE OF HIS, AND THAT MEANS WE MUST COUNT ON YOU.
COUNT ON ME?
TO MARRY AND MARRY WELL.
NO.
YES. YOU ALWAYS THROW IT IN MY FACE THAT HE'S YOUR FATHER, TOO, AND THAT MEANS HIS DEBTS ARE YOURS.
I DON'T BET ON PONIES OR GO TO GAMING HELLS. I DON'T VISIT--
SILENCE!
BESIDES, WHO WOULD WANT TO MARRY ME? I'M THE WRONG COLOR. YOU'VE TOLD ME SO OFTEN ENOUGH.
YOU'RE YOUNG AND PRETTY AND UNTOUCHED. OR WOULD YOU RATHER CAROLINE MARRY? MR. FISHER IS A BARONET, AND HE SAID SHE WAS CHARMING...
BUT HE'S SEVENTY!
THEN IT REALLY IS UP TO YOU, ISN'T IT? TRY IT ON. PRACTICE SMILING, FOR ONCE.
YOU'LL BE PRESENTED AT THE GRAND BALL AT THE CRYSTAL PALACE, AND YOU WILL BRING HOME A TITLED HUSBAND.
OR I'LL SELL CAROLINE OFF TO THE HIGHEST BIDDER.

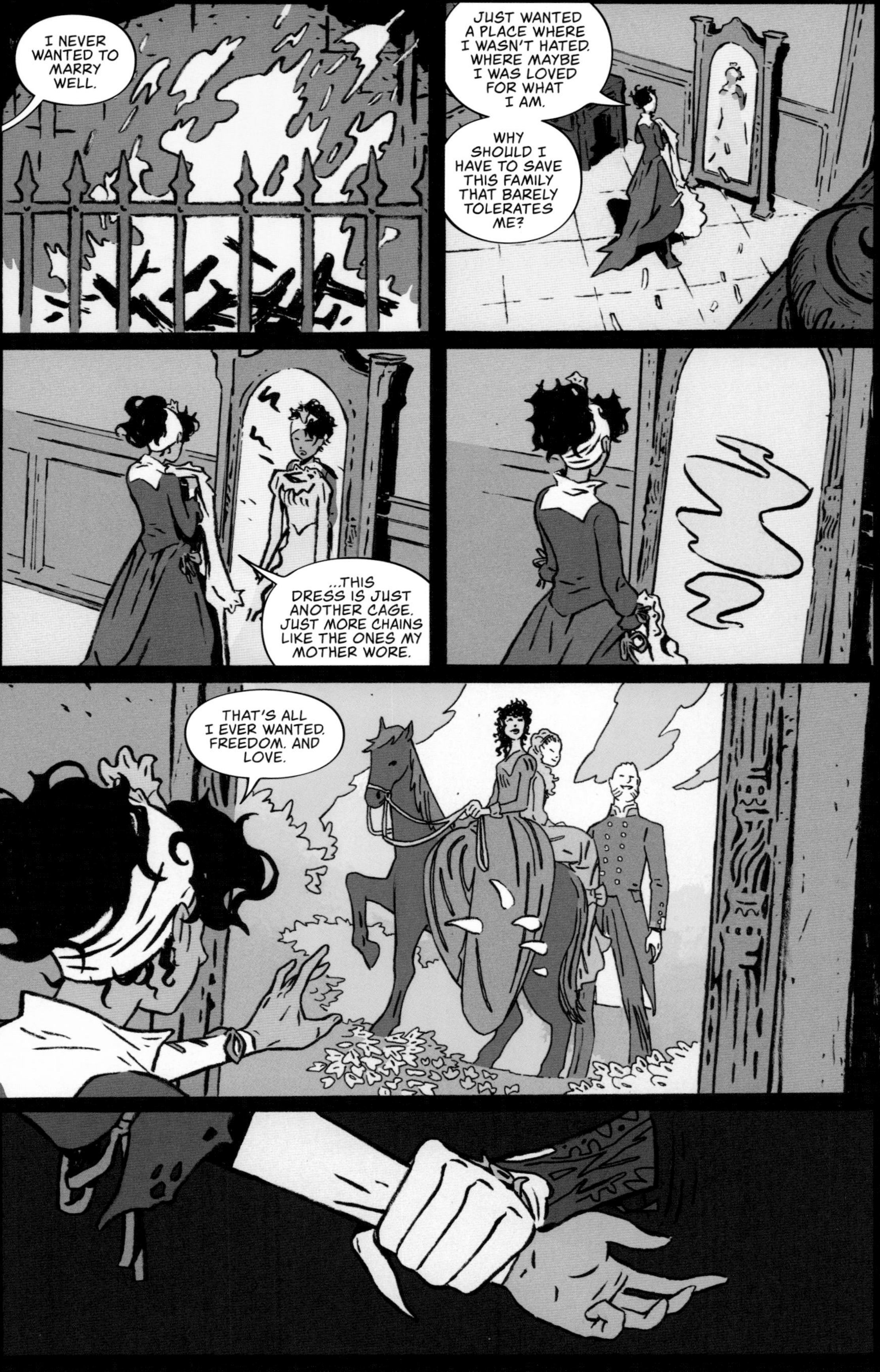
I NEVER WANTED TO MARRY WELL.
JUST WANTED A PLACE WHERE I WASN'T HATED. WHERE MAYBE I WAS LOVED FOR WHAT I AM.
WHY SHOULD I HAVE TO SAVE THIS FAMILY THAT BARELY TOLERATES ME?
...THIS DRESS IS JUST ANOTHER CAGE. JUST MORE CHAINS LIKE THE ONES MY MOTHER WORE.
THAT'S ALL I EVER WANTED. FREEDOM. AND LOVE.

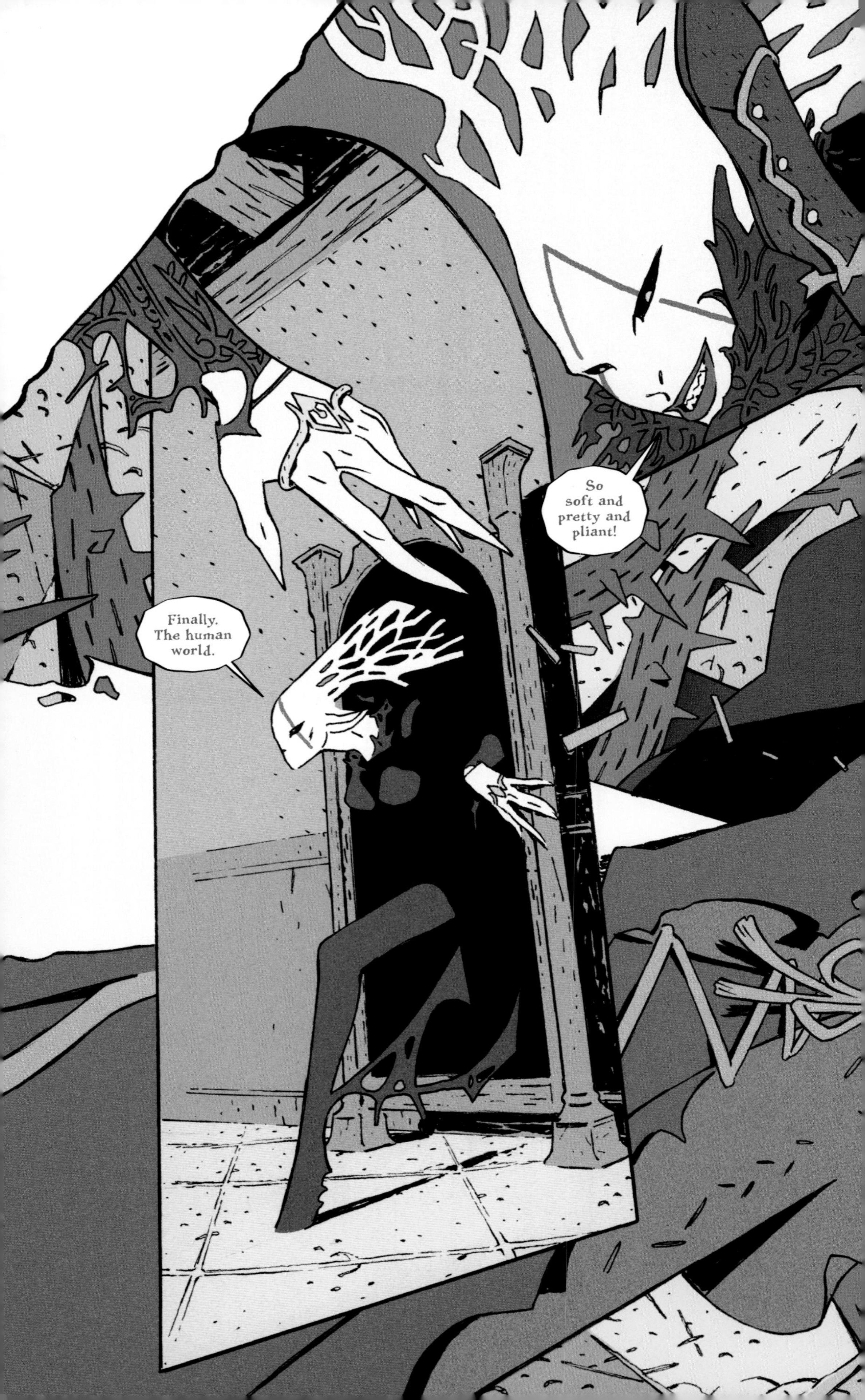
Finally. The human world.
So soft and pretty and pliant!

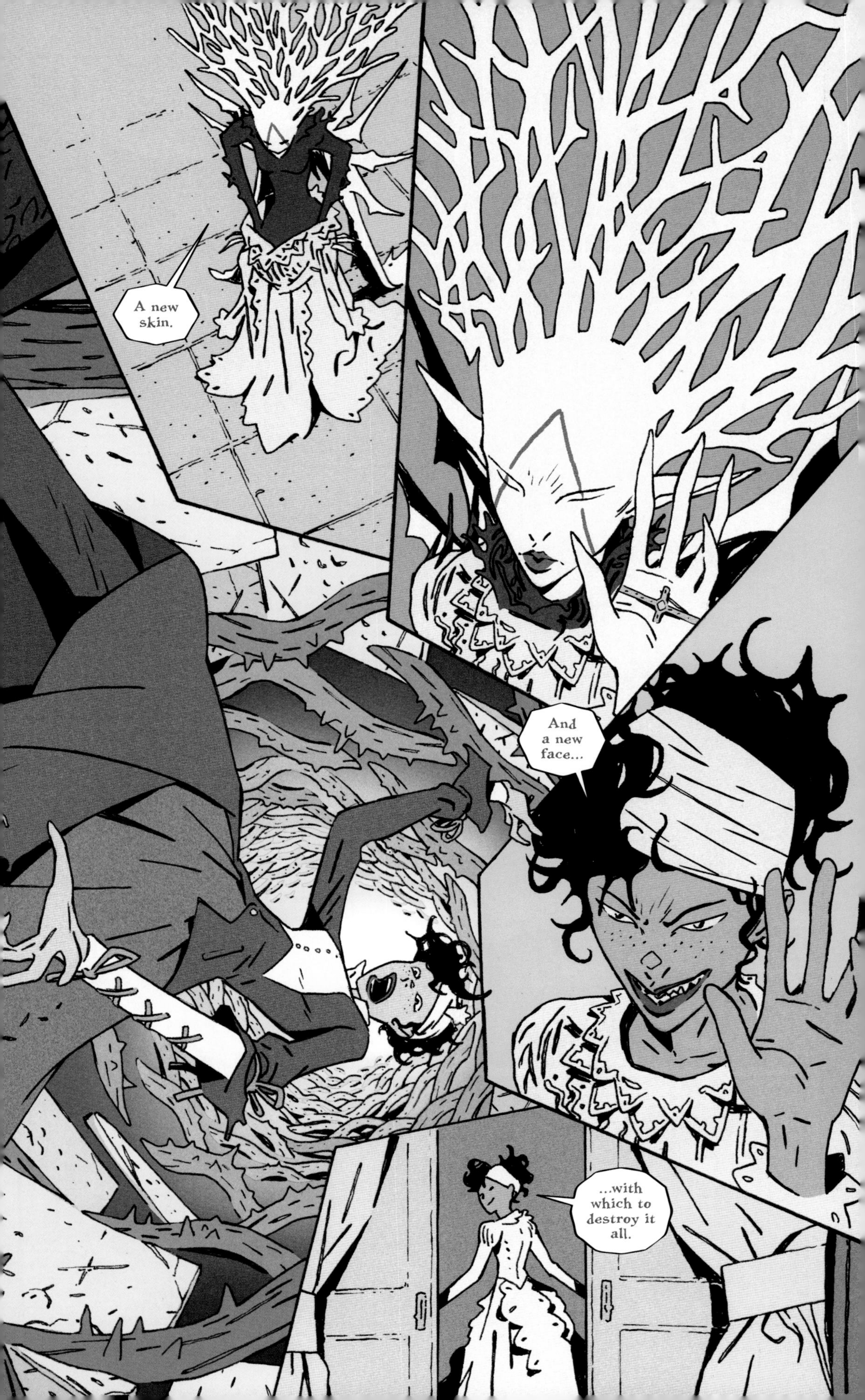
A new skin.
And a new face...
...with which to destroy it all.

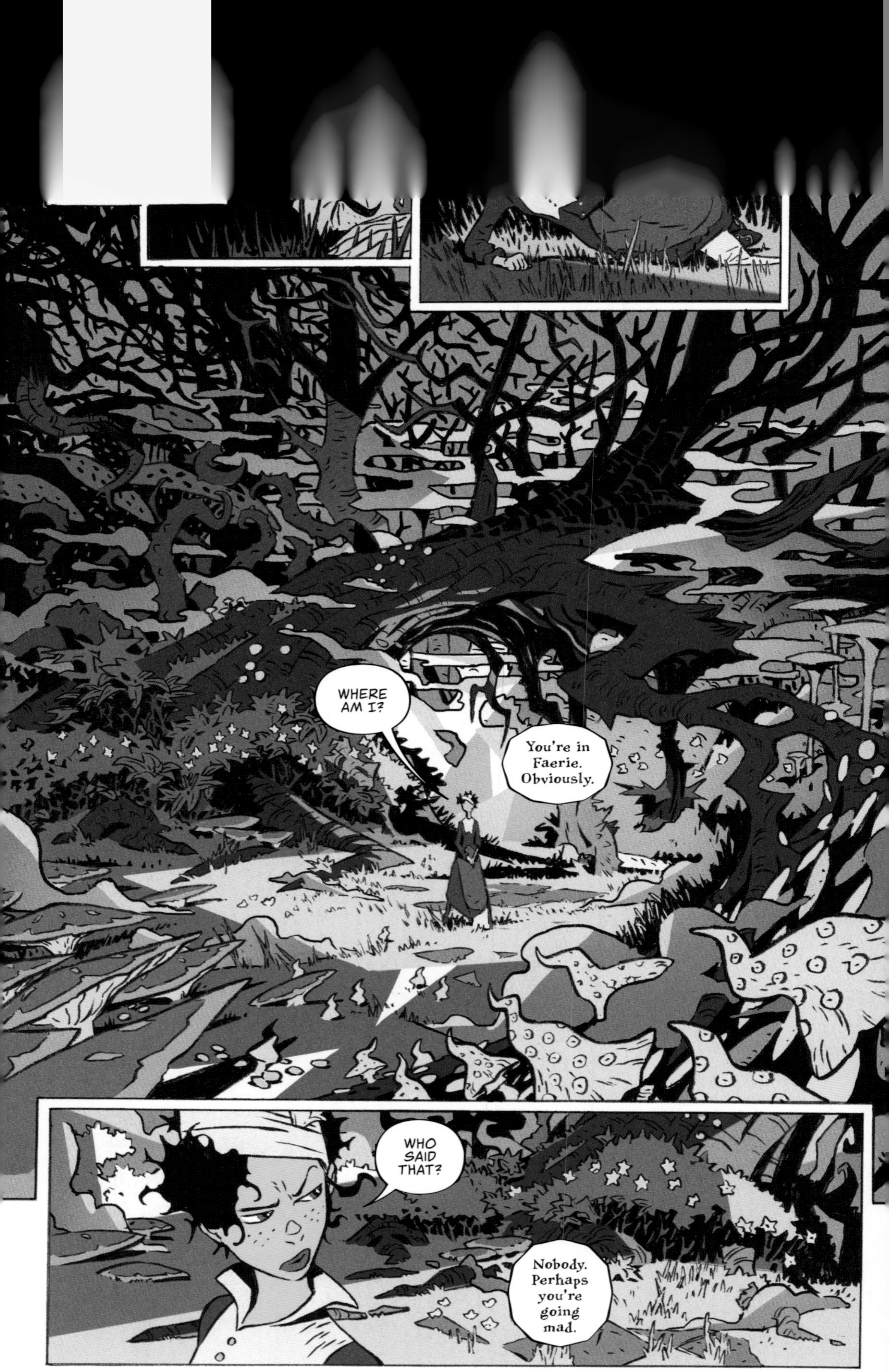
WHERE AM I?
You're in Faerie. Obviously.
WHO SAID THAT?
Nobody. Perhaps you're going mad.

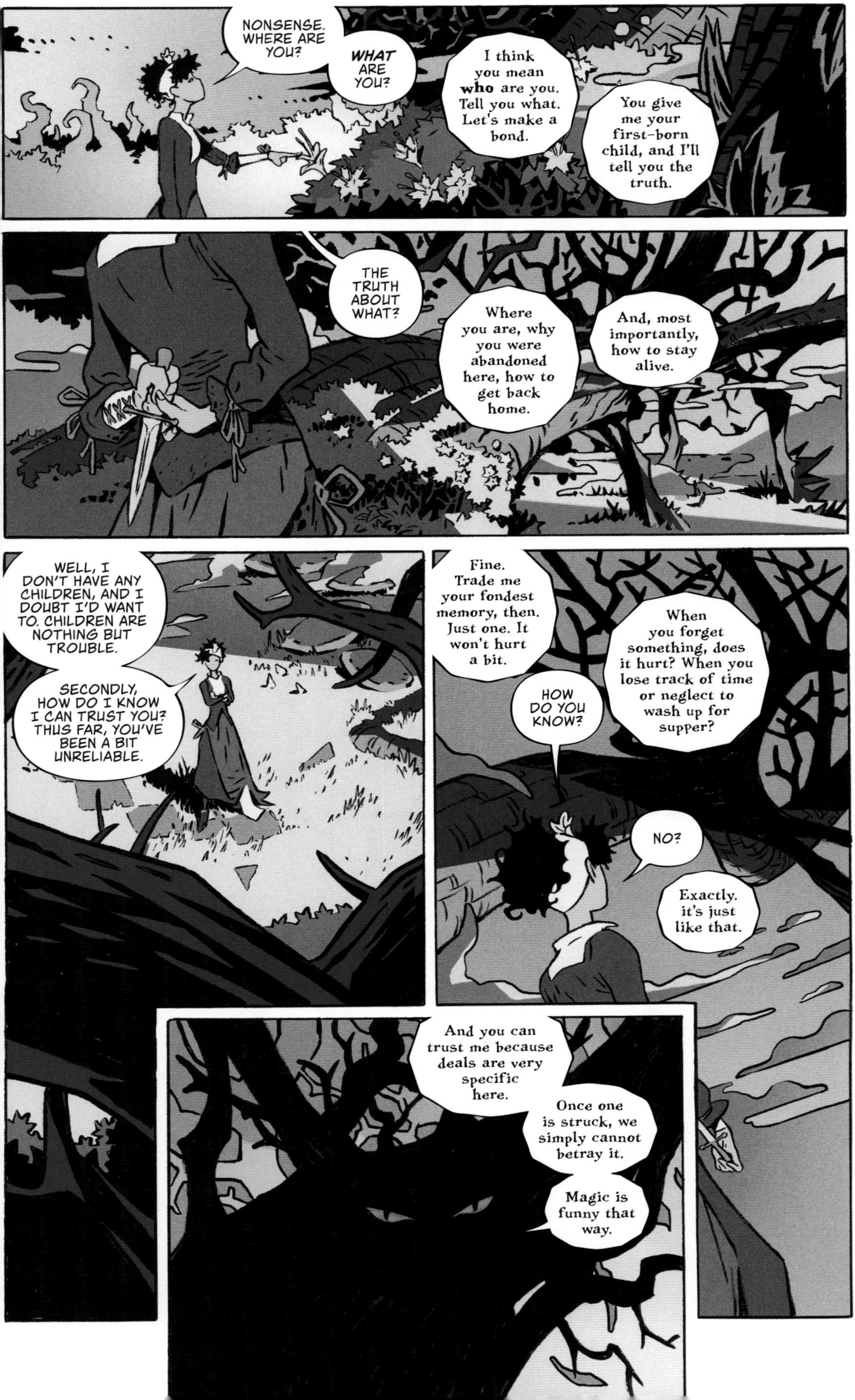
NONSENSE. WHERE ARE YOU?
WHAT ARE YOU?
I think you mean who are you. Tell you what. Let's make a bond.
You give me your first-born child, and I'll tell you the truth.
THE TRUTH ABOUT WHAT?
Where you are, why you were abandoned here, how to get back home.
And, most importantly, how to stay alive.
WELL, I DON'T HAVE ANY CHILDREN, AND I DOUBT I'D WANT TO. CHILDREN ARE NOTHING BUT TROUBLE.
SECONDLY, HOW DO I KNOW I CAN TRUST YOU? THUS FAR, YOU'VE BEEN A BIT UNRELIABLE.
Fine. Trade me your fondest memory, then. Just one. It won't hurt a bit.
HOW DO YOU KNOW?
When you forget something, does it hurt? When you lose track of time or neglect to wash up for supper?
NO?
Exactly. it's just like that.
And you can trust me because deals are very specific here.
Once one is struck, we simply cannot betray it.
Magic is funny that way.

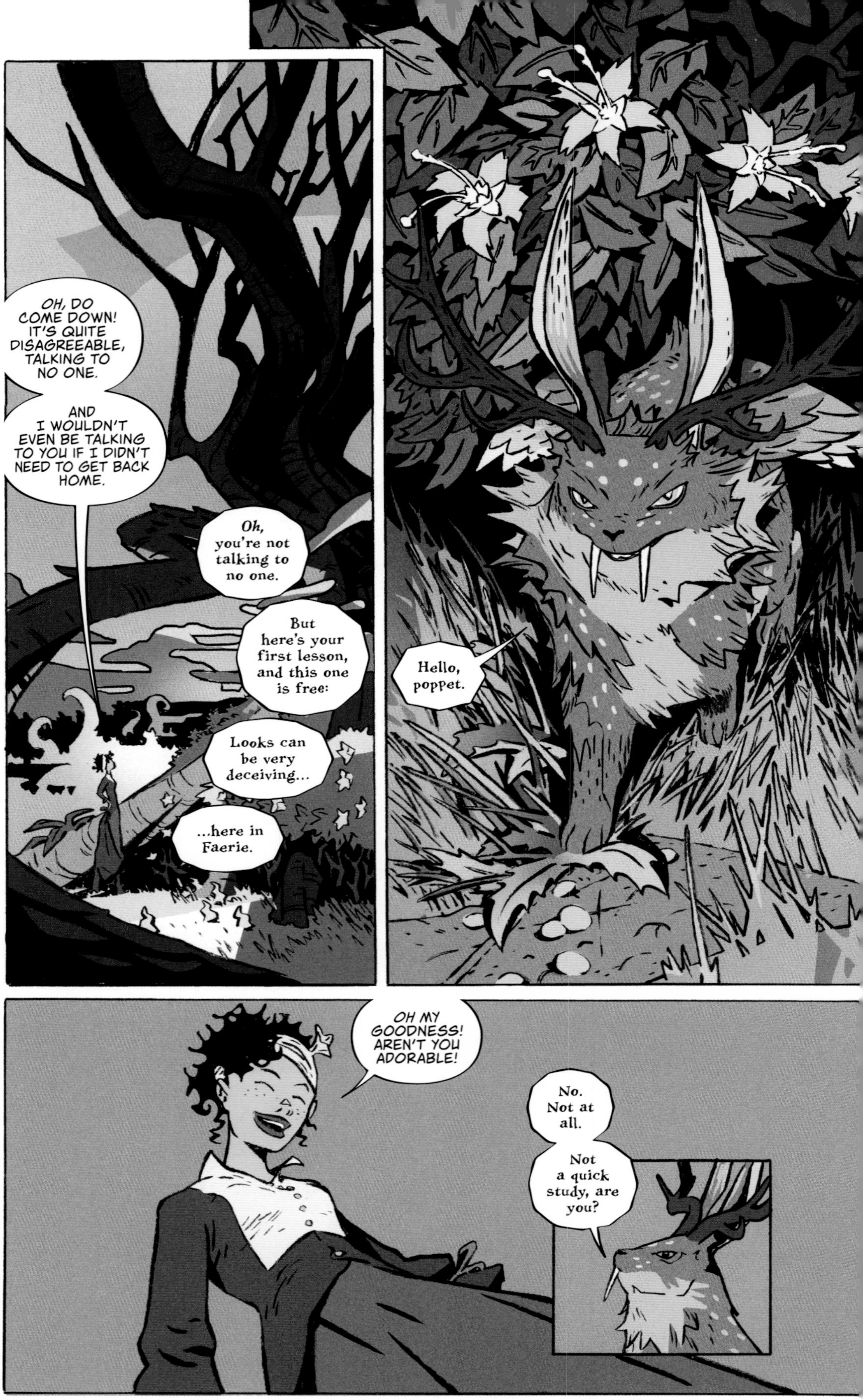
OH, DO COME DOWN! IT'S QUITE DISAGREEABLE, TALKING TO NO ONE.
AND I WOULDN'T EVEN BE TALKING TO YOU IF I DIDN'T NEED TO GET BACK HOME.
Oh, you're not talking to no one.
But here's your first lesson, and this one is free:
Looks can be very deceiving...
...here in Faerie.
Hello, poppet.
OH MY GOODNESS! AREN'T YOU ADORABLE!
No. Not at all.
Not a quick study, are you?

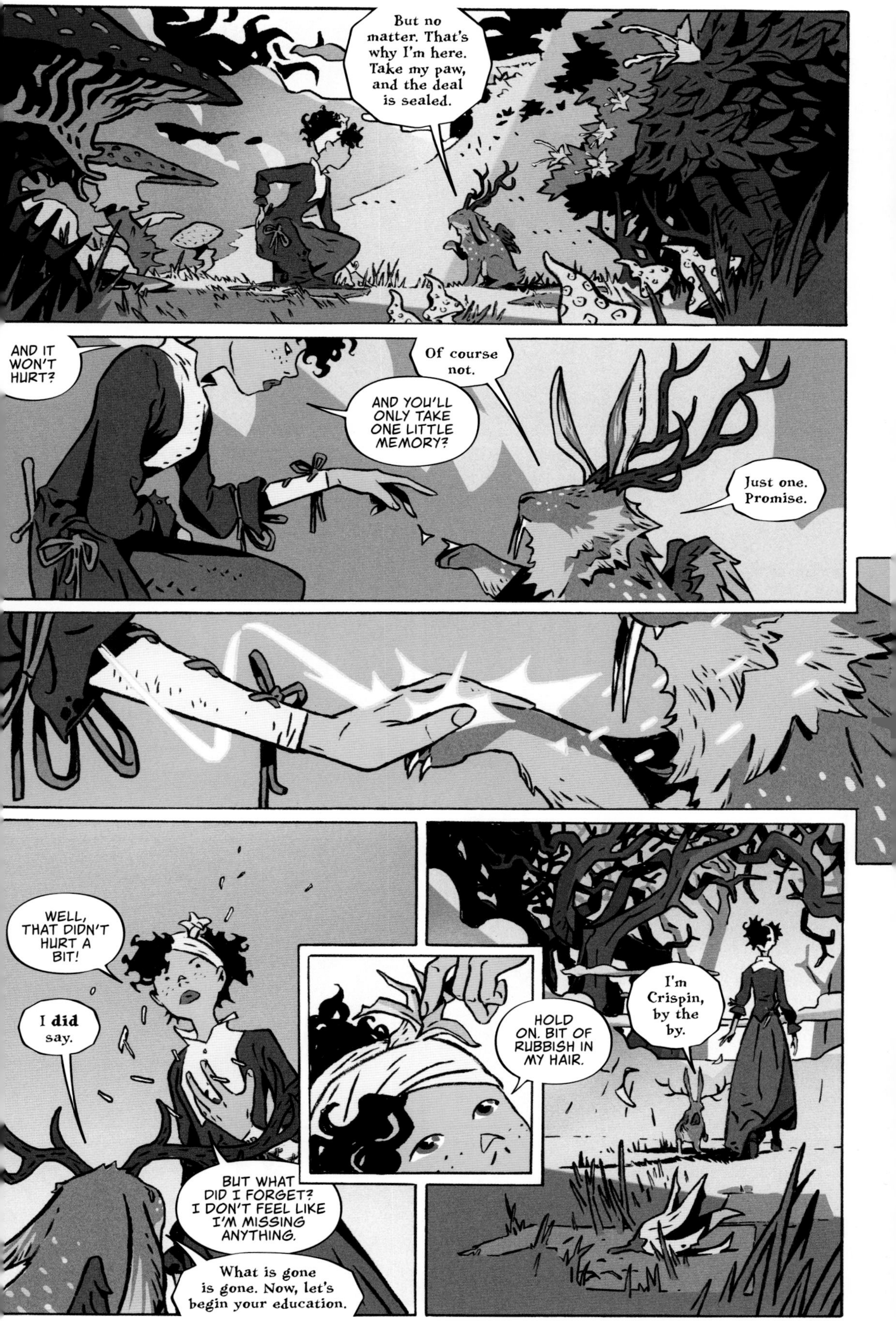
But no matter. That's why I'm here. Take my paw, and the deal is sealed.
AND IT WON'T HURT?
Of course not.
AND YOU'LL ONLY TAKE ONE LITTLE MEMORY?
Just one. Promise.
WELL, THAT DIDN'T HURT A BIT!
I **did** say.
BUT WHAT DID I FORGET? I DON'T FEEL LIKE I'M MISSING ANYTHING.
What is gone is gone. Now, let's begin your education.
HOLD ON. BIT OF RUBBISH IN MY HAIR.
I'm Crispin, by the by.

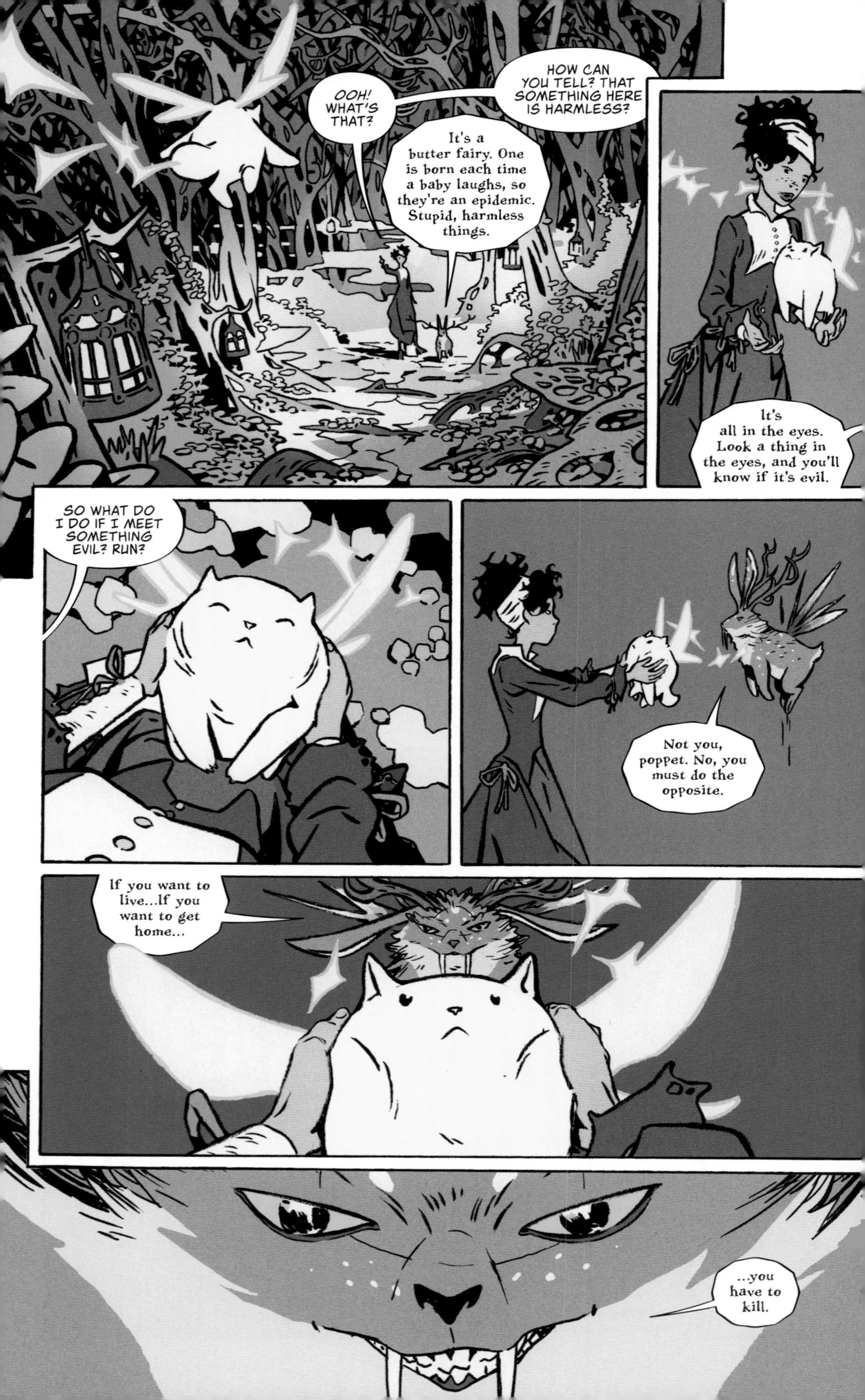
OOH! WHAT'S THAT?
HOW CAN YOU TELL? THAT SOMETHING HERE IS HARMLESS?
It's a butter fairy. One is born each time a baby laughs, so they're an epidemic. Stupid, harmless things.
It's all in the eyes. Look a thing in the eyes, and you'll know if it's evil.
SO WHAT DO I DO IF I MEET SOMETHING EVIL? RUN?
Not you, poppet. No, you must do the opposite.
If you want to live...If you want to get home...
...you have to kill.

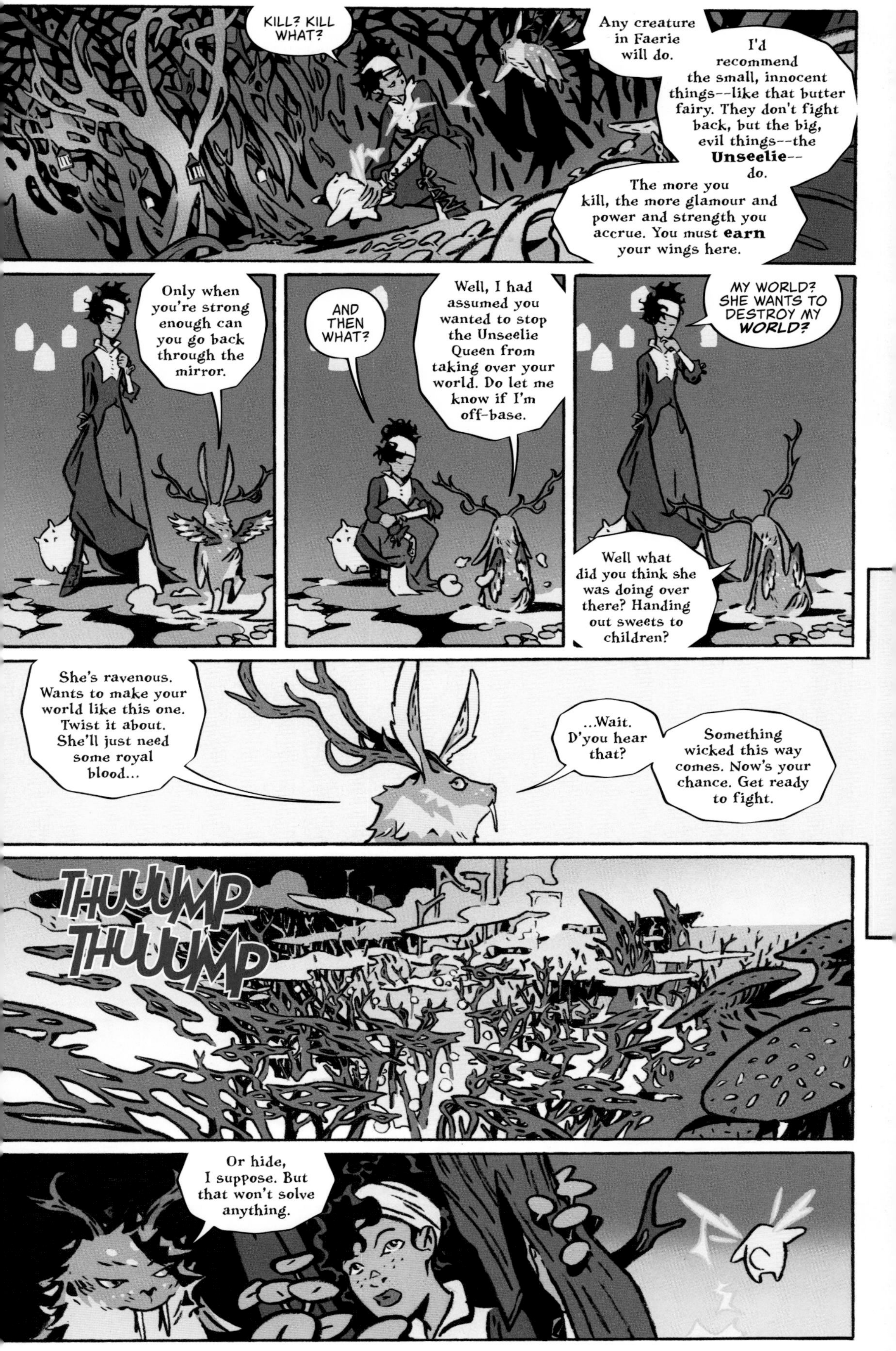
KILL? KILL WHAT?
Any creature in Faerie will do.
I'd recommend the small, innocent things--like that butter fairy. They don't fight back, but the big, evil things--the **Unseelie**--do.
The more you kill, the more glamour and power and strength you accrue. You must **earn** your wings here.
Only when you're strong enough can you go back through the mirror.
AND THEN WHAT?
Well, I had assumed you wanted to stop the Unseelie Queen from taking over your world. Do let me know if I'm off-base.
MY WORLD? SHE WANTS TO DESTROY MY *WORLD?*
Well what did you think she was doing over there? Handing out sweets to children?
She's ravenous. Wants to make your world like this one. Twist it about. She'll just need some royal blood...
...Wait. D'you hear that?
Something wicked this way comes. Now's your chance. Get ready to fight.
THUUUMP THUUUMP
Or hide, I suppose. But that won't solve anything.

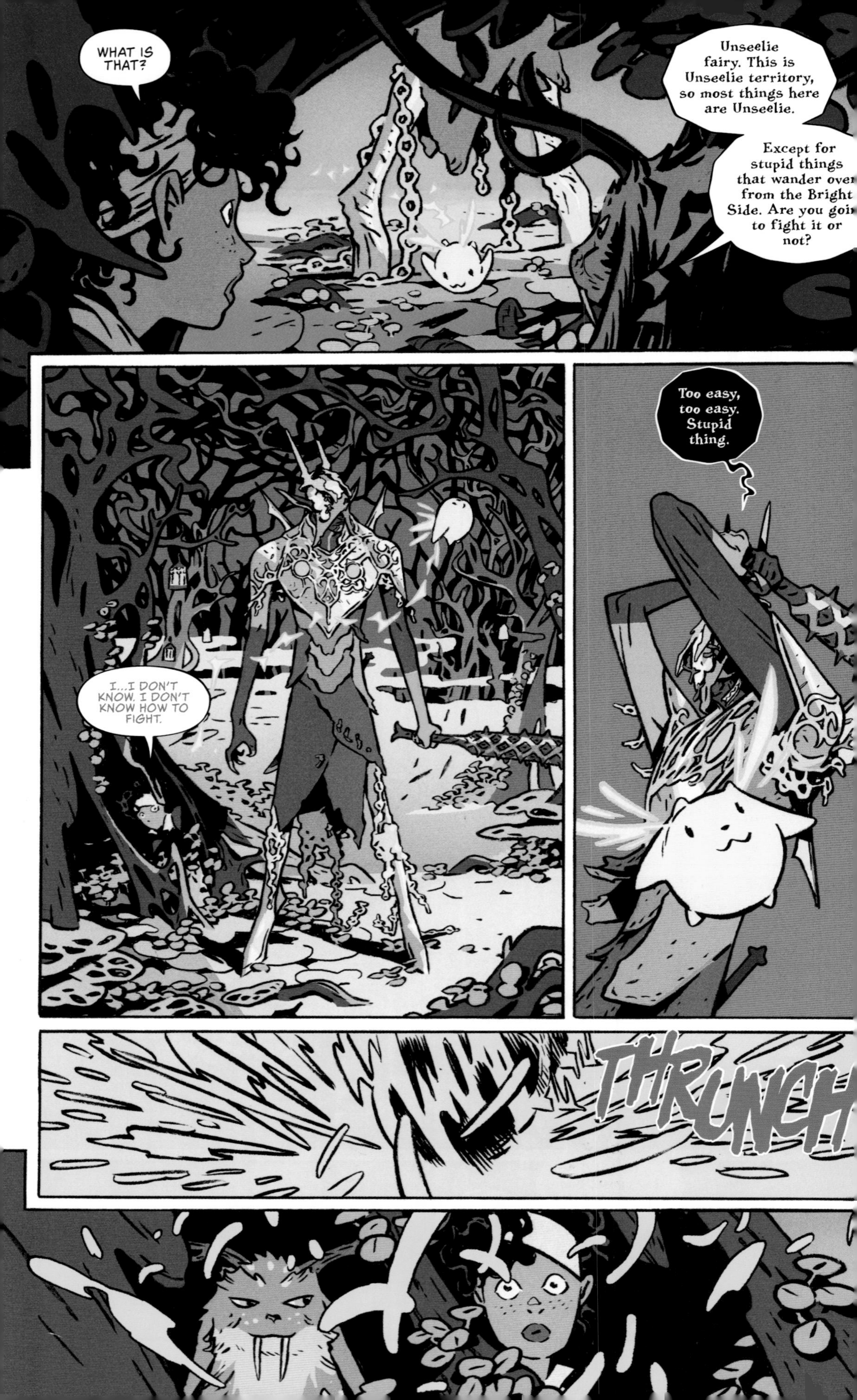
WHAT IS THAT?
Unseelie fairy. This is Unseelie territory, so most things here are Unseelie.
Except for stupid things that wander ove from the Bright Side. Are you goi to fight it or not?
I...I DON'T KNOW. I DON'T KNOW HOW TO FIGHT.
Too easy, too easy. Stupid thing.
THRUNCH

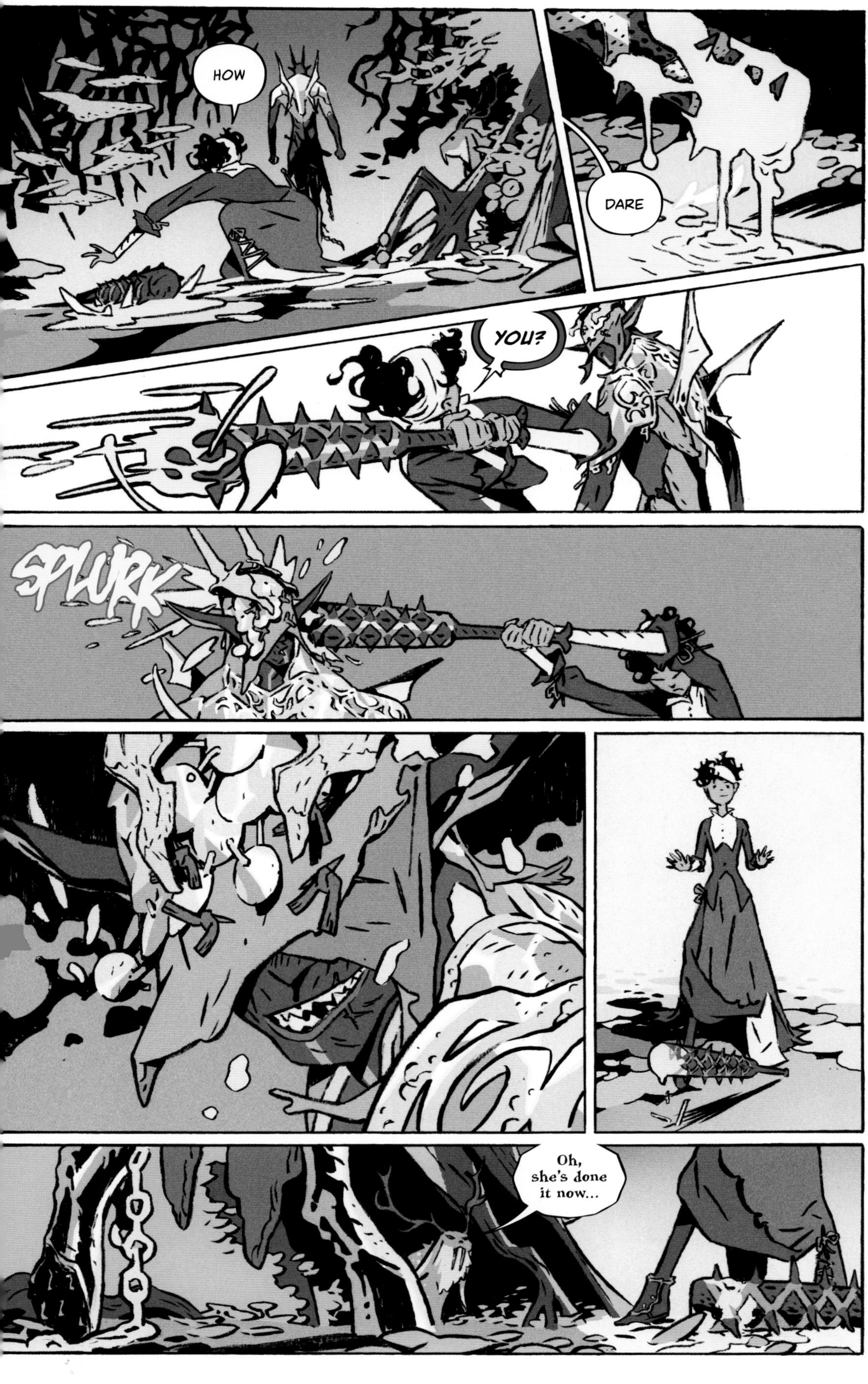
HOW
DARE
YOU?
SPLURK
Oh, she's done it now...

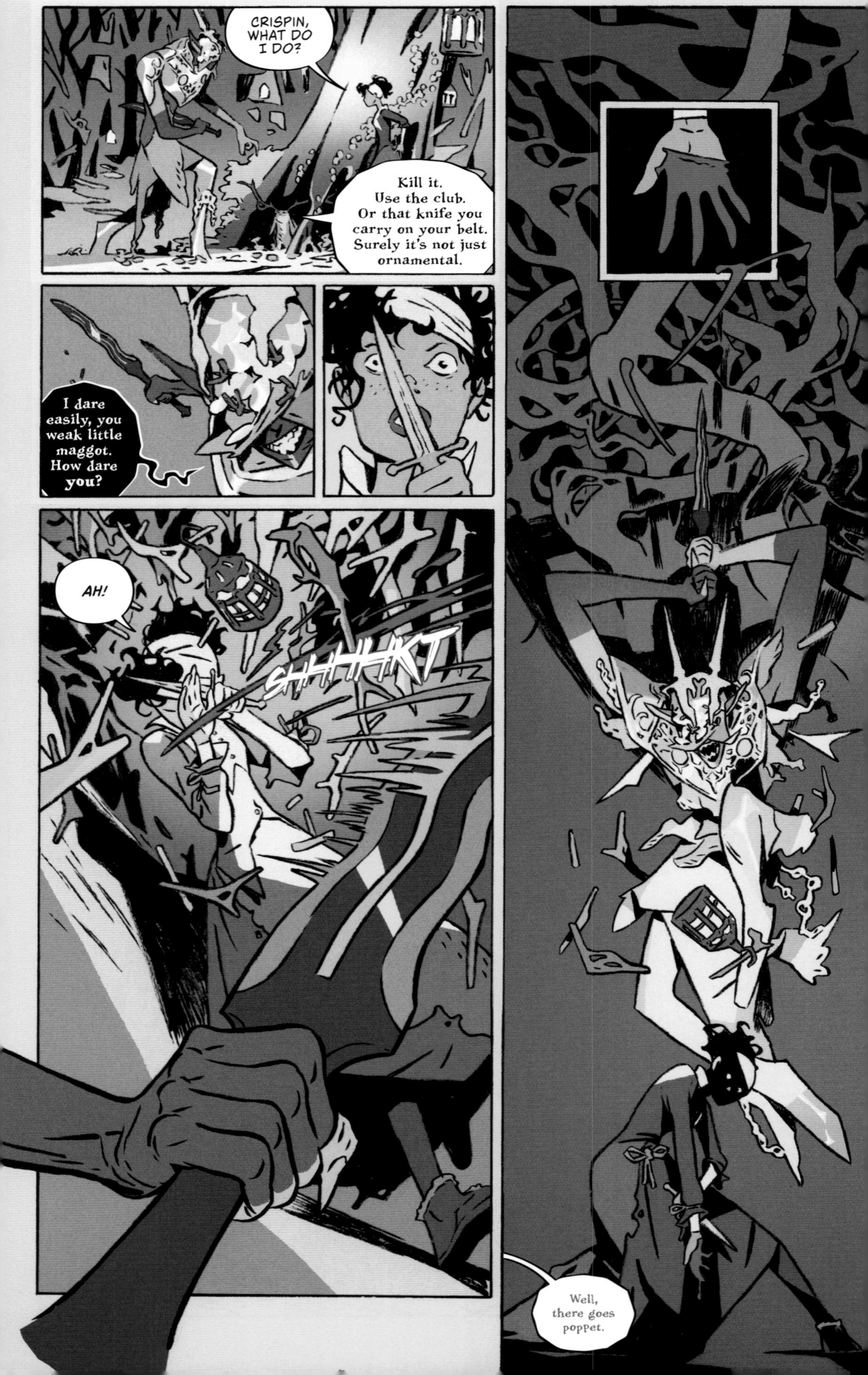
CRISPIN, WHAT DO I DO?
Kill it. Use the club. Or that knife you carry on your belt. Surely it's not just ornamental.
I dare easily, you weak little maggot. How dare you?
AH!
SHHHHHKT
Well, there goes poppet.

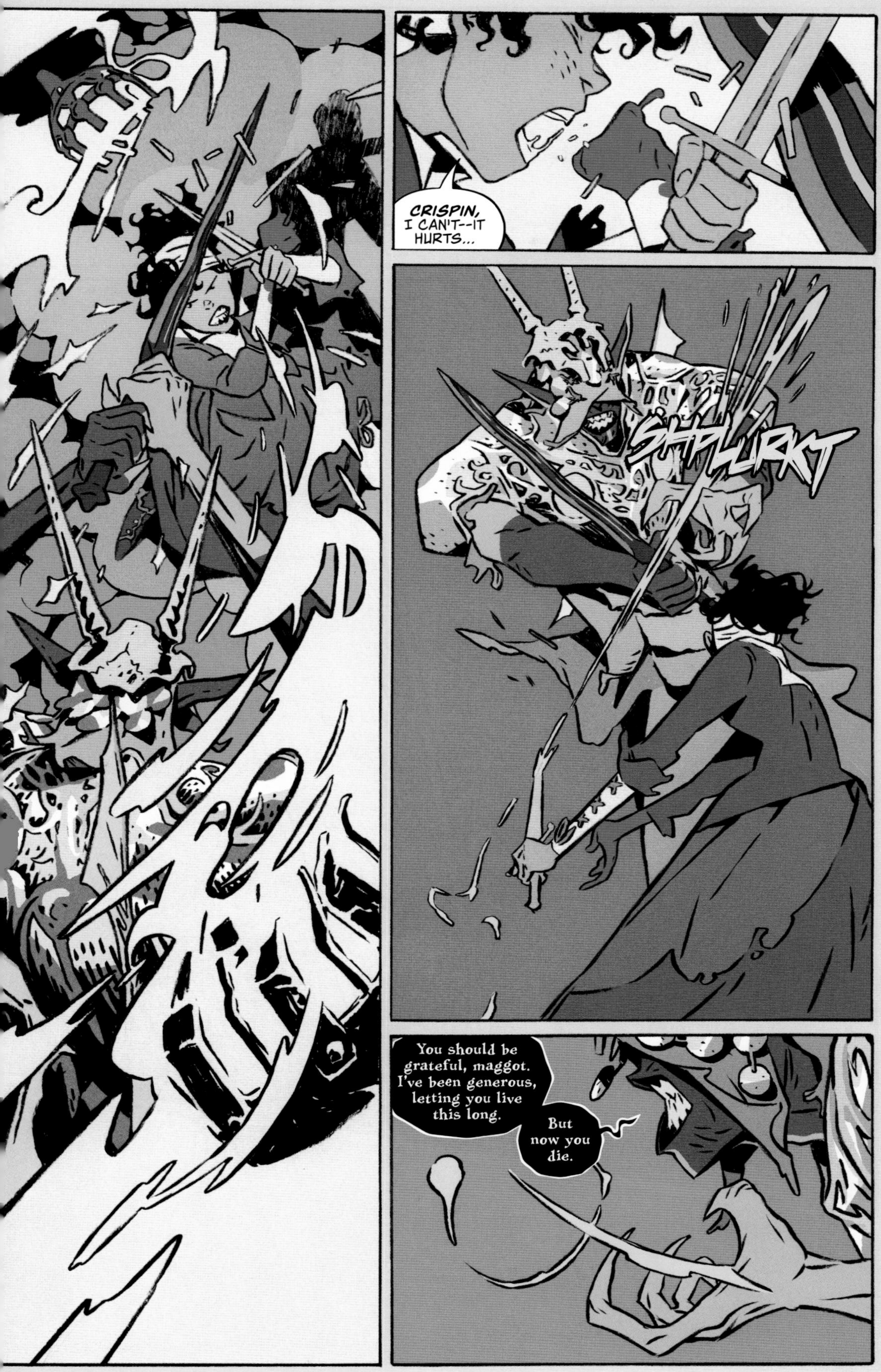
CRISPIN, I CAN'T--IT HURTS...
SHPLURKT
You should be grateful, maggot. I've been generous, letting you live this long.
But now you die.

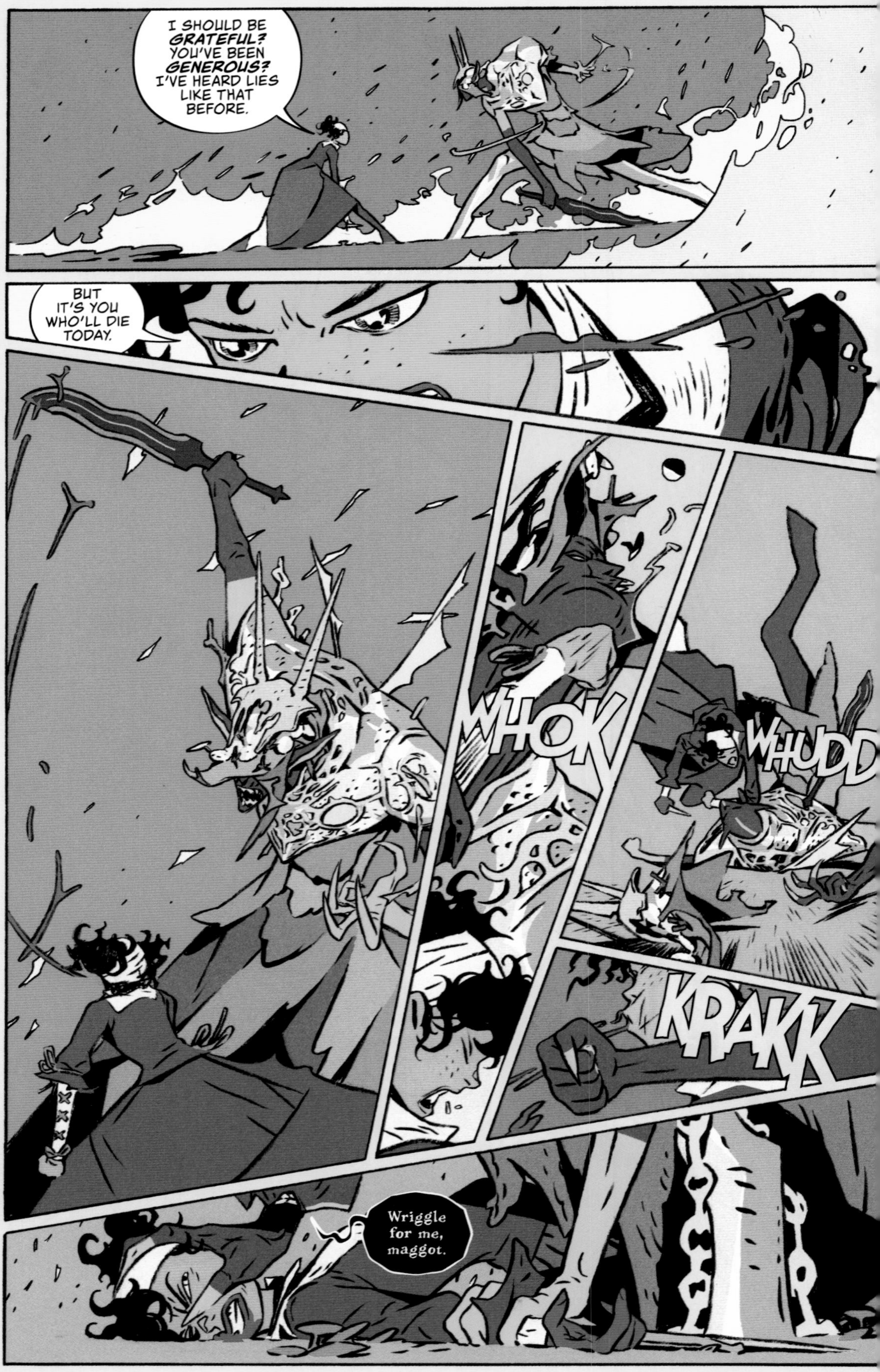
I SHOULD BE GRATEFUL? YOU'VE BEEN GENEROUS? I'VE HEARD LIES LIKE THAT BEFORE.
BUT IT'S YOU WHO'LL DIE TODAY.
WHOK
WHUDD
KRAKK
Wriggle for me, maggot.

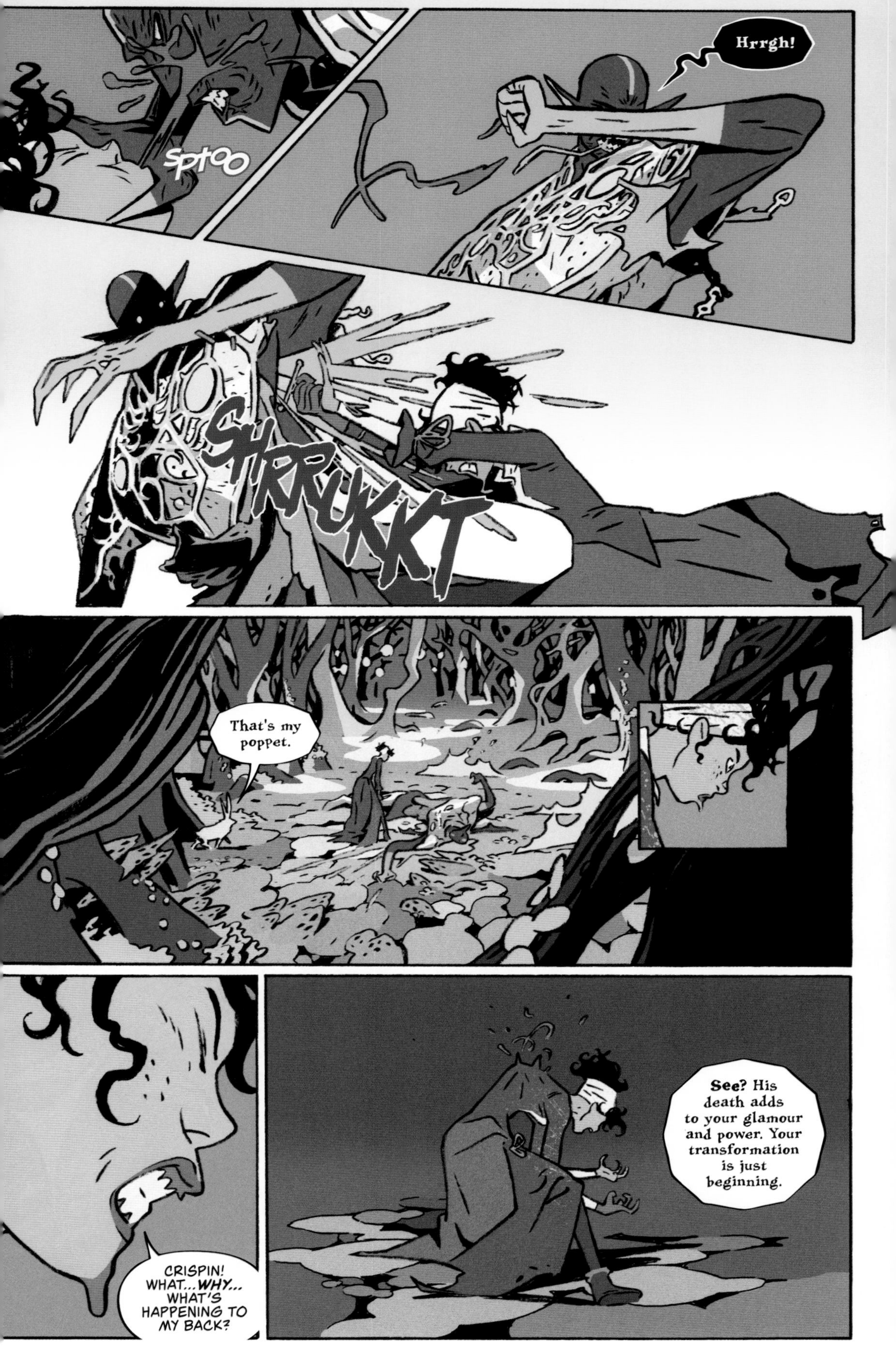
SPTOO
Hrrgh!
SHRRUKKT
That's my poppet.
CRISPIN! WHAT... WHY... WHAT'S HAPPENING TO MY BACK?
See? His death adds to your glamour and power. Your transformation is just beginning.

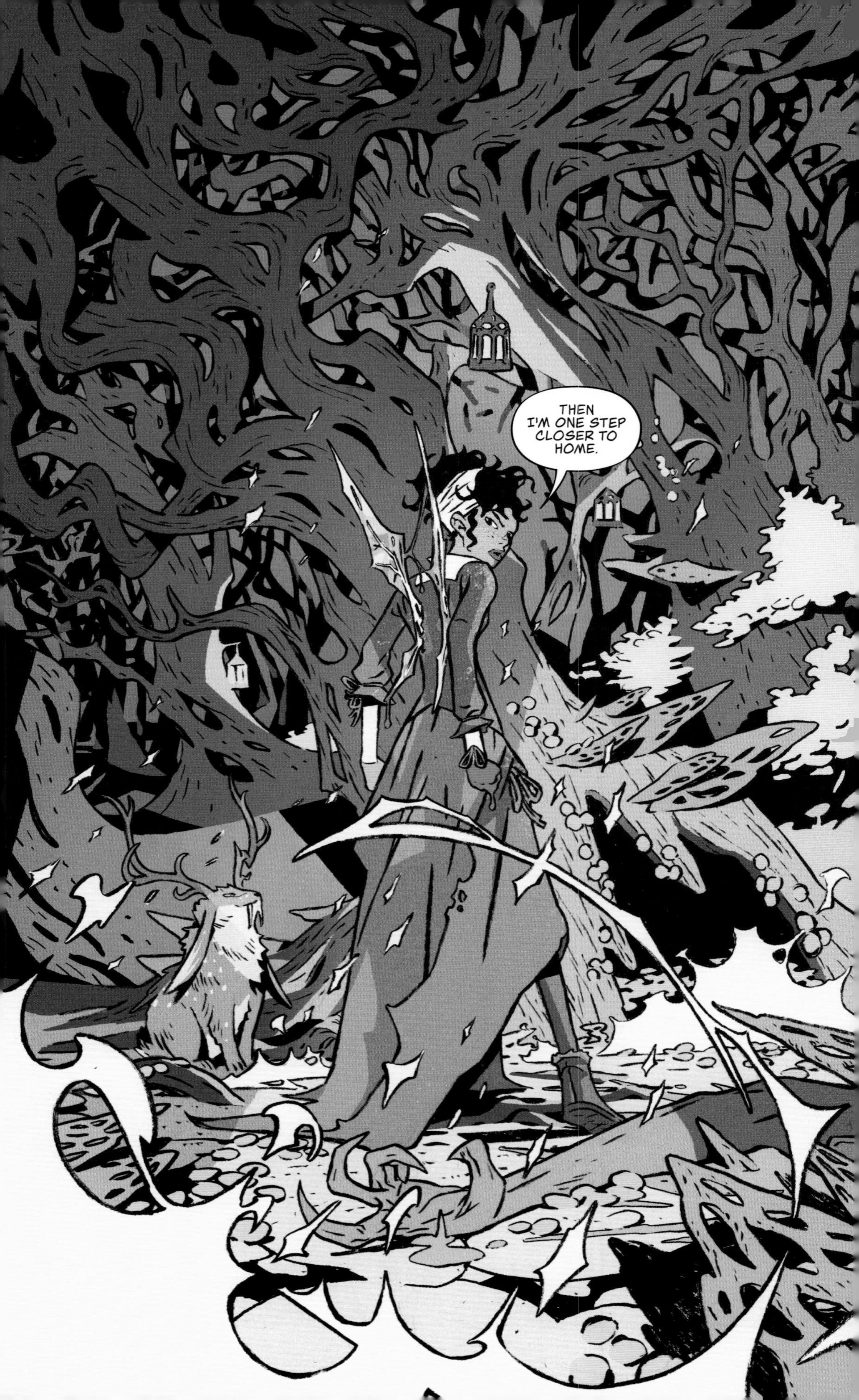
THEN I'M ONE STEP CLOSER TO HOME.

SPARROWHAWK #1 COVER BY

STEPHANIE HANS

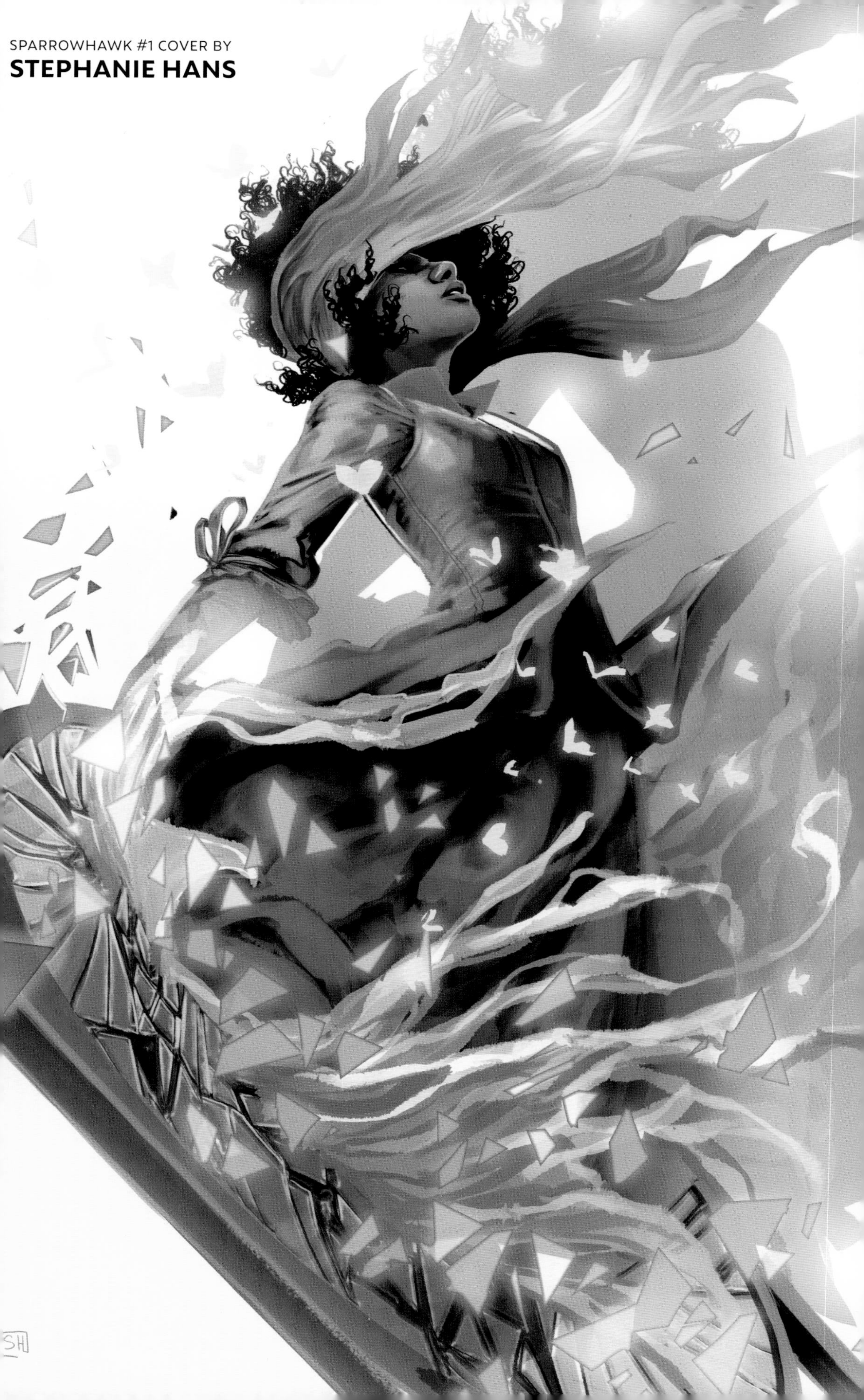
SH

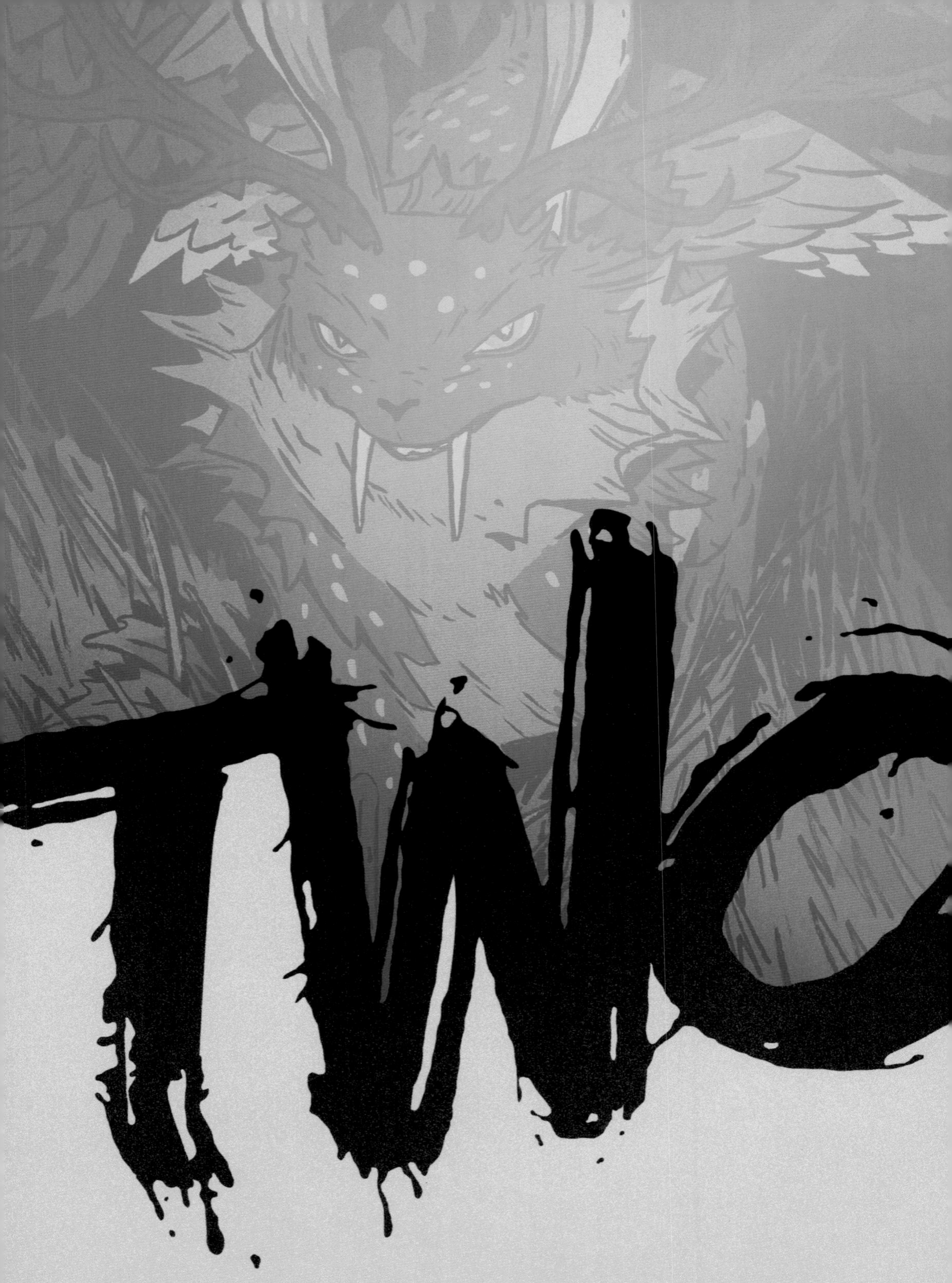

TWO

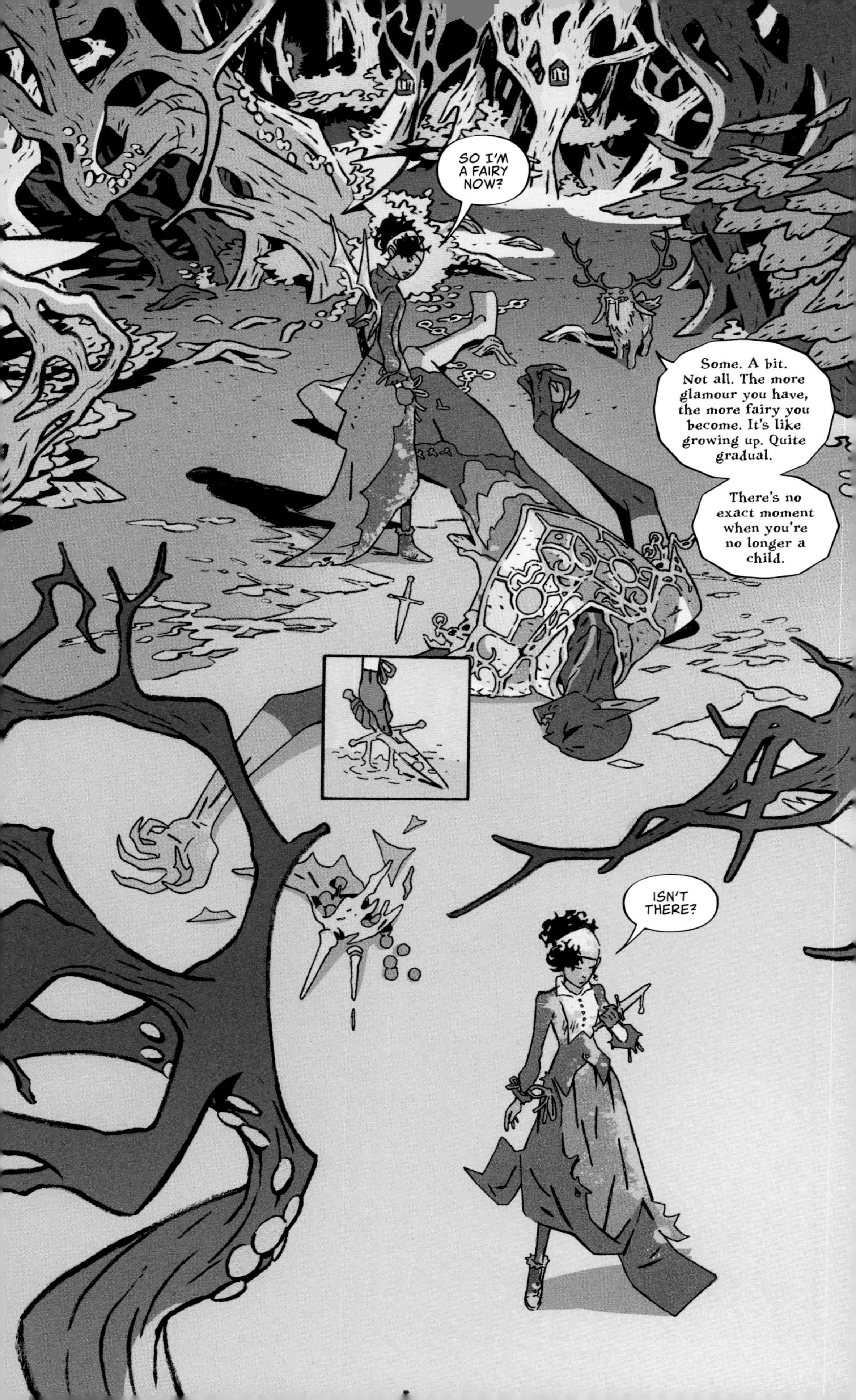
SO I'M A FAIRY NOW?
Some. A bit. Not all. The more glamour you have, the more fairy you become. It's like growing up. Quite gradual.
There's no exact moment when you're no longer a child.
ISN'T THERE?

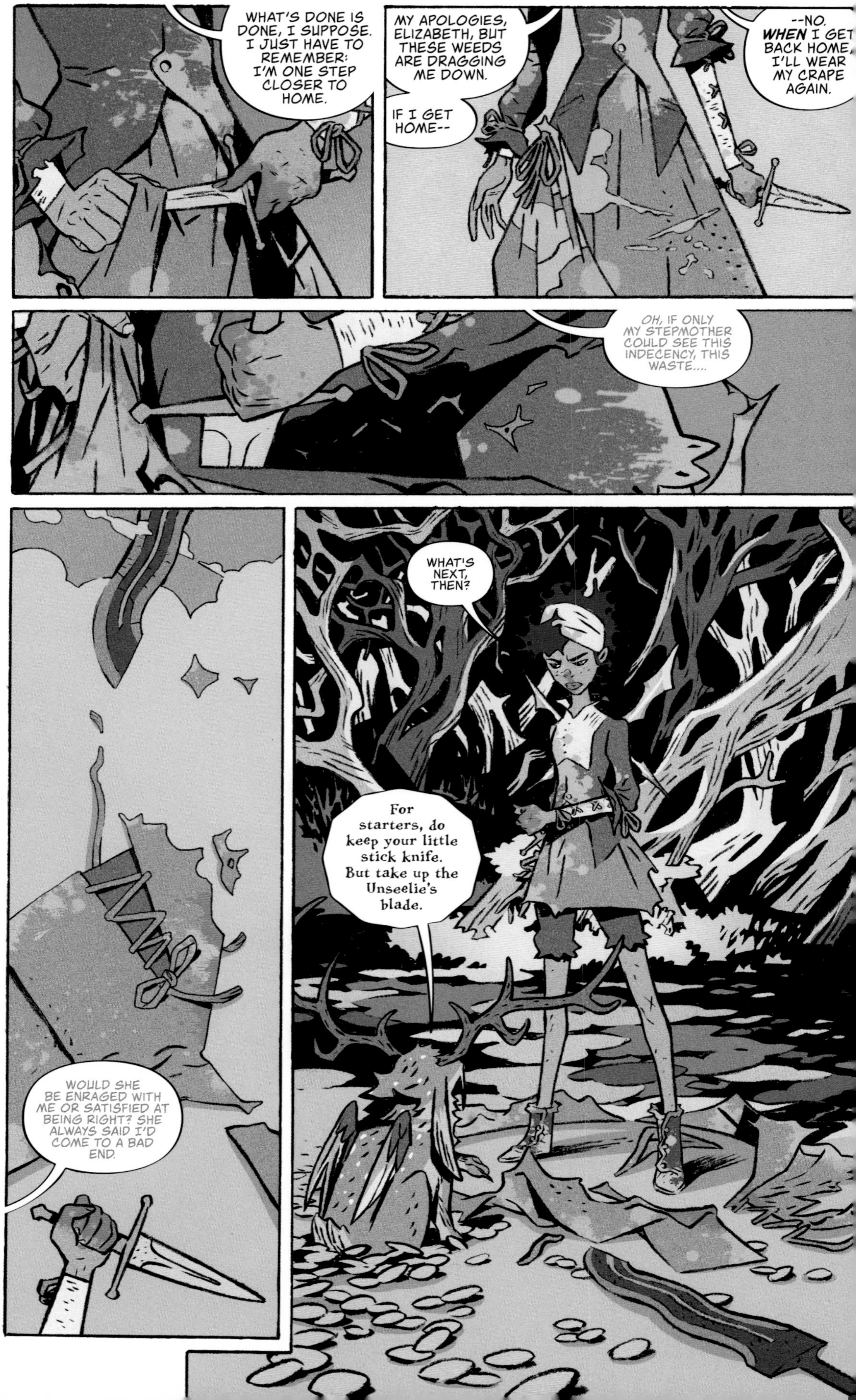
WHAT'S DONE IS DONE, I SUPPOSE. I JUST HAVE TO REMEMBER: I'M ONE STEP CLOSER TO HOME.
MY APOLOGIES, ELIZABETH, BUT THESE WEEDS ARE DRAGGING ME DOWN.
IF I GET HOME--
--NO. WHEN I GET BACK HOME, I'LL WEAR MY CRAPE AGAIN.
OH, IF ONLY MY STEPMOTHER COULD SEE THIS INDECENCY, THIS WASTE....
WOULD SHE BE ENRAGED WITH ME OR SATISFIED AT BEING RIGHT? SHE ALWAYS SAID I'D COME TO A BAD END.
WHAT'S NEXT, THEN?
For starters, do keep your little stick knife. But take up the Unseelie's blade.

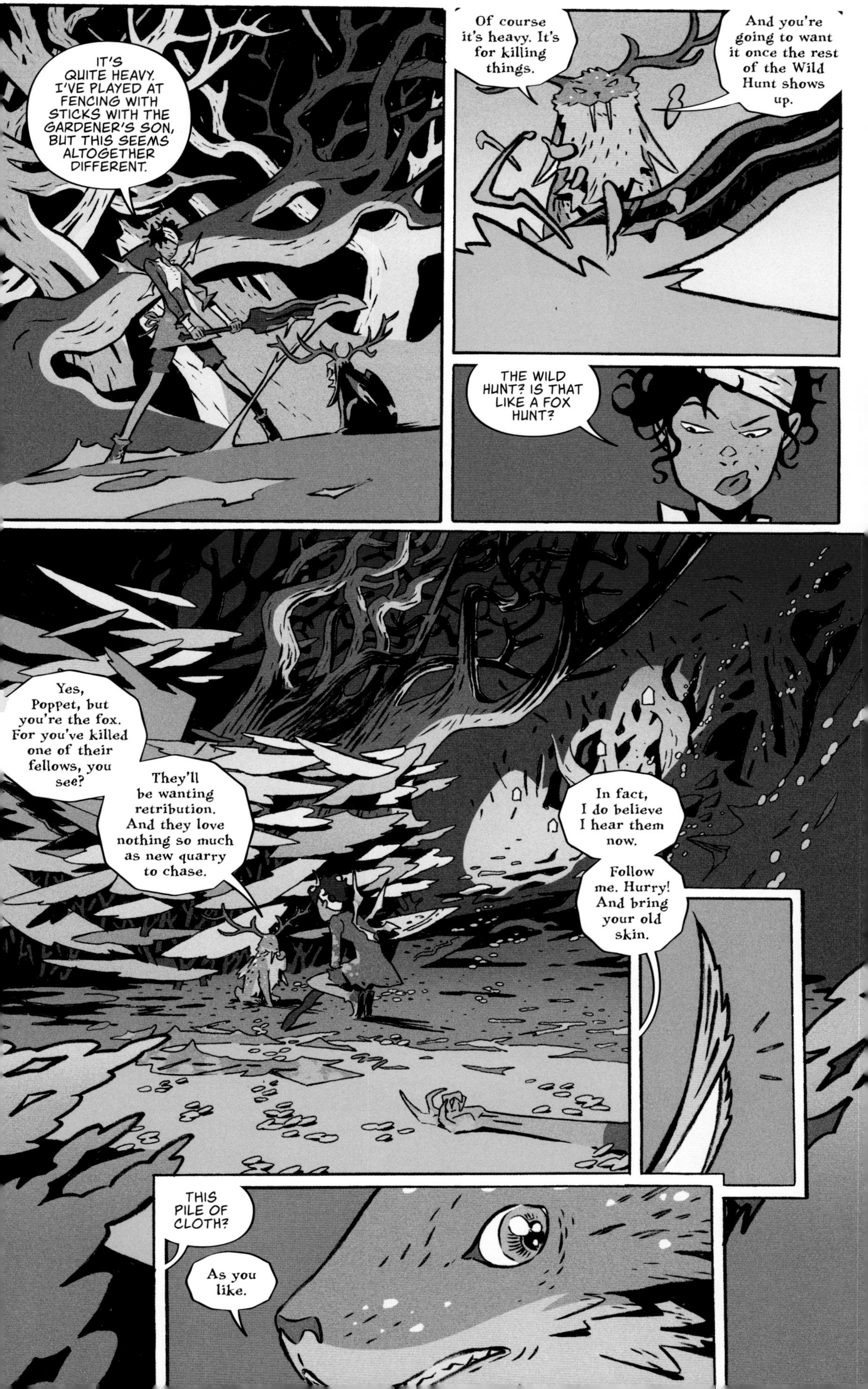
IT'S QUITE HEAVY. I'VE PLAYED AT FENCING WITH STICKS WITH THE GARDENER'S SON, BUT THIS SEEMS ALTOGETHER DIFFERENT.
Of course it's heavy. It's for killing things.
And you're going to want it once the rest of the Wild Hunt shows up.
THE WILD HUNT? IS THAT LIKE A FOX HUNT?
Yes, Poppet, but you're the fox. For you've killed one of their fellows, you see?
They'll be wanting retribution. And they love nothing so much as new quarry to chase.
In fact, I do believe I hear them now.
Follow me. Hurry! And bring your old skin.
THIS PILE OF CLOTH?
As you like.

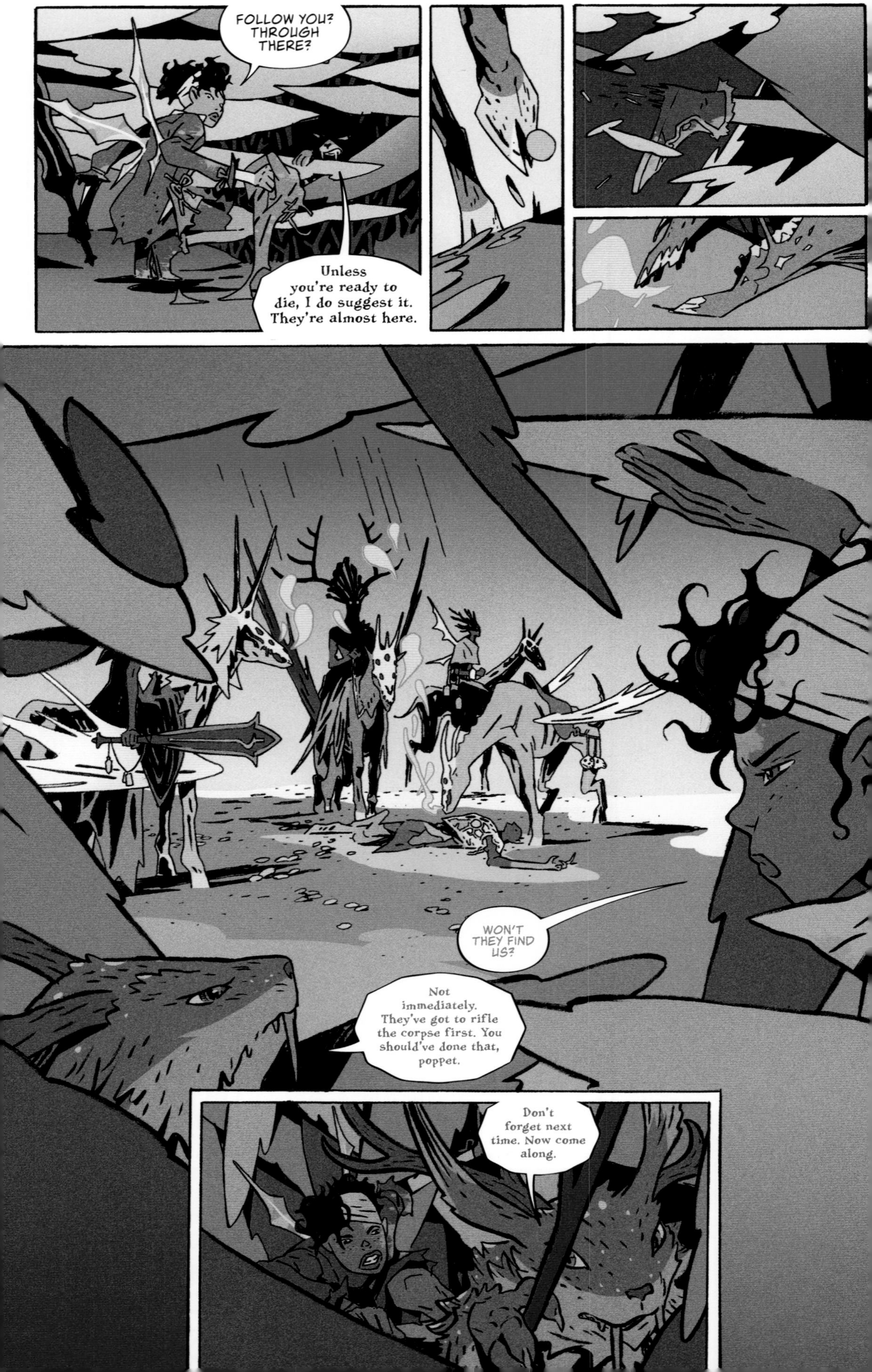
FOLLOW YOU? THROUGH THERE?
Unless you're ready to die, I do suggest it. They're almost here.
WON'T THEY FIND US?
Not immediately. They've got to rifle the corpse first. You should've done that, poppet.
Don't forget next time. Now come along.

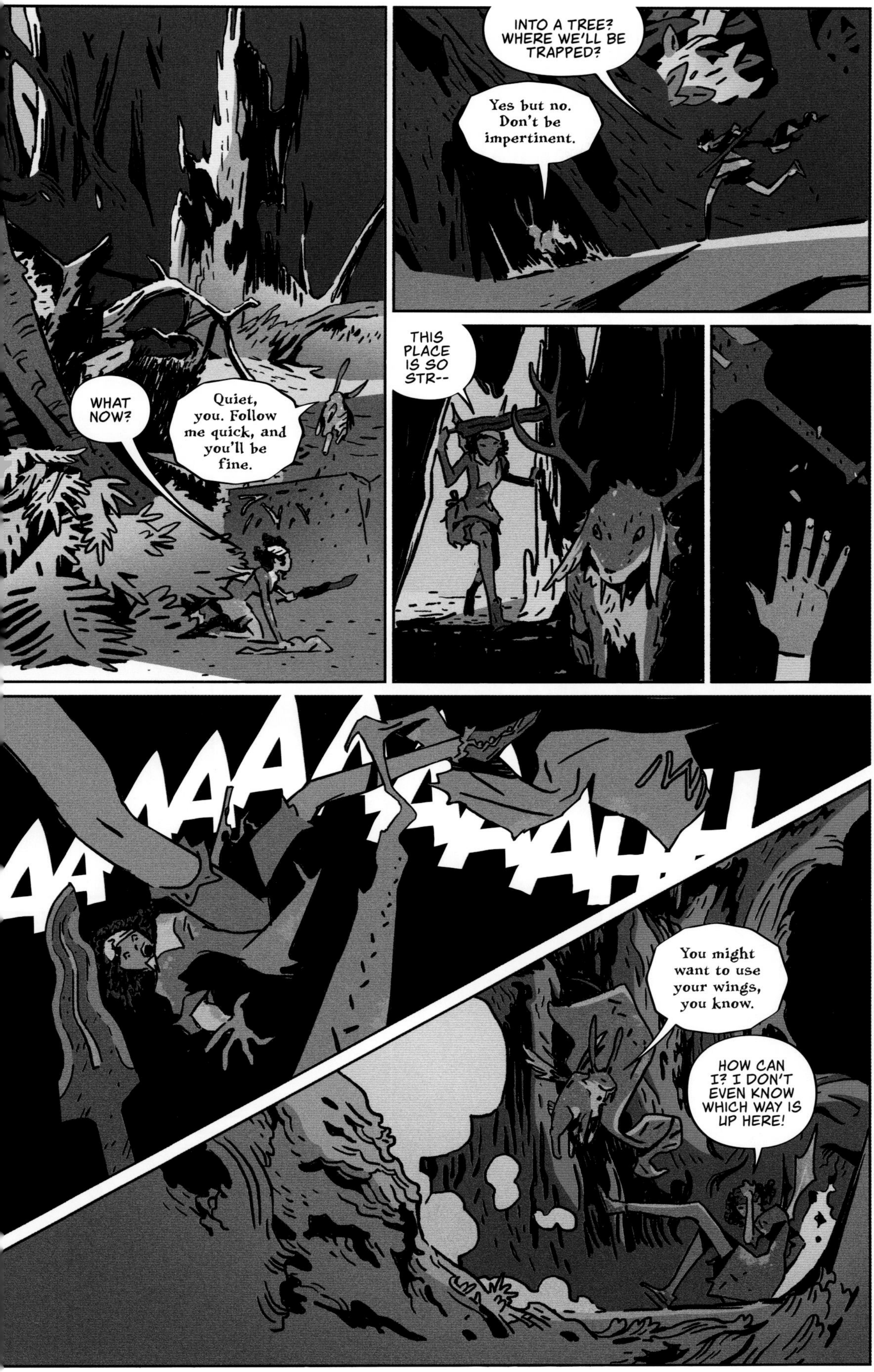
WHAT NOW?
Quiet, you. Follow me quick, and you'll be fine.
INTO A TREE? WHERE WE'LL BE TRAPPED?
Yes but no. Don't be impertinent.
THIS PLACE IS SO STR--
AAAAAAAAAHHH
You might want to use your wings, you know.
HOW CAN I? I DON'T EVEN KNOW WHICH WAY IS UP HERE!

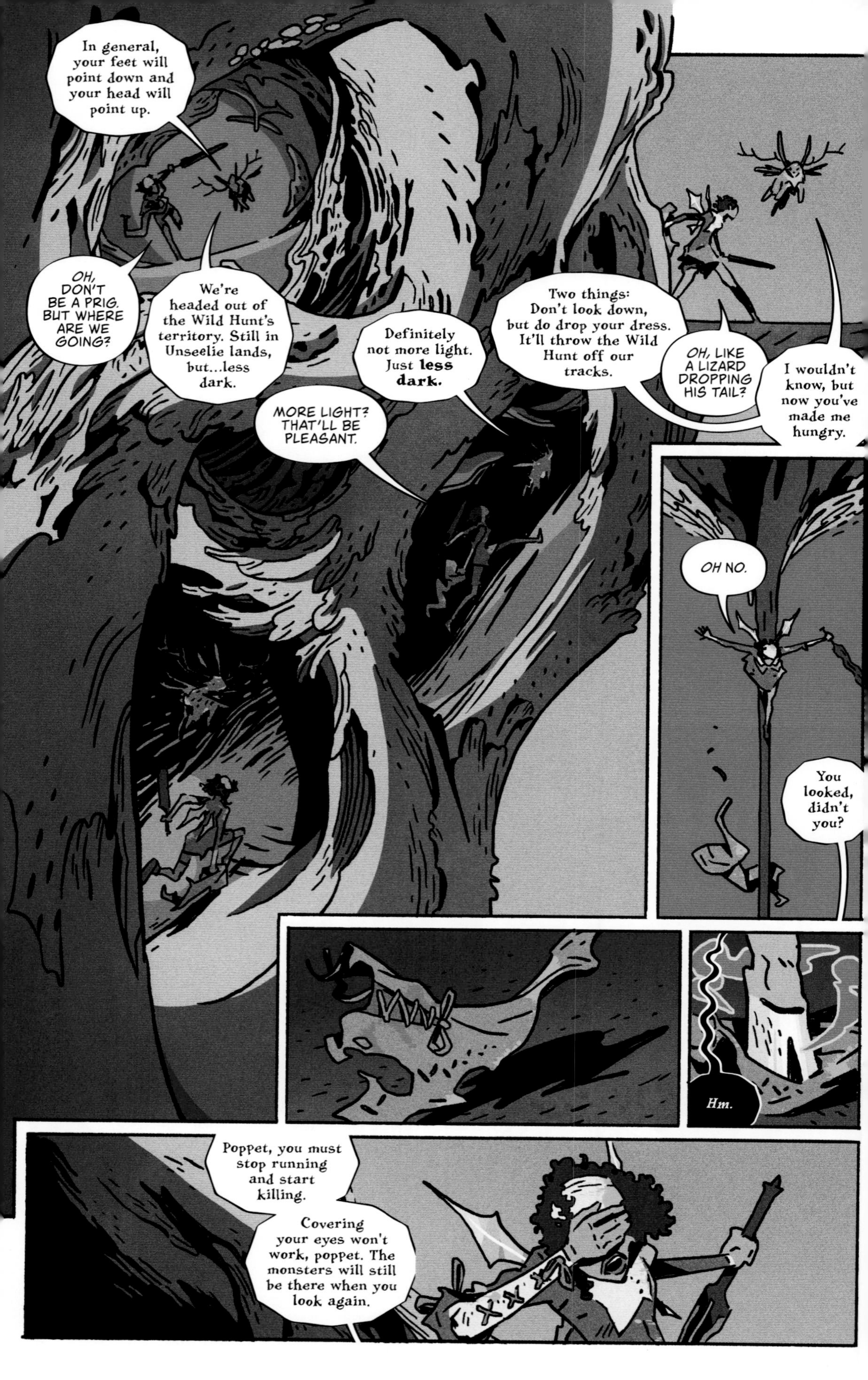
In general, your feet will point down and your head will point up.
OH, DON'T BE A PRIG. BUT WHERE ARE WE GOING?
We're headed out of the Wild Hunt's territory. Still in Unseelie lands, but...less dark.
MORE LIGHT? THAT'LL BE PLEASANT.
Definitely not more light. Just **less dark.**
Two things: Don't look down, but do drop your dress. It'll throw the Wild Hunt off our tracks.
OH, LIKE A LIZARD DROPPING HIS TAIL?
I wouldn't know, but now you've made me hungry.
OH NO.
You looked, didn't you?
Hm.
Poppet, you must stop running and start killing.
Covering your eyes won't work, poppet. The monsters will still be there when you look again.

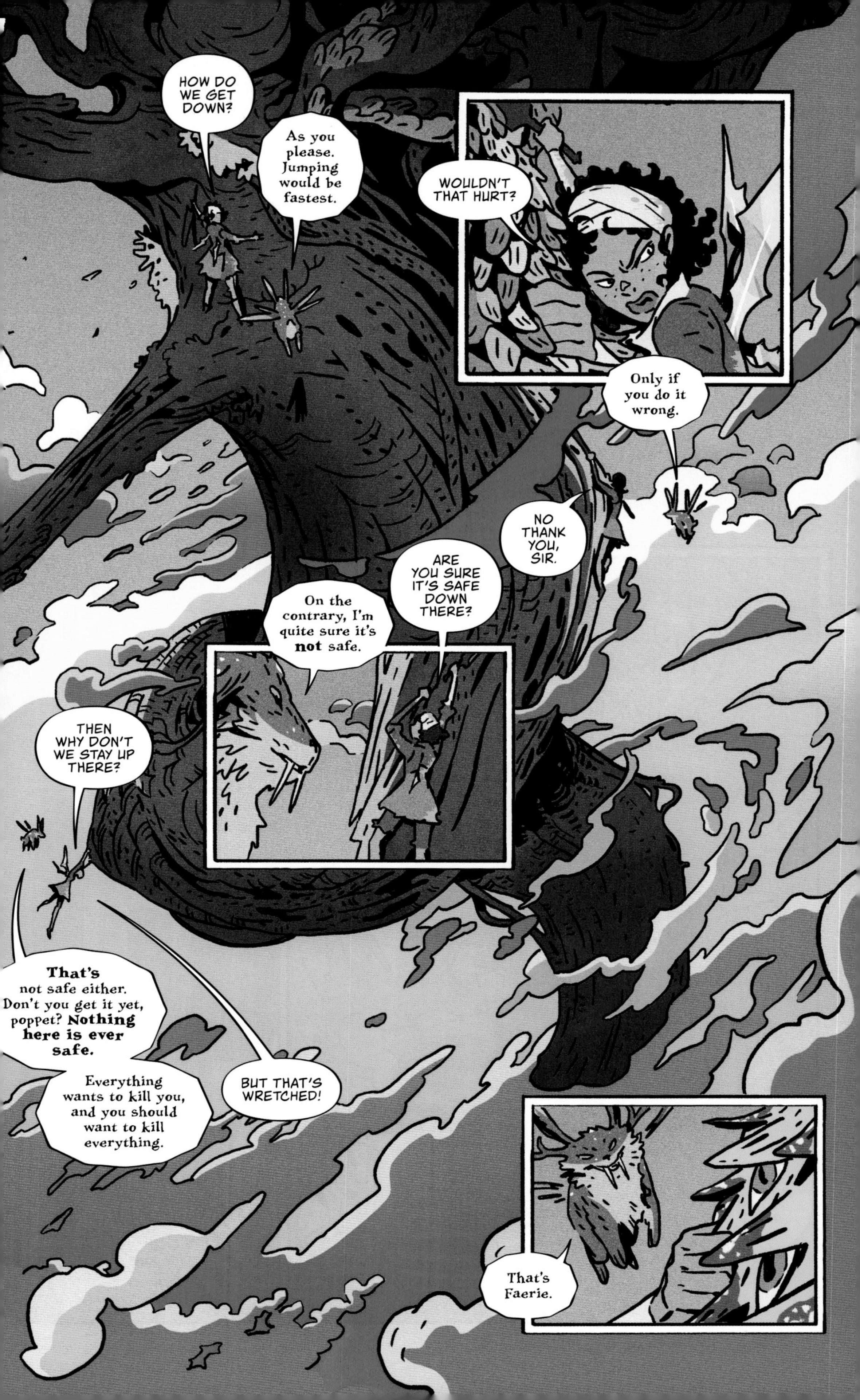
HOW DO WE GET DOWN?
As you please. Jumping would be fastest.
WOULDN'T THAT HURT?
Only if you do it wrong.
NO THANK YOU, SIR.
ARE YOU SURE IT'S SAFE DOWN THERE?
On the contrary, I'm quite sure it's **not** safe.
THEN WHY DON'T WE STAY UP THERE?
That's not safe either. Don't you get it yet, poppet? **Nothing here is ever safe.**
Everything wants to kill you, and you should want to kill everything.
BUT THAT'S WRETCHED!
That's Faerie.

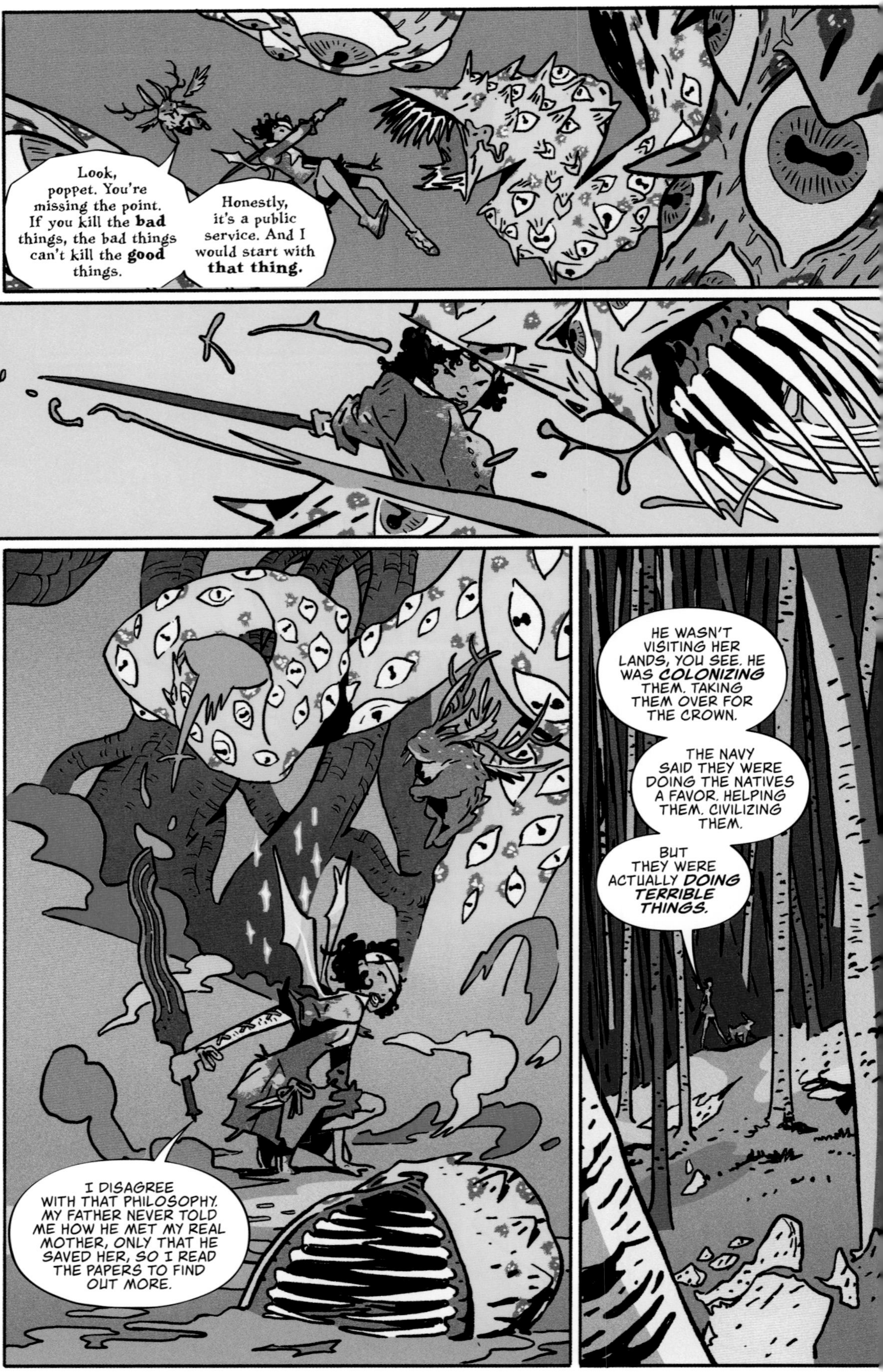
Look, poppet. You're missing the point. If you kill the bad things, the bad things can't kill the good things.
Honestly, it's a public service. And I would start with that thing.
I DISAGREE WITH THAT PHILOSOPHY. MY FATHER NEVER TOLD ME HOW HE MET MY REAL MOTHER, ONLY THAT HE SAVED HER, SO I READ THE PAPERS TO FIND OUT MORE.
HE WASN'T VISITING HER LANDS, YOU SEE. HE WAS COLONIZING THEM. TAKING THEM OVER FOR THE CROWN.
THE NAVY SAID THEY WERE DOING THE NATIVES A FAVOR. HELPING THEM. CIVILIZING THEM.
BUT THEY WERE ACTUALLY DOING TERRIBLE THINGS.

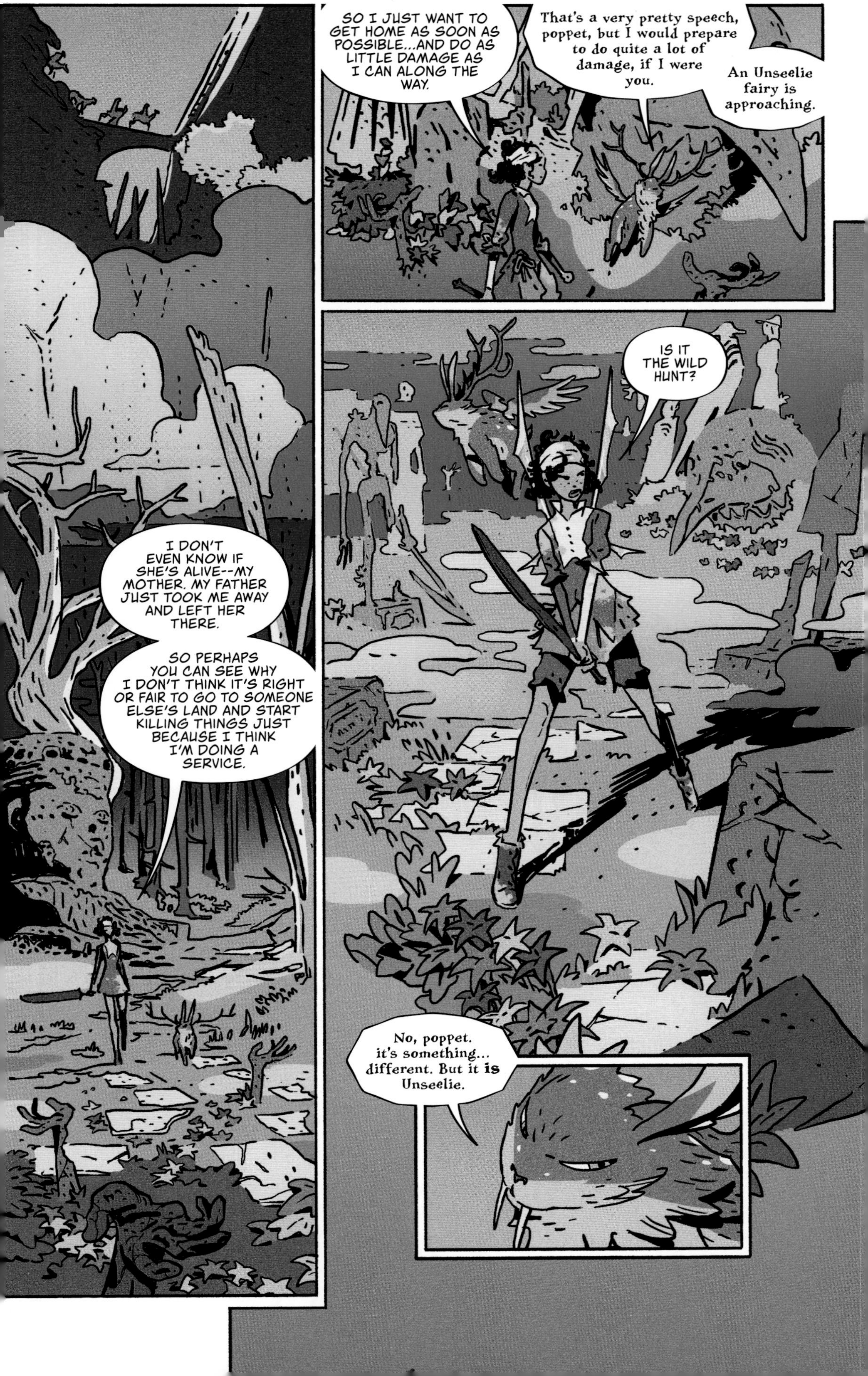
I DON'T EVEN KNOW IF SHE'S ALIVE--MY MOTHER. MY FATHER JUST TOOK ME AWAY AND LEFT HER THERE.
SO PERHAPS YOU CAN SEE WHY I DON'T THINK IT'S RIGHT OR FAIR TO GO TO SOMEONE ELSE'S LAND AND START KILLING THINGS JUST BECAUSE I THINK I'M DOING A SERVICE.
SO I JUST WANT TO GET HOME AS SOON AS POSSIBLE...AND DO AS LITTLE DAMAGE AS I CAN ALONG THE WAY.
That's a very pretty speech, poppet, but I would prepare to do quite a lot of damage, if I were you.
An Unseelie fairy is approaching.
IS IT THE WILD HUNT?
No, poppet. it's something... different. But it **is** Unseelie.

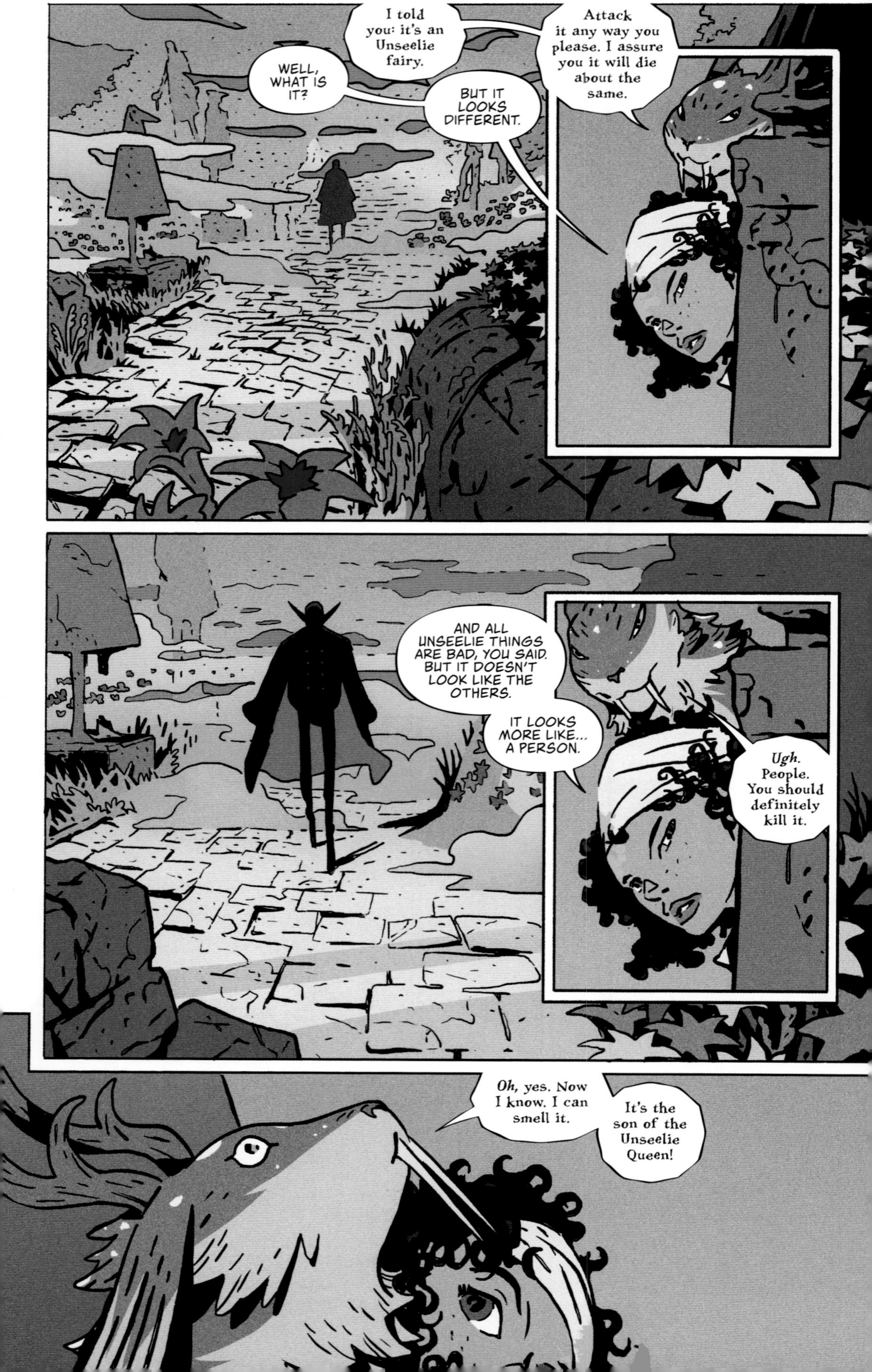
WELL, WHAT IS IT?
I told you: it's an Unseelie fairy.
BUT IT LOOKS DIFFERENT.
Attack it any way you please. I assure you it will die about the same.
AND ALL UNSEELIE THINGS ARE BAD, YOU SAID. BUT IT DOESN'T LOOK LIKE THE OTHERS.
IT LOOKS MORE LIKE... A PERSON.
Ugh. People. You should definitely kill it.
Oh, yes. Now I know. I can smell it.
It's the son of the Unseelie Queen!

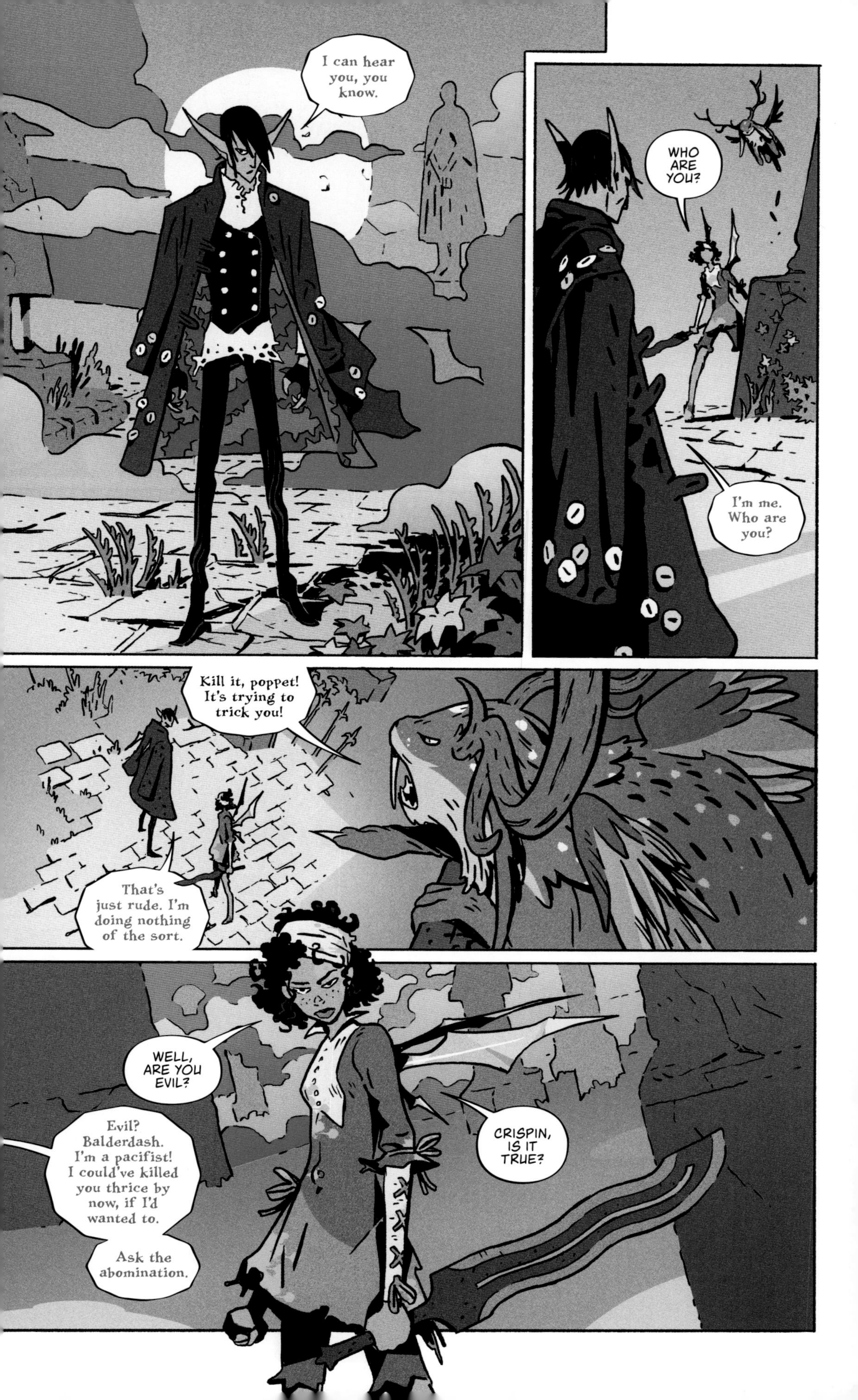
I can hear you, you know.
WHO ARE YOU?
I'm me. Who are you?
Kill it, poppet! It's trying to trick you!
That's just rude. I'm doing nothing of the sort.
WELL, ARE YOU EVIL?
Evil? Balderdash. I'm a pacifist! I could've killed you thrice by now, if I'd wanted to.
Ask the abomination.
CRISPIN, IS IT TRUE?

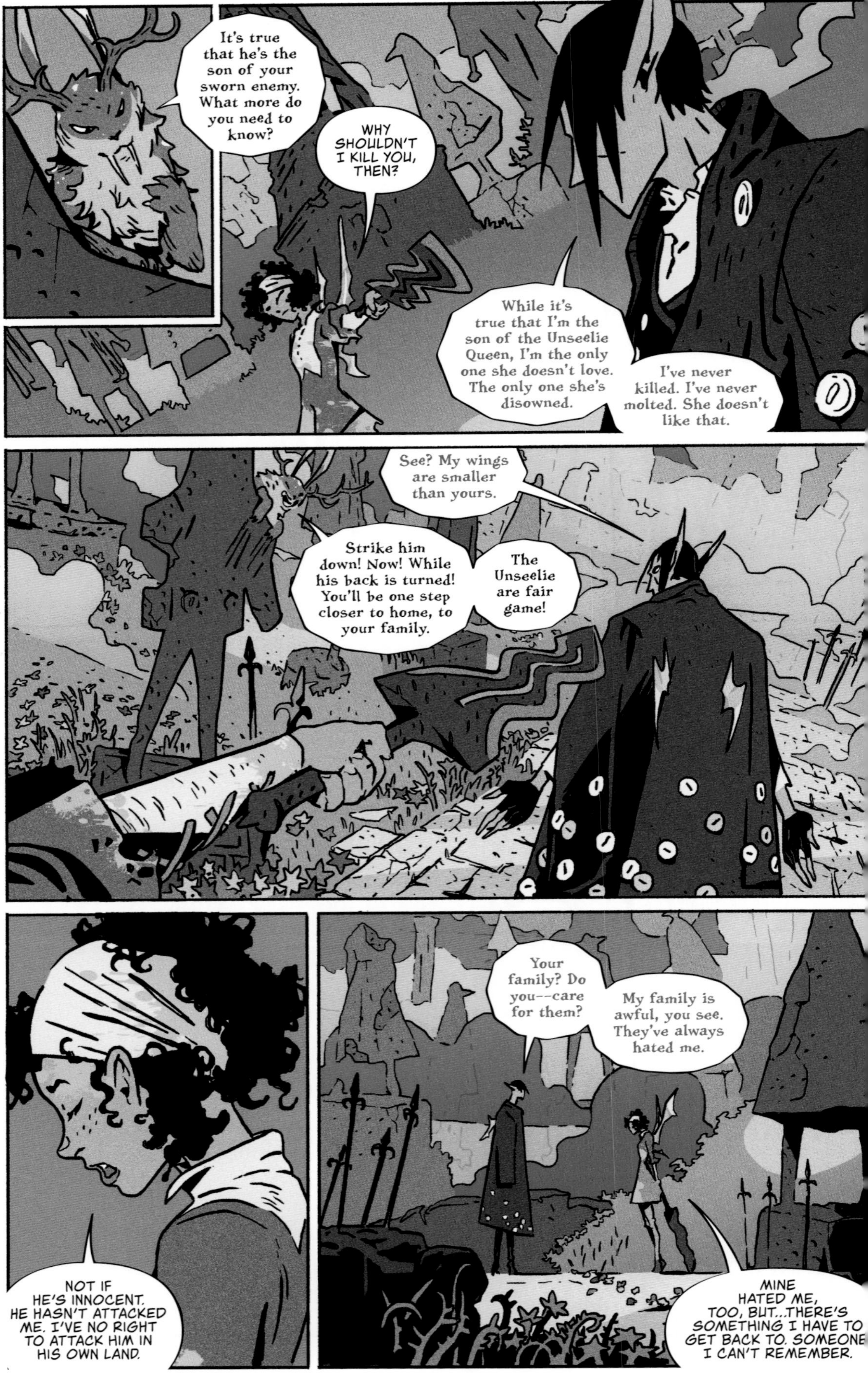
It's true that he's the son of your sworn enemy. What more do you need to know?
WHY SHOULDN'T I KILL YOU, THEN?
While it's true that I'm the son of the Unseelie Queen, I'm the only one she doesn't love. The only one she's disowned.
I've never killed. I've never molted. She doesn't like that.
See? My wings are smaller than yours.
Strike him down! Now! While his back is turned! You'll be one step closer to home, to your family.
The Unseelie are fair game!
NOT IF HE'S INNOCENT. HE HASN'T ATTACKED ME. I'VE NO RIGHT TO ATTACK HIM IN HIS OWN LAND.
Your family? Do you--care for them?
My family is awful, you see. They've always hated me.
MINE HATED ME, TOO, BUT...THERE'S SOMETHING I HAVE TO GET BACK TO. SOMEONE I CAN'T REMEMBER.

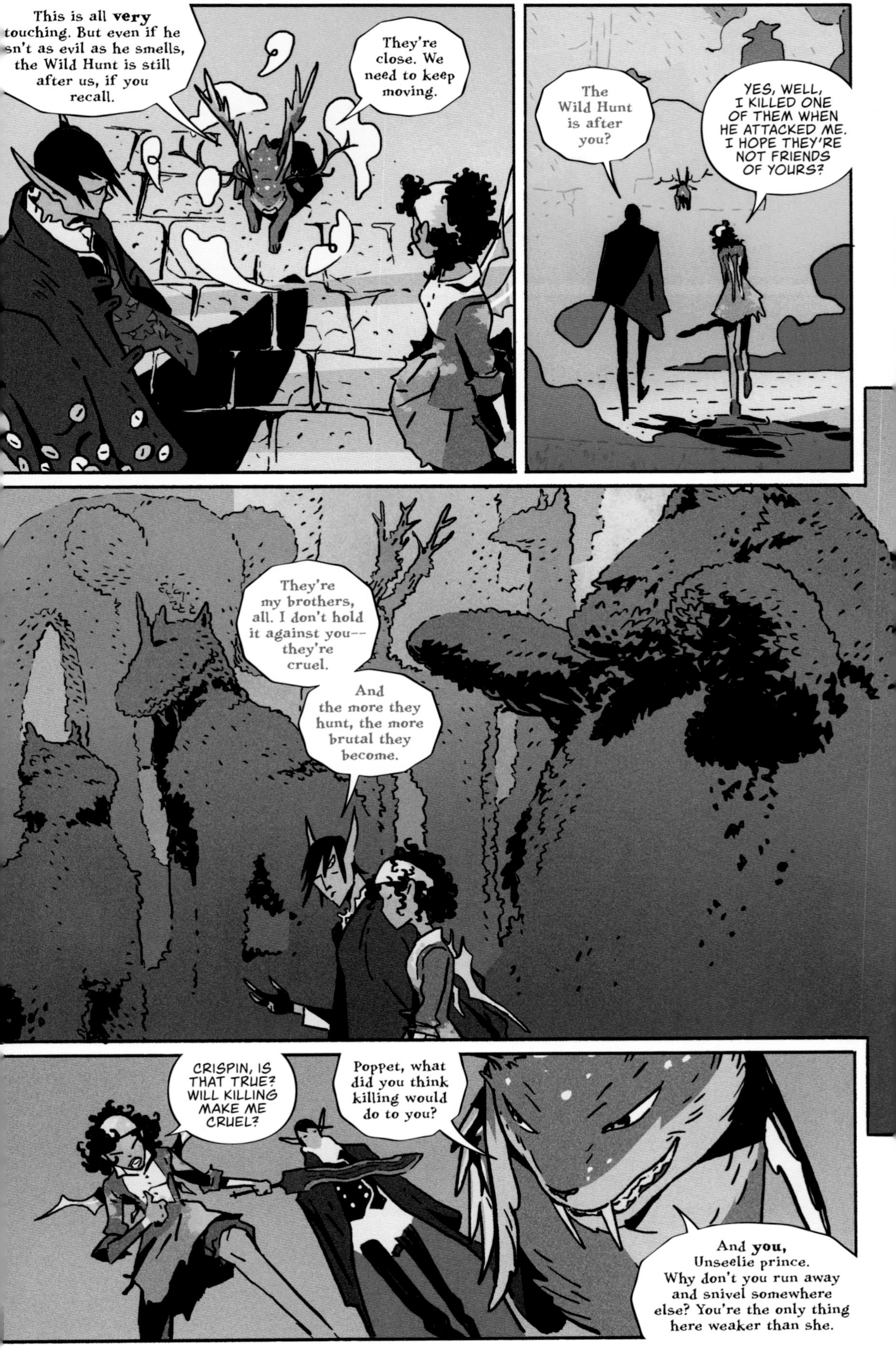
This is all very touching. But even if he isn't as evil as he smells, the Wild Hunt is still after us, if you recall.
They're close. We need to keep moving.
The Wild Hunt is after you?
YES, WELL, I KILLED ONE OF THEM WHEN HE ATTACKED ME. I HOPE THEY'RE NOT FRIENDS OF YOURS?
They're my brothers, all. I don't hold it against you-- they're cruel.
And the more they hunt, the more brutal they become.
CRISPIN, IS THAT TRUE? WILL KILLING MAKE ME CRUEL?
Poppet, what did you think killing would do to you?
And you, Unseelie prince. Why don't you run away and snivel somewhere else? You're the only thing here weaker than she.

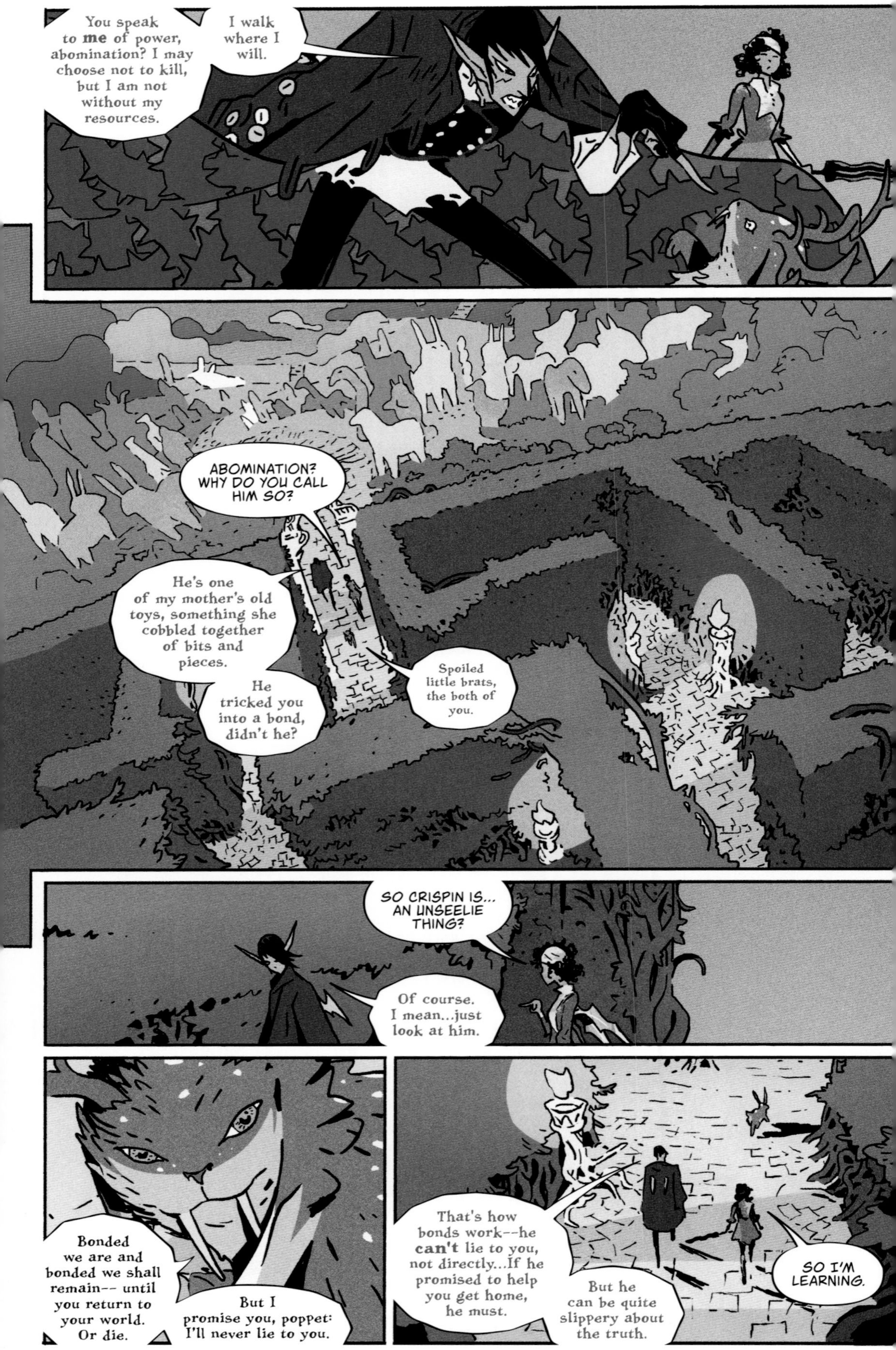
You speak to **me** of power, abomination? I may choose not to kill, but I am not without my resources.
I walk where I will.
ABOMINATION? WHY DO YOU CALL HIM SO?
He's one of my mother's old toys, something she cobbled together of bits and pieces.
He tricked you into a bond, didn't he?
Spoiled little brats, the both of you.
SO CRISPIN IS... AN UNSEELIE THING?
Of course. I mean...just look at him.
Bonded we are and bonded we shall remain-- until you return to your world. Or die.
But I promise you, poppet: I'll never lie to you.
That's how bonds work--he **can't** lie to you, not directly...If he promised to help you get home, he must.
But he can be quite slippery about the truth.
SO I'M LEARNING.

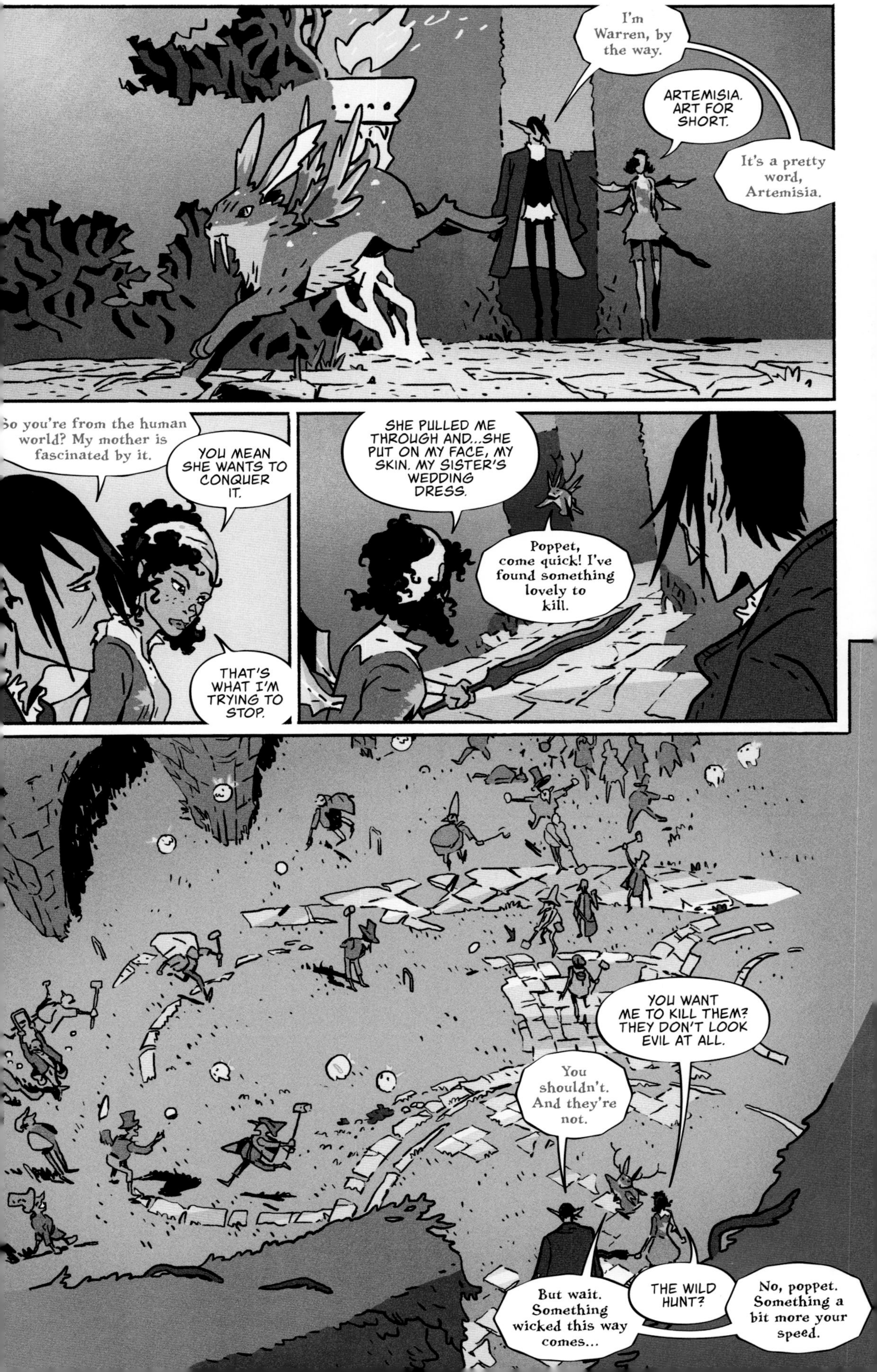
I'm Warren, by the way.
ARTEMISIA. ART FOR SHORT.
It's a pretty word, Artemisia.
So you're from the human world? My mother is fascinated by it.
YOU MEAN SHE WANTS TO CONQUER IT.
THAT'S WHAT I'M TRYING TO STOP.
SHE PULLED ME THROUGH AND...SHE PUT ON MY FACE, MY SKIN. MY SISTER'S WEDDING DRESS.
Poppet, come quick! I've found something lovely to kill.
YOU WANT ME TO KILL THEM? THEY DON'T LOOK EVIL AT ALL.
You shouldn't. And they're not.
But wait. Something wicked this way comes...
THE WILD HUNT?
No, poppet. Something a bit more your speed.

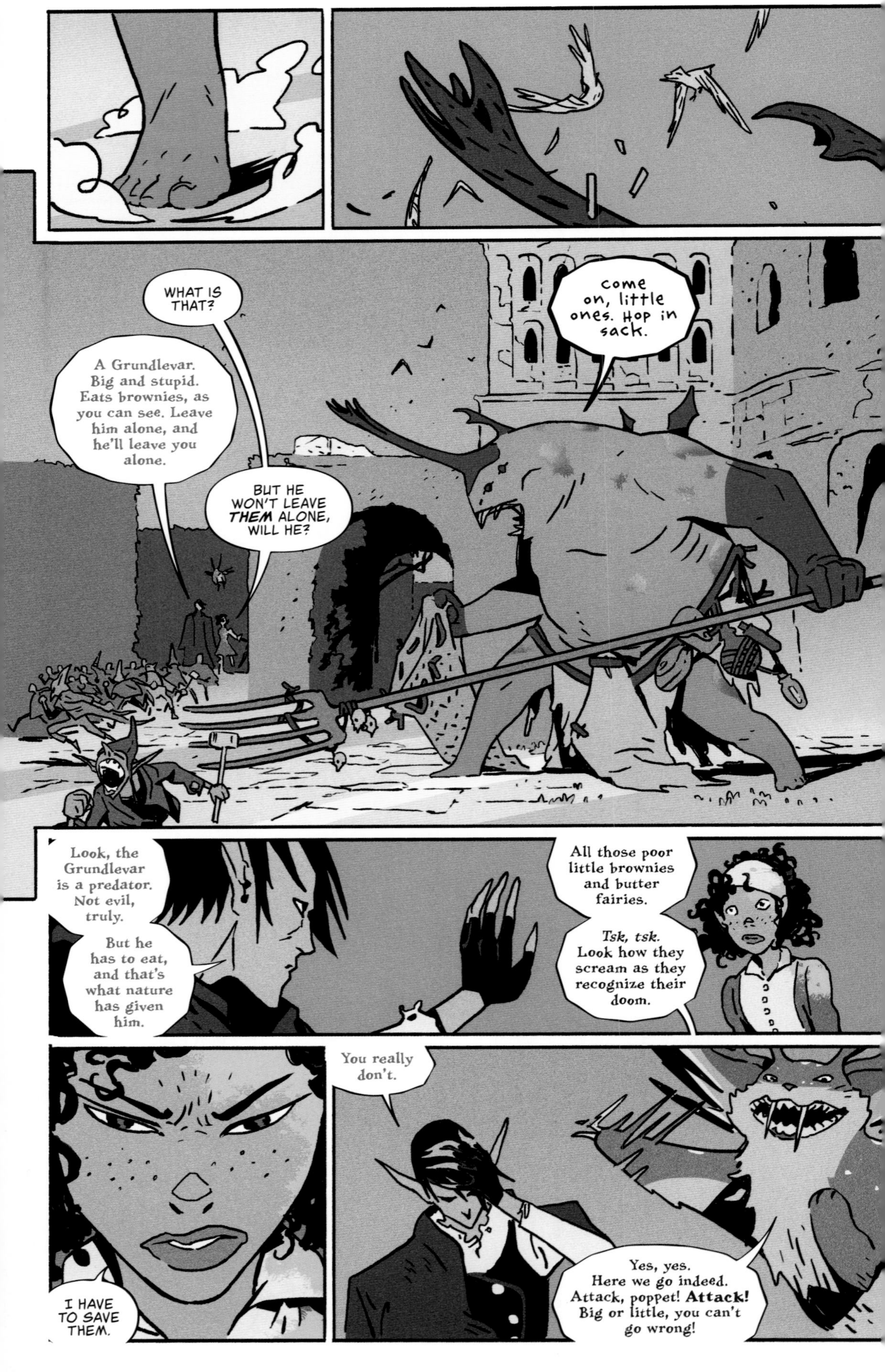

WHAT IS THAT?
A Grundlevar. Big and stupid. Eats brownies, as you can see. Leave him alone, and he'll leave you alone.
BUT HE WON'T LEAVE *THEM* ALONE, WILL HE?
come on, little ones. Hop in sack.
Look, the Grundlevar is a predator. Not evil, truly.
But he has to eat, and that's what nature has given him.
All those poor little brownies and butter fairies.
Tsk, tsk. Look how they scream as they recognize their doom.
I HAVE TO SAVE THEM.
You really don't.
Yes, yes. Here we go indeed. Attack, poppet! **Attack!** Big or little, you can't go wrong!

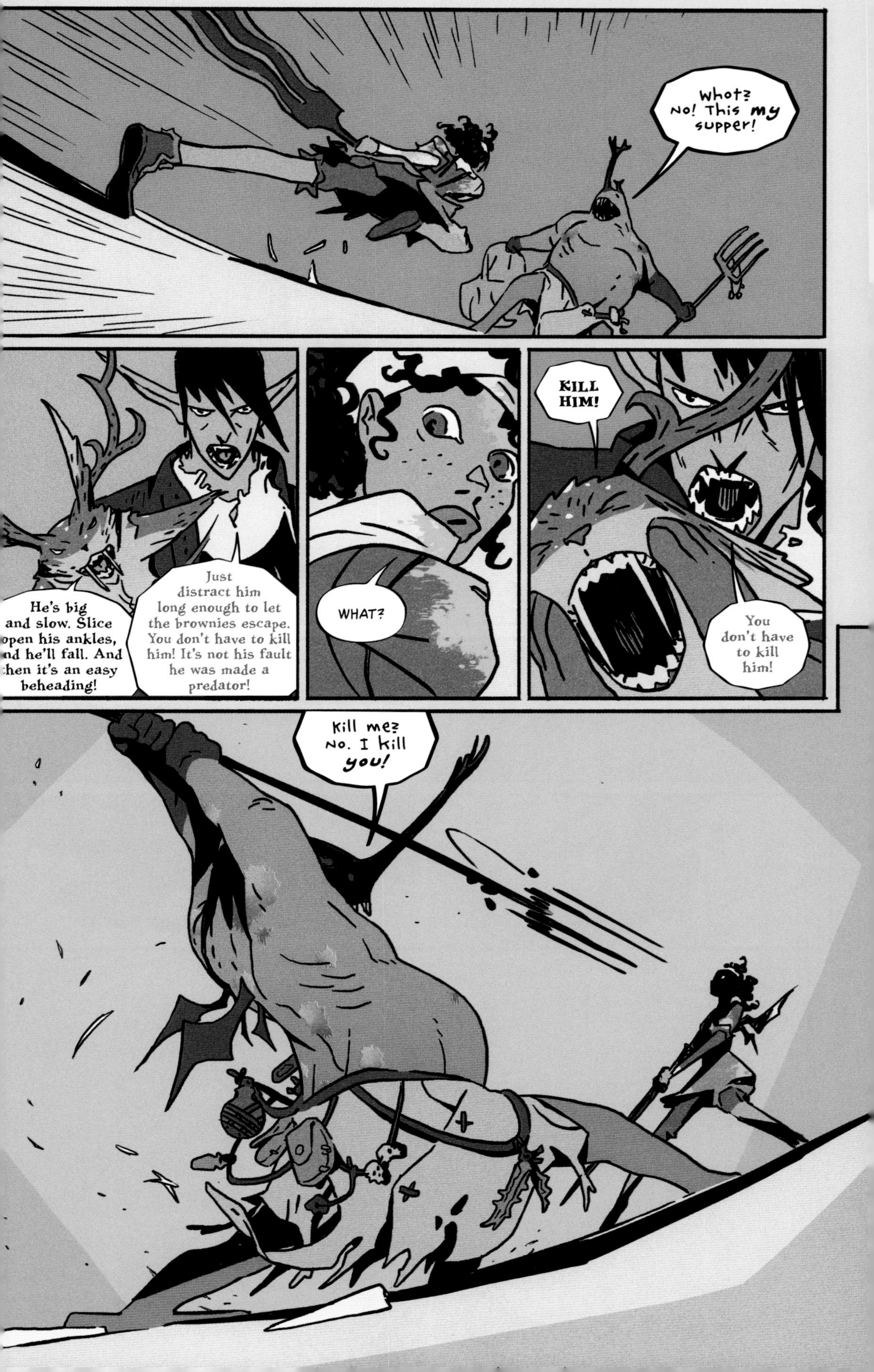
Whot? No! This my supper!
He's big and slow. Slice open his ankles, nd he'll fall. And hen it's an easy beheading!
Just distract him long enough to let the brownies escape. You don't have to kill him! It's not his fault he was made a predator!
WHAT?
KILL HIM!
You don't have to kill him!
Kill me? No. I kill you!

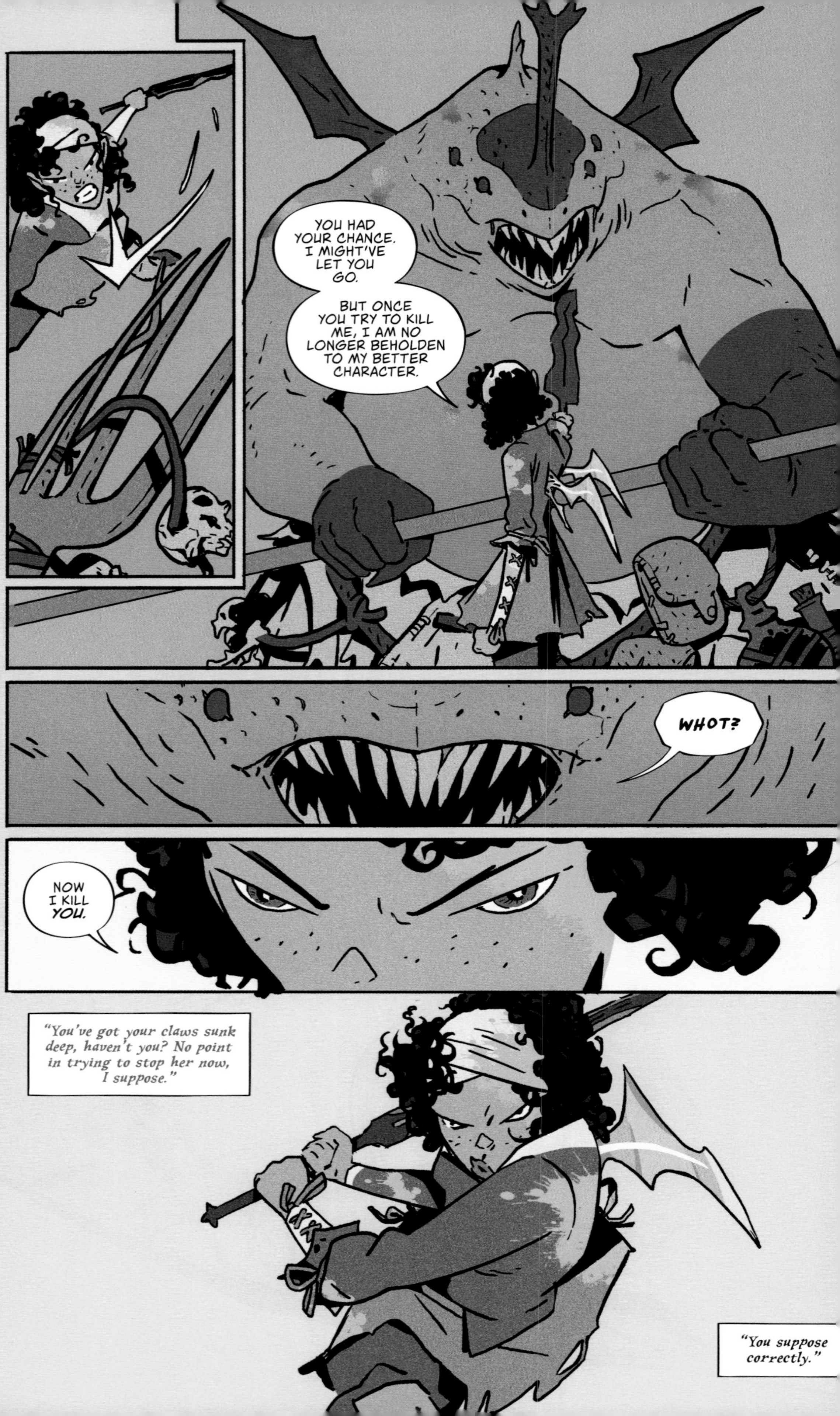
YOU HAD YOUR CHANCE. I MIGHT'VE LET YOU GO.
BUT ONCE YOU TRY TO KILL ME, I AM NO LONGER BEHOLDEN TO MY BETTER CHARACTER.
WHOT?
NOW I KILL *YOU.*
"You've got your claws sunk deep, haven't you? No point in trying to stop her now, I suppose."
"You suppose correctly."

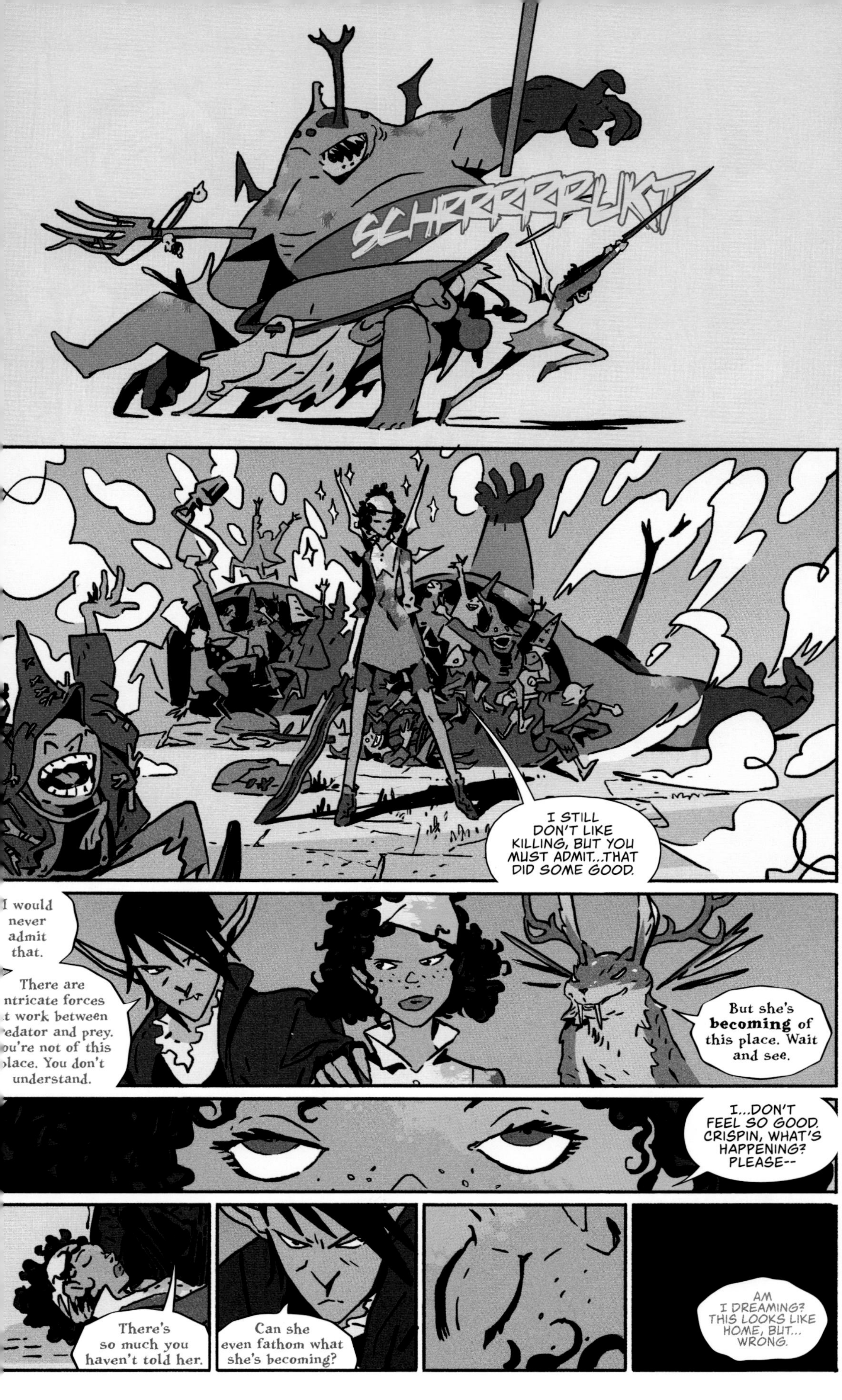
SCHRRRRRLKT
I STILL DON'T LIKE KILLING, BUT YOU MUST ADMIT...THAT DID SOME GOOD.
I would never admit that.
There are ntricate forces t work between edator and prey. ou're not of this lace. You don't understand.
But she's becoming of this place. Wait and see.
I...DON'T FEEL SO GOOD. CRISPIN, WHAT'S HAPPENING? PLEASE--
There's so much you haven't told her.
Can she even fathom what she's becoming?
AM I DREAMING? THIS LOOKS LIKE HOME, BUT... WRONG.

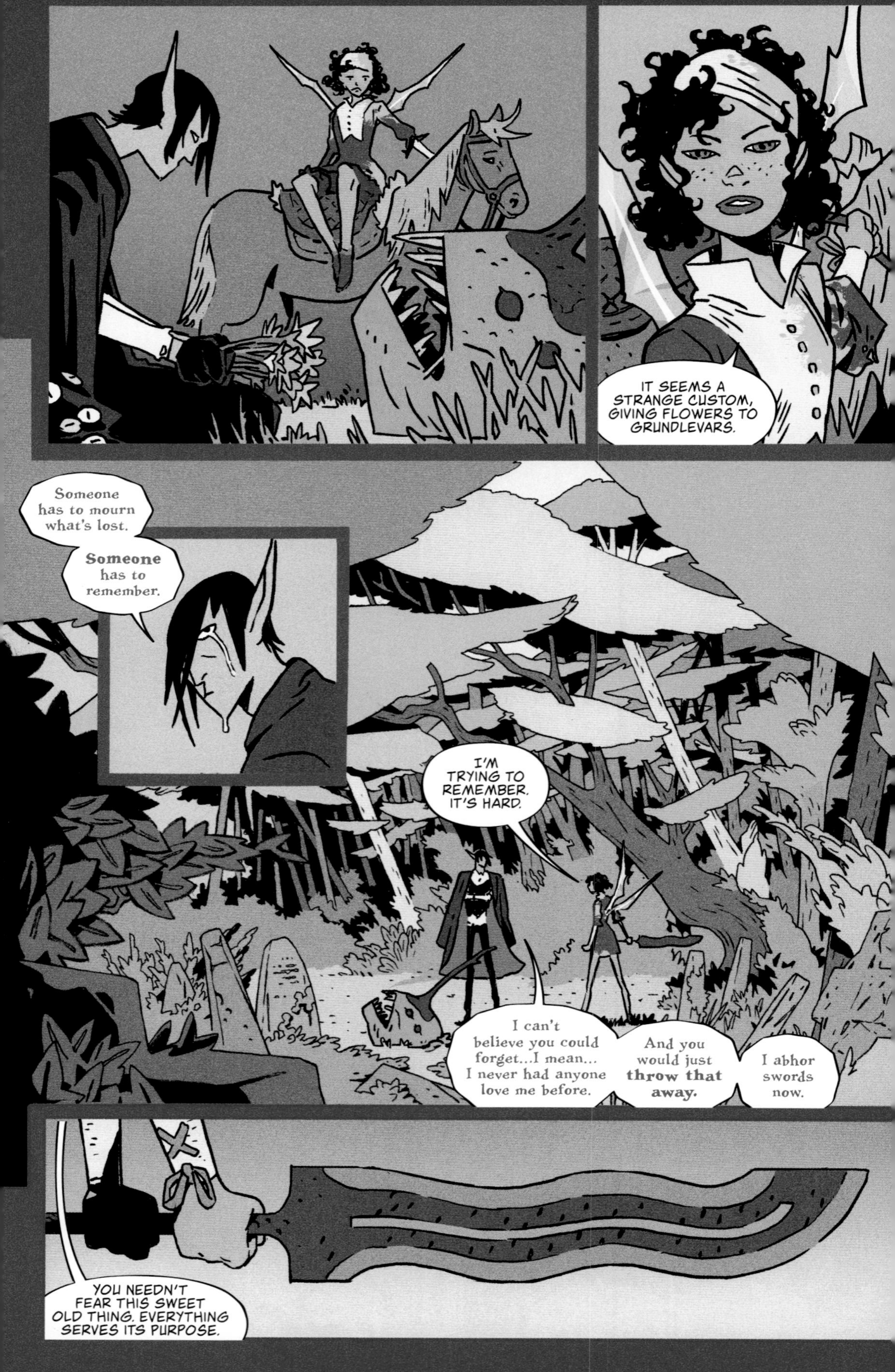
IT SEEMS A STRANGE CUSTOM, GIVING FLOWERS TO GRUNDLEVARS.
Someone has to mourn what's lost.
Someone has to remember.
I'M TRYING TO REMEMBER. IT'S HARD.
I can't believe you could forget...I mean... I never had anyone love me before.
And you would just **throw that away.**
I abhor swords now.
YOU NEEDN'T FEAR THIS SWEET OLD THING. EVERYTHING SERVES ITS PURPOSE.

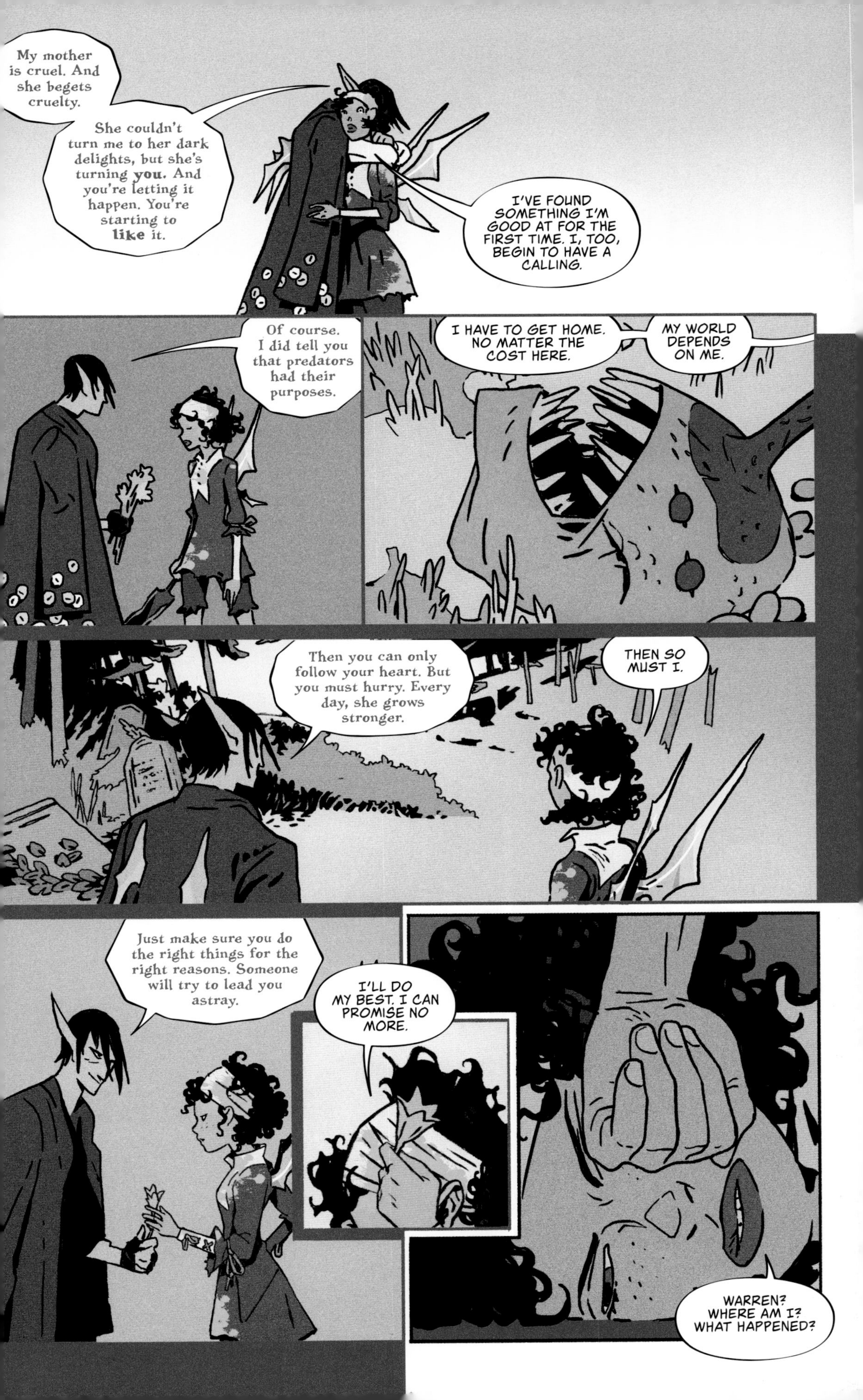
My mother is cruel. And she begets cruelty.
She couldn't turn me to her dark delights, but she's turning **you**. And you're letting it happen. You're starting to **like** it.
I'VE FOUND SOMETHING I'M GOOD AT FOR THE FIRST TIME. I, TOO, BEGIN TO HAVE A CALLING.
Of course. I did tell you that predators had their purposes.
I HAVE TO GET HOME. NO MATTER THE COST HERE.
MY WORLD DEPENDS ON ME.
Then you can only follow your heart. But you must hurry. Every day, she grows stronger.
THEN SO MUST I.
Just make sure you do the right things for the right reasons. Someone will try to lead you astray.
I'LL DO MY BEST. I CAN PROMISE NO MORE.
WARREN? WHERE AM I? WHAT HAPPENED?

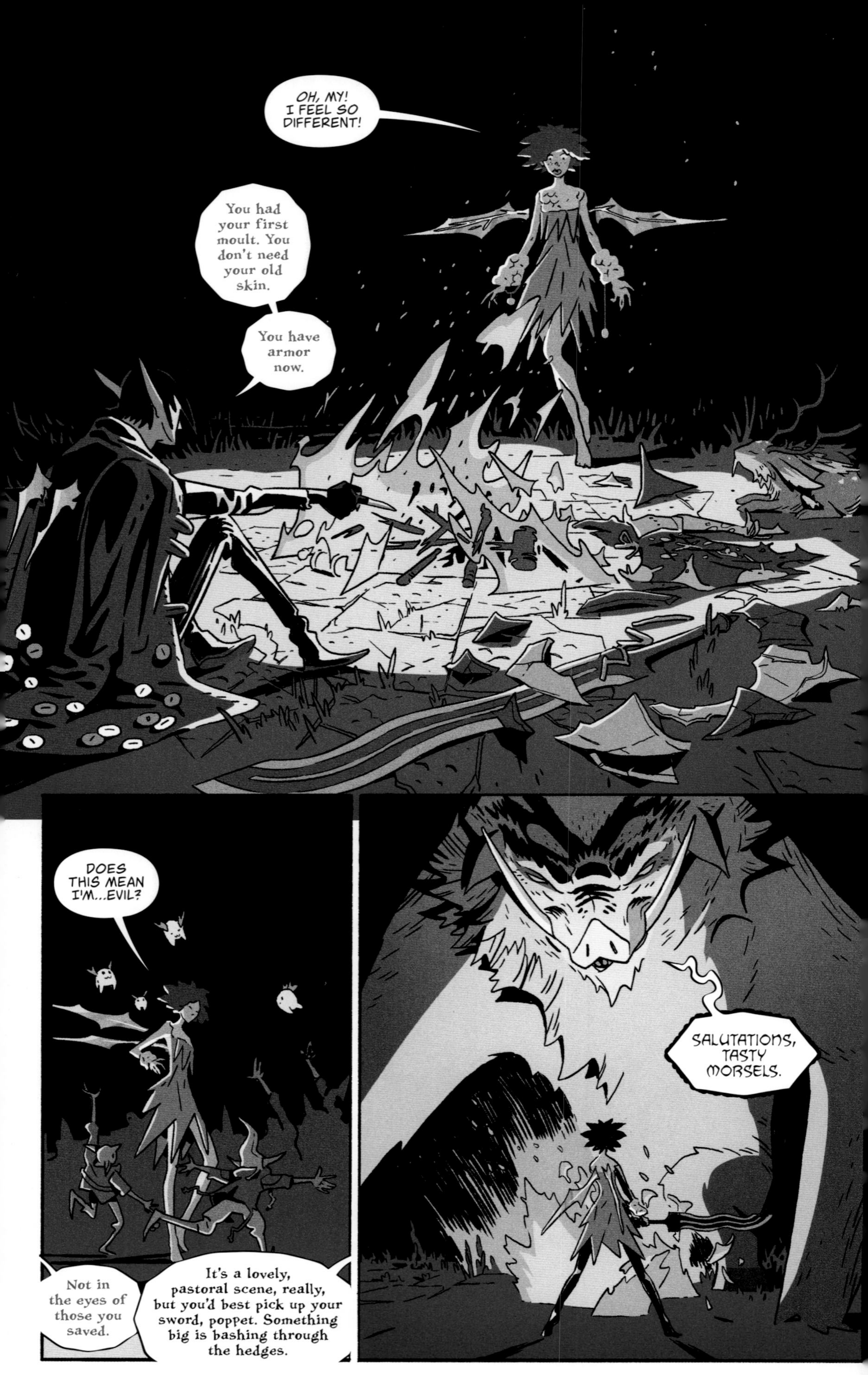
OH, MY! I FEEL SO DIFFERENT!
You had your first moult. You don't need your old skin.
You have armor now.
DOES THIS MEAN I'M...EVIL?
Not in the eyes of those you saved.
It's a lovely, pastoral scene, really, but you'd best pick up your sword, poppet. Something big is bashing through the hedges.
SALUTATIONS, TASTY MORSELS.

SPARROWHAWK #2 COVER BY
MIGUEL MERCADO

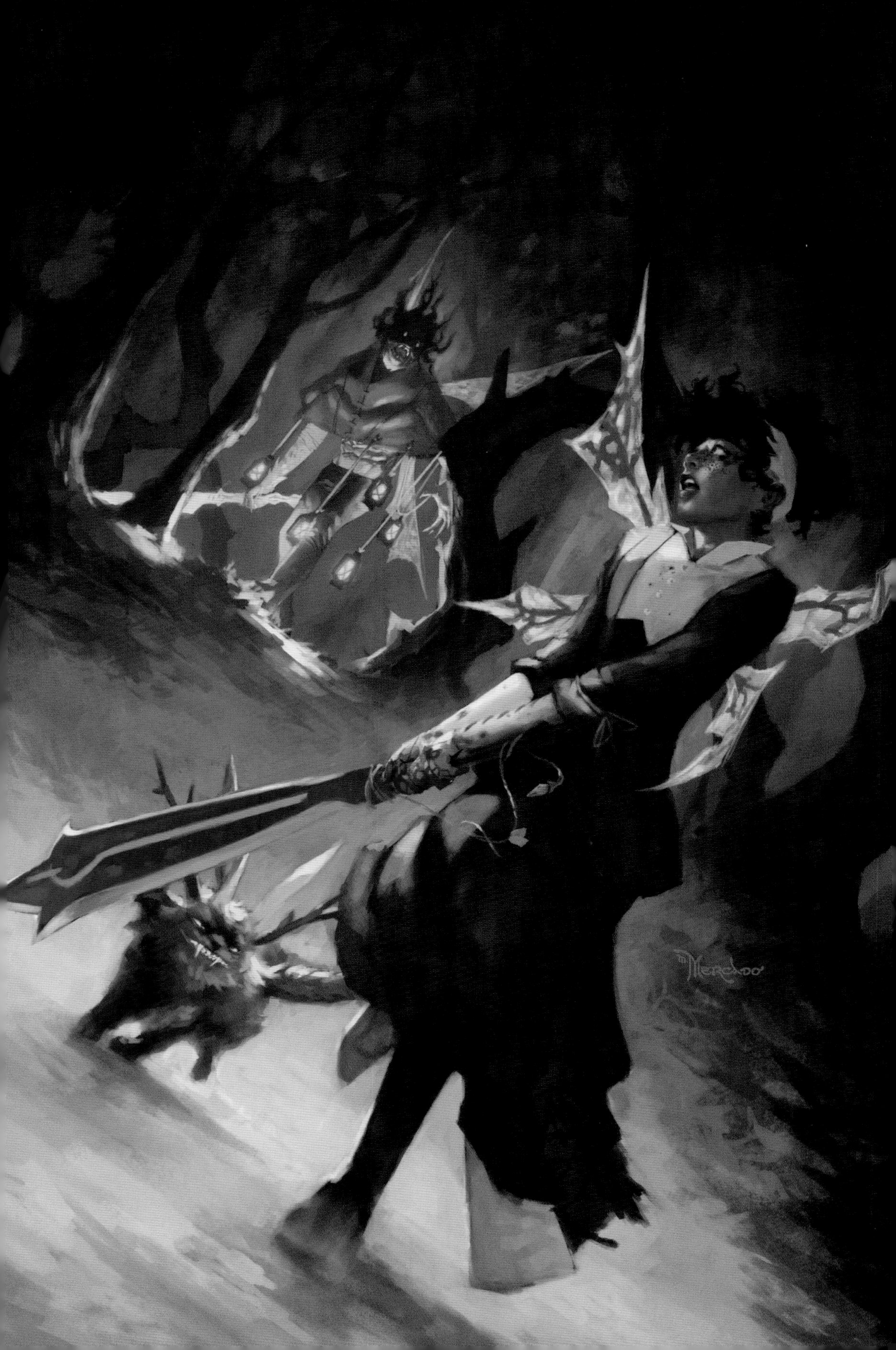

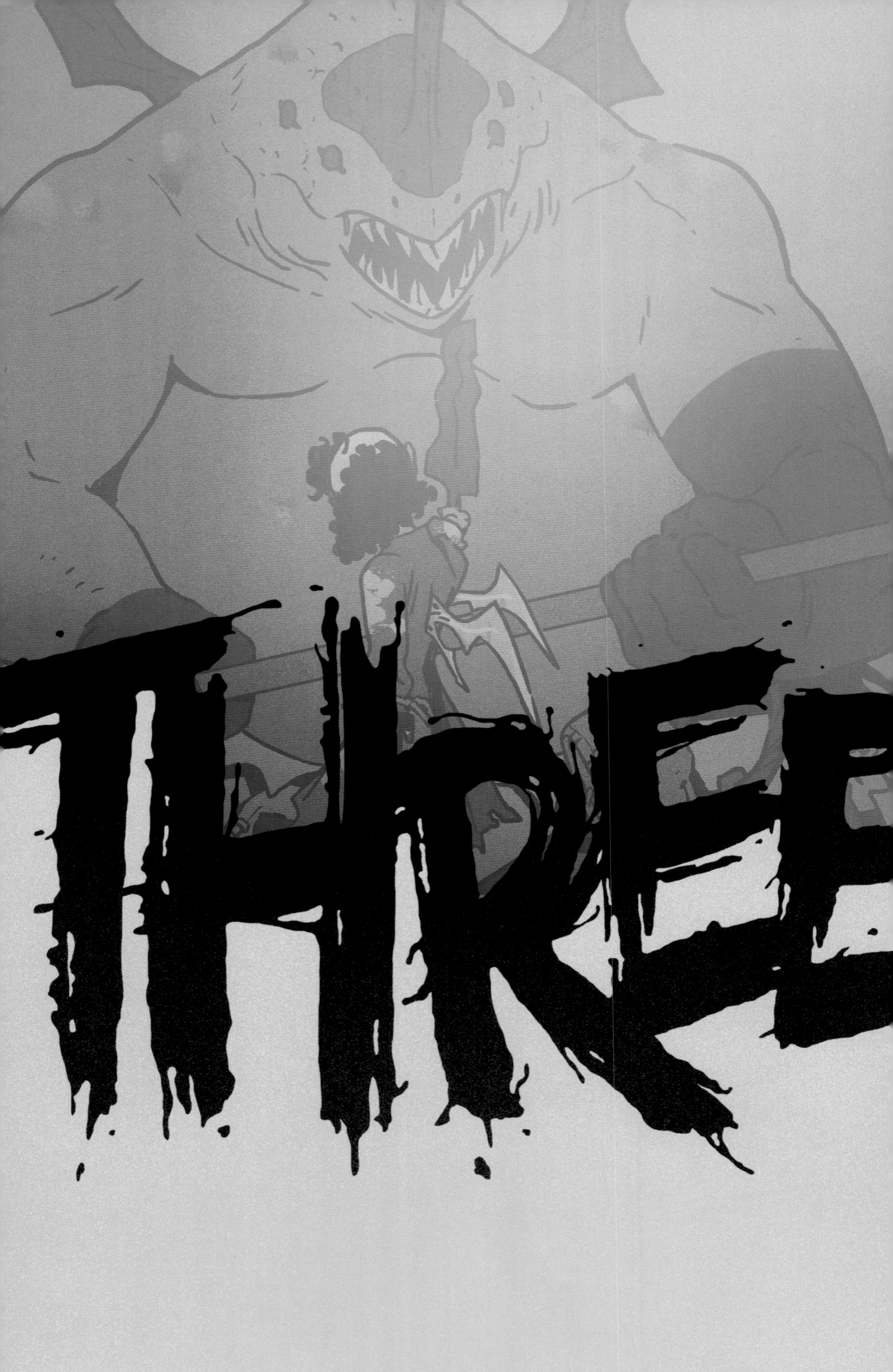
THRE

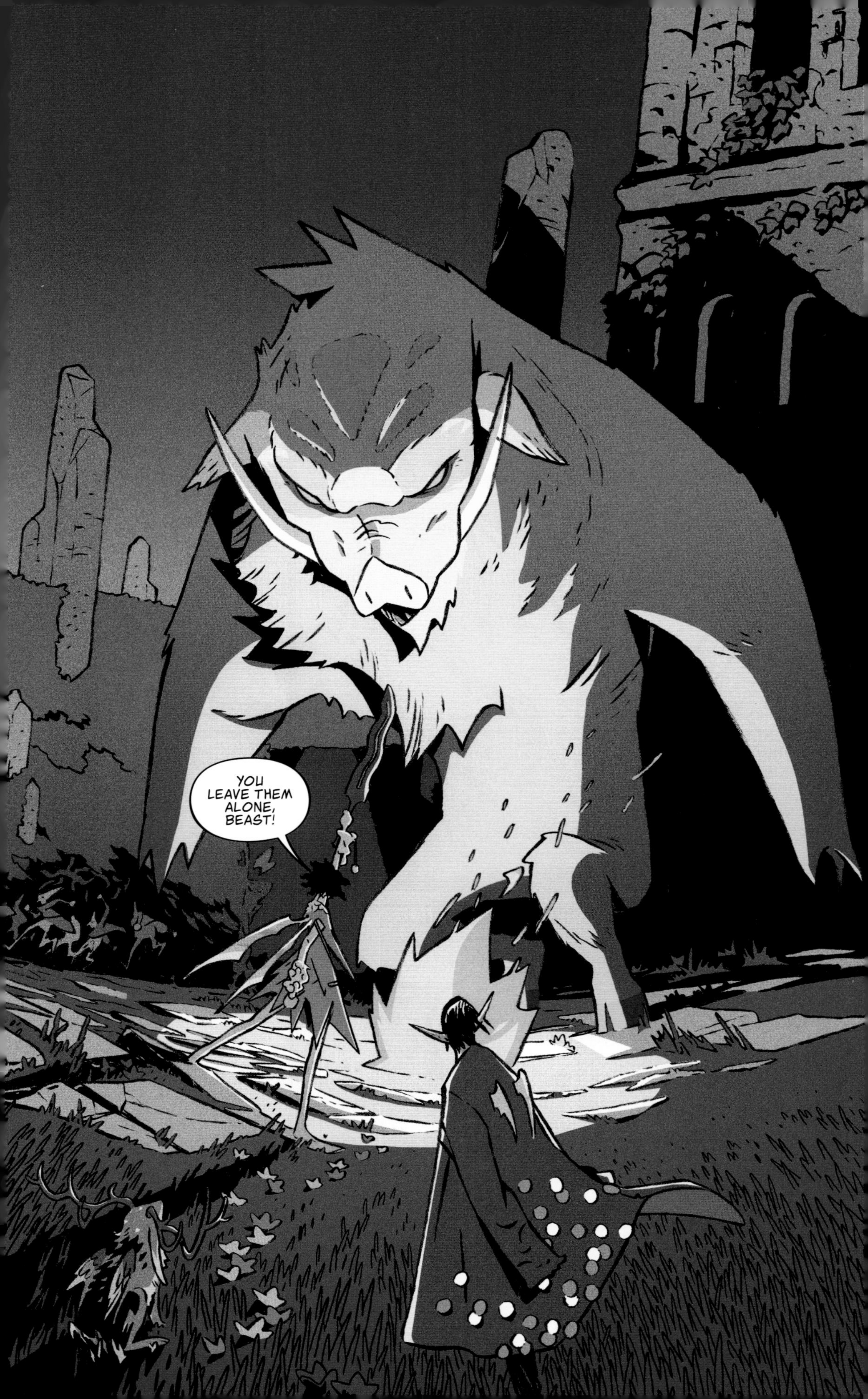
YOU LEAVE THEM ALONE, BEAST!

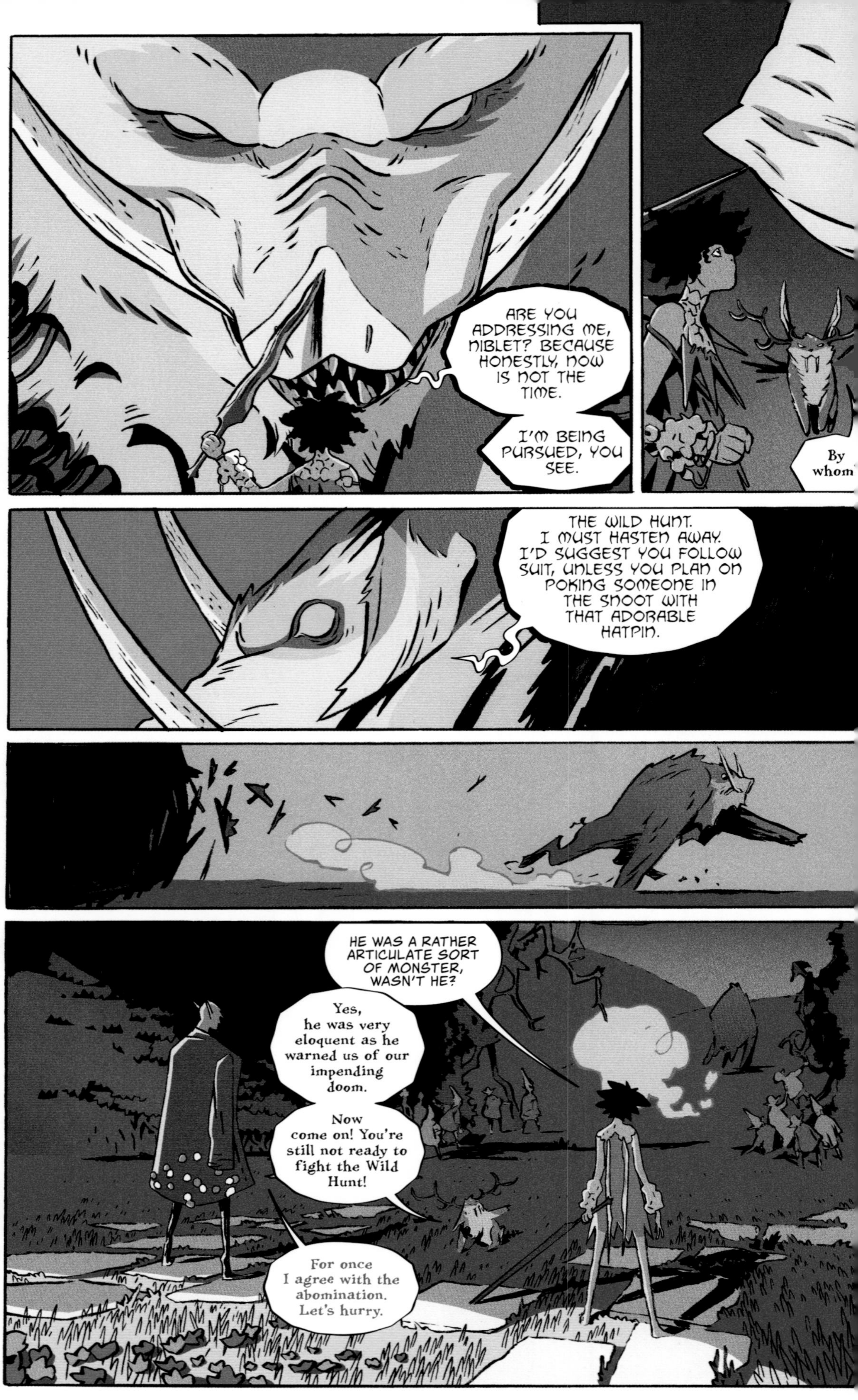
ARE YOU ADDRESSING ME, NIBLET? BECAUSE HONESTLY, NOW IS NOT THE TIME.
I'M BEING PURSUED, YOU SEE.
By whom
THE WILD HUNT. I MUST HASTEN AWAY. I'D SUGGEST YOU FOLLOW SUIT, UNLESS YOU PLAN ON POKING SOMEONE IN THE SNOOT WITH THAT ADORABLE HATPIN.
HE WAS A RATHER ARTICULATE SORT OF MONSTER, WASN'T HE?
Yes, he was very eloquent as he warned us of our impending doom.
Now come on! You're still not ready to fight the Wild Hunt!
For once I agree with the abomination. Let's hurry.

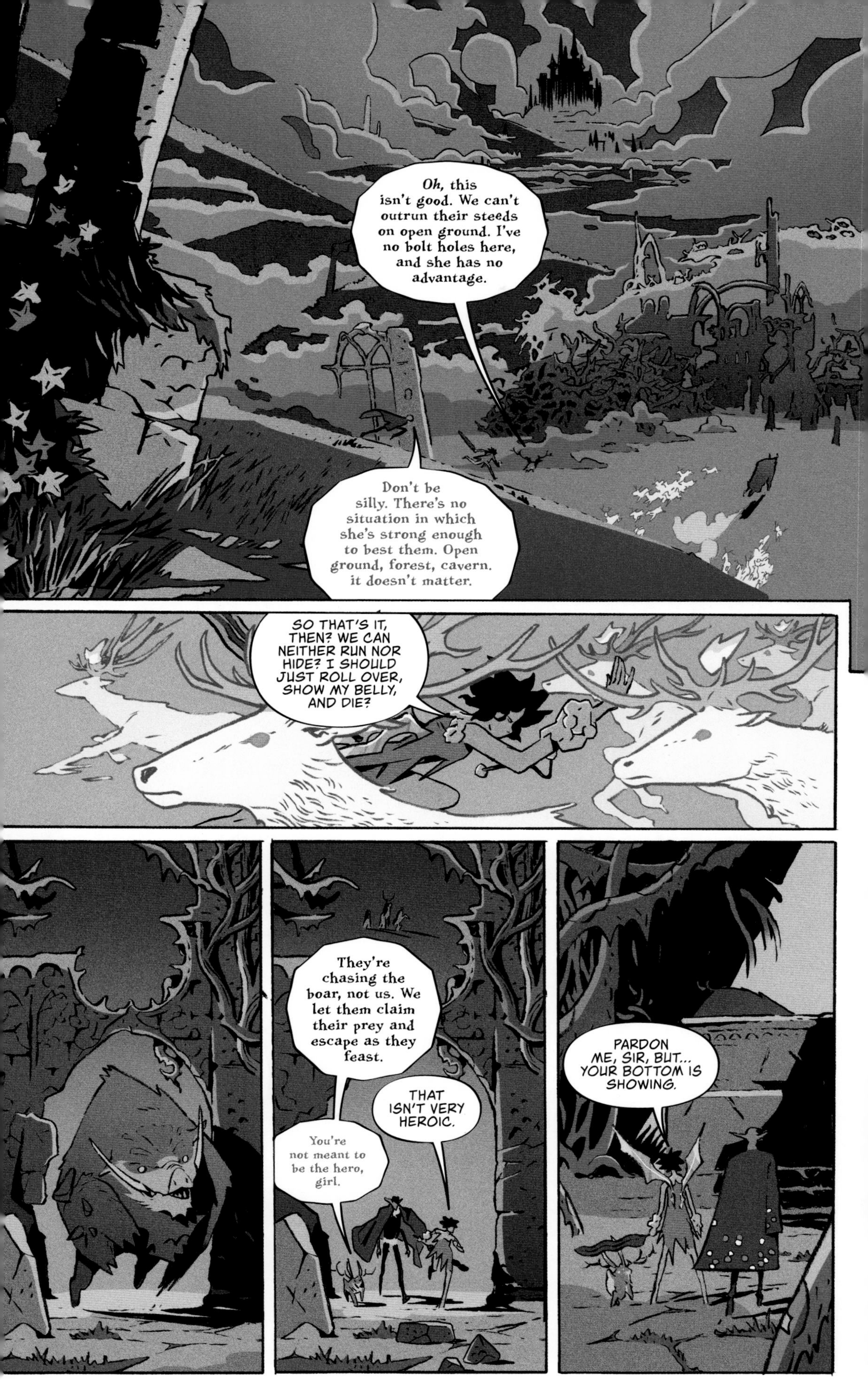
Oh, this isn't good. We can't outrun their steeds on open ground. I've no bolt holes here, and she has no advantage.
Don't be silly. There's no situation in which she's strong enough to best them. Open ground, forest, cavern. it doesn't matter.
SO THAT'S IT, THEN? WE CAN NEITHER RUN NOR HIDE? I SHOULD JUST ROLL OVER, SHOW MY BELLY, AND DIE?
They're chasing the boar, not us. We let them claim their prey and escape as they feast.
THAT ISN'T VERY HEROIC.
You're not meant to be the hero, girl.
PARDON ME, SIR, BUT... YOUR BOTTOM IS SHOWING.

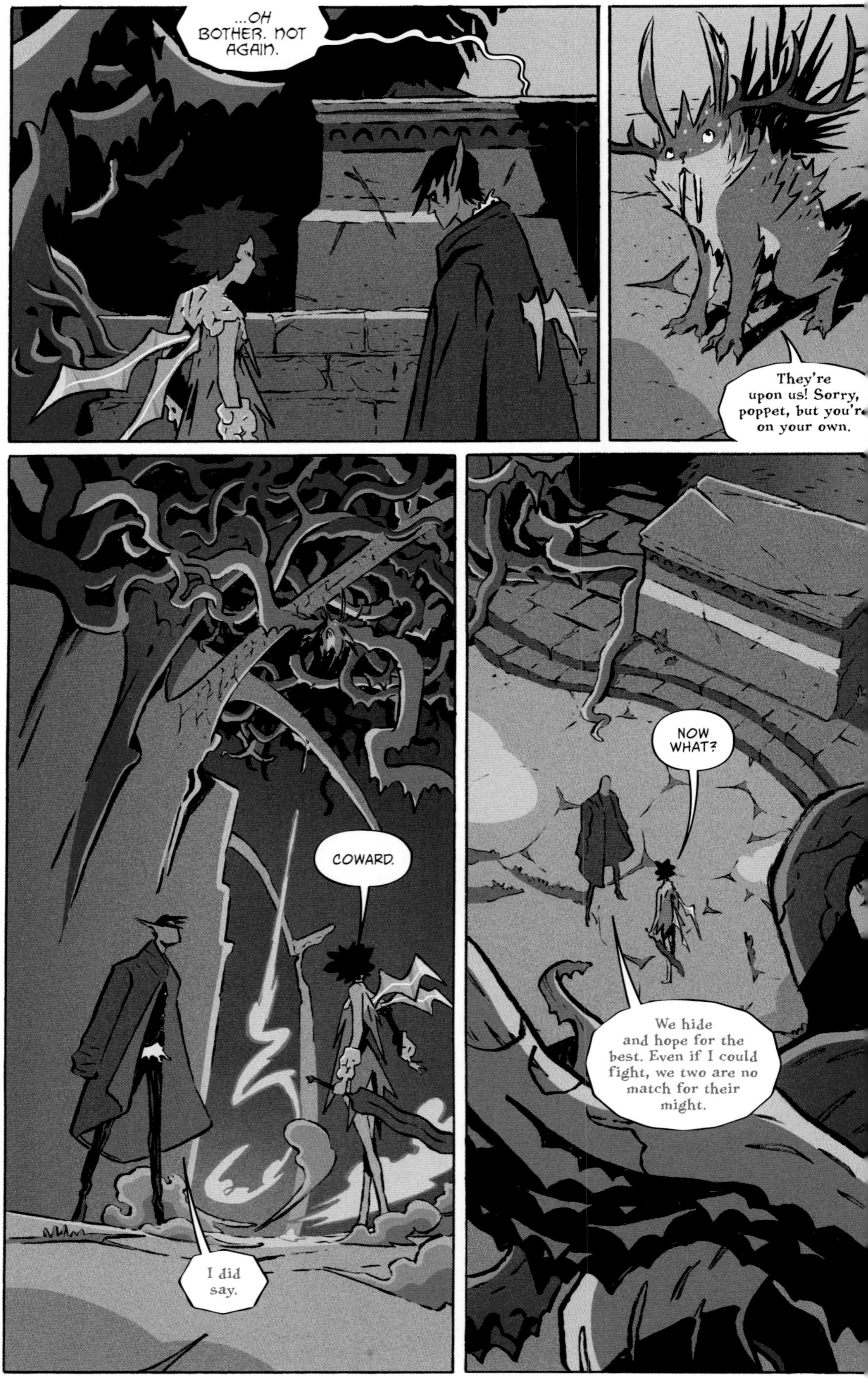
...OH BOTHER. NOT AGAIN.
They're upon us! Sorry, poppet, but you're on your own.
COWARD.
I did say.
NOW WHAT?
We hide and hope for the best. Even if I could fight, we two are no match for their might.

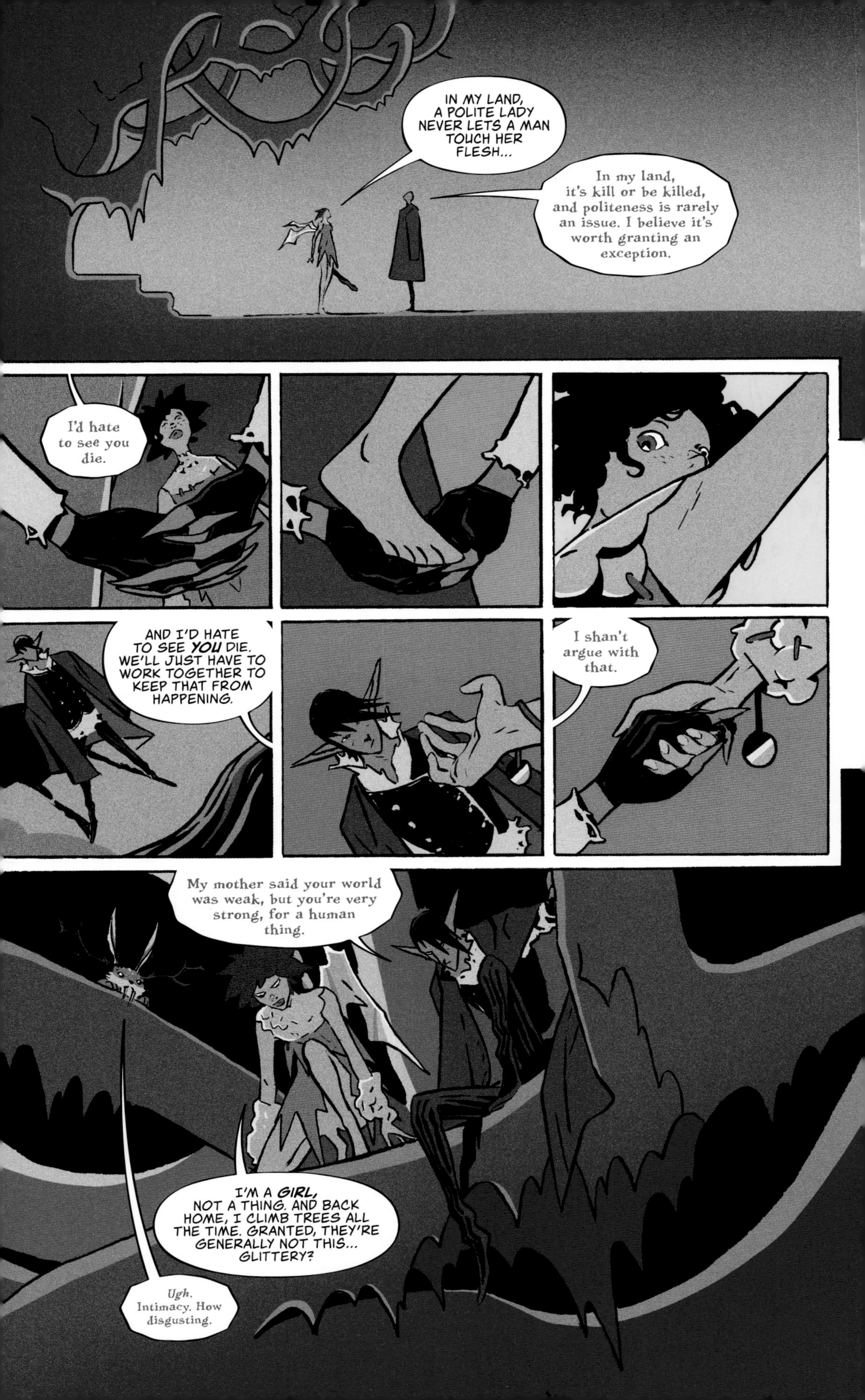
IN MY LAND, A POLITE LADY NEVER LETS A MAN TOUCH HER FLESH...
In my land, it's kill or be killed, and politeness is rarely an issue. I believe it's worth granting an exception.
I'd hate to see you die.
AND I'D HATE TO SEE YOU DIE. WE'LL JUST HAVE TO WORK TOGETHER TO KEEP THAT FROM HAPPENING.
I shan't argue with that.
My mother said your world was weak, but you're very strong, for a human thing.
I'M A GIRL, NOT A THING. AND BACK HOME, I CLIMB TREES ALL THE TIME. GRANTED, THEY'RE GENERALLY NOT THIS... GLITTERY?
Ugh. Intimacy. How disgusting.

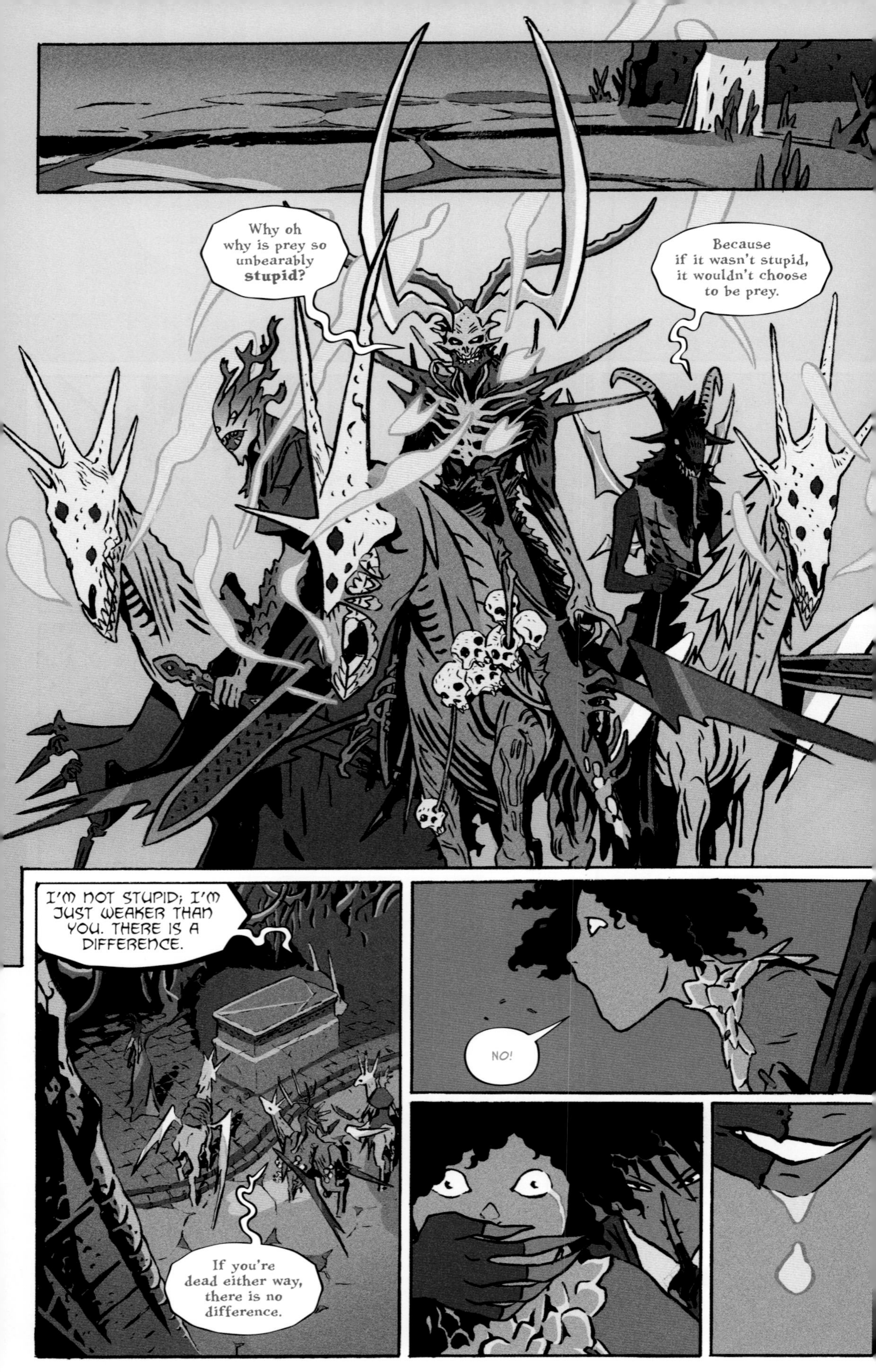
Why oh why is prey so unbearably **stupid?**
Because if it wasn't stupid, it wouldn't choose to be prey.
I'M NOT STUPID; I'M JUST WEAKER THAN YOU. THERE IS A DIFFERENCE.
If you're dead either way, there is no difference.
NO!

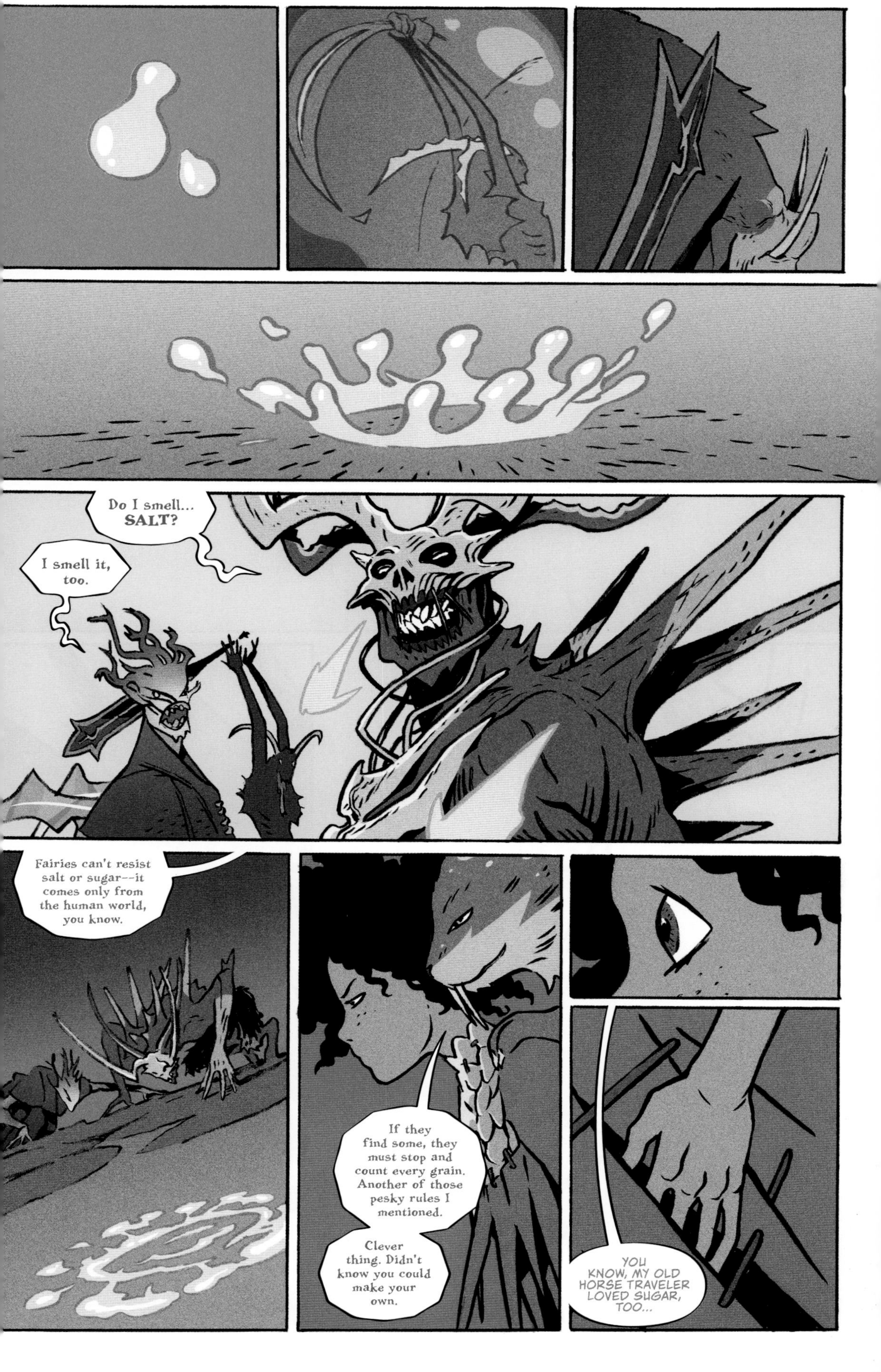
Do I smell... SALT?
I smell it, too.
Fairies can't resist salt or sugar--it comes only from the human world, you know.
If they find some, they must stop and count every grain. Another of those pesky rules I mentioned.
Clever thing. Didn't know you could make your own.
YOU KNOW, MY OLD HORSE TRAVELER LOVED SUGAR, TOO...

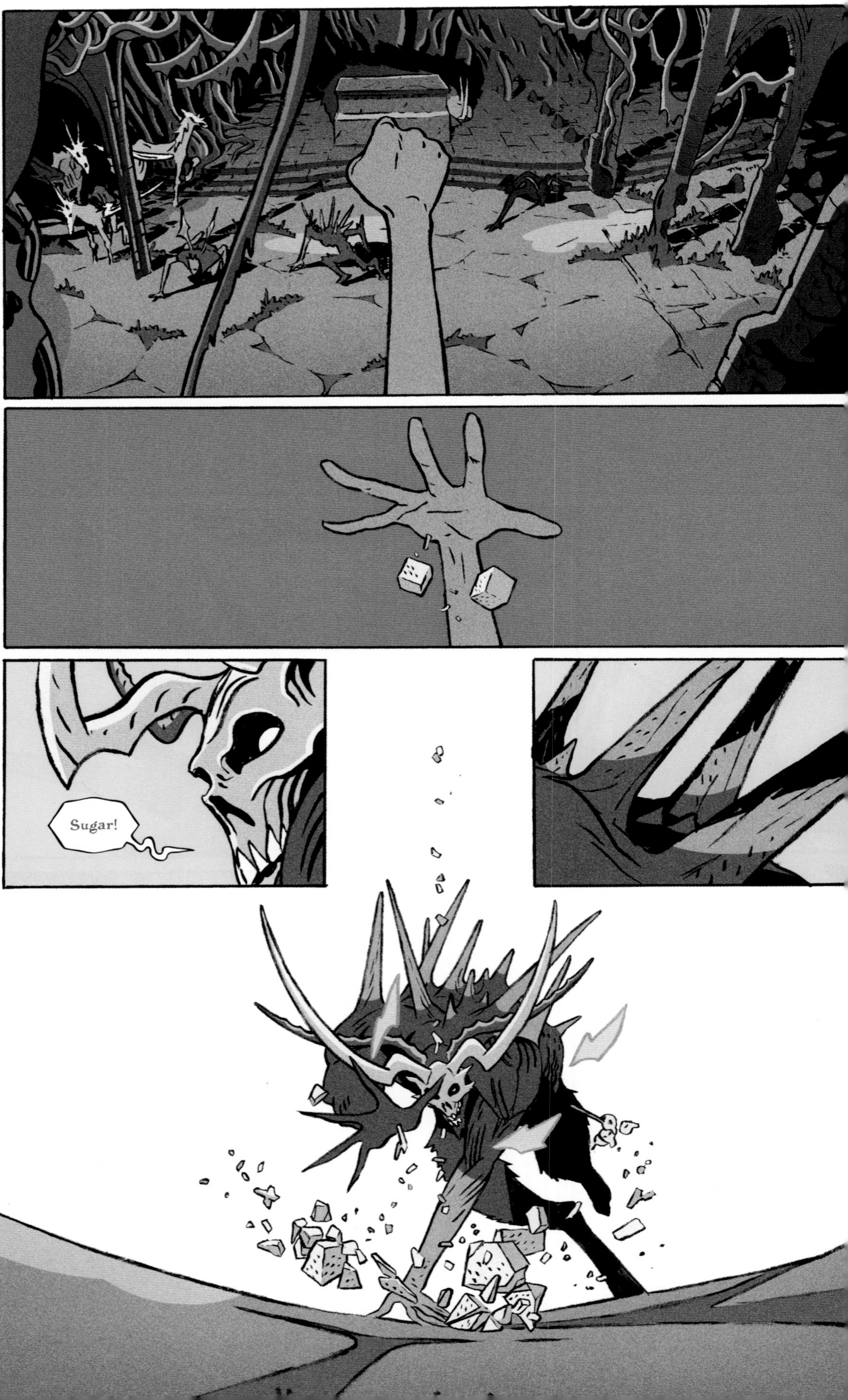
Sugar!

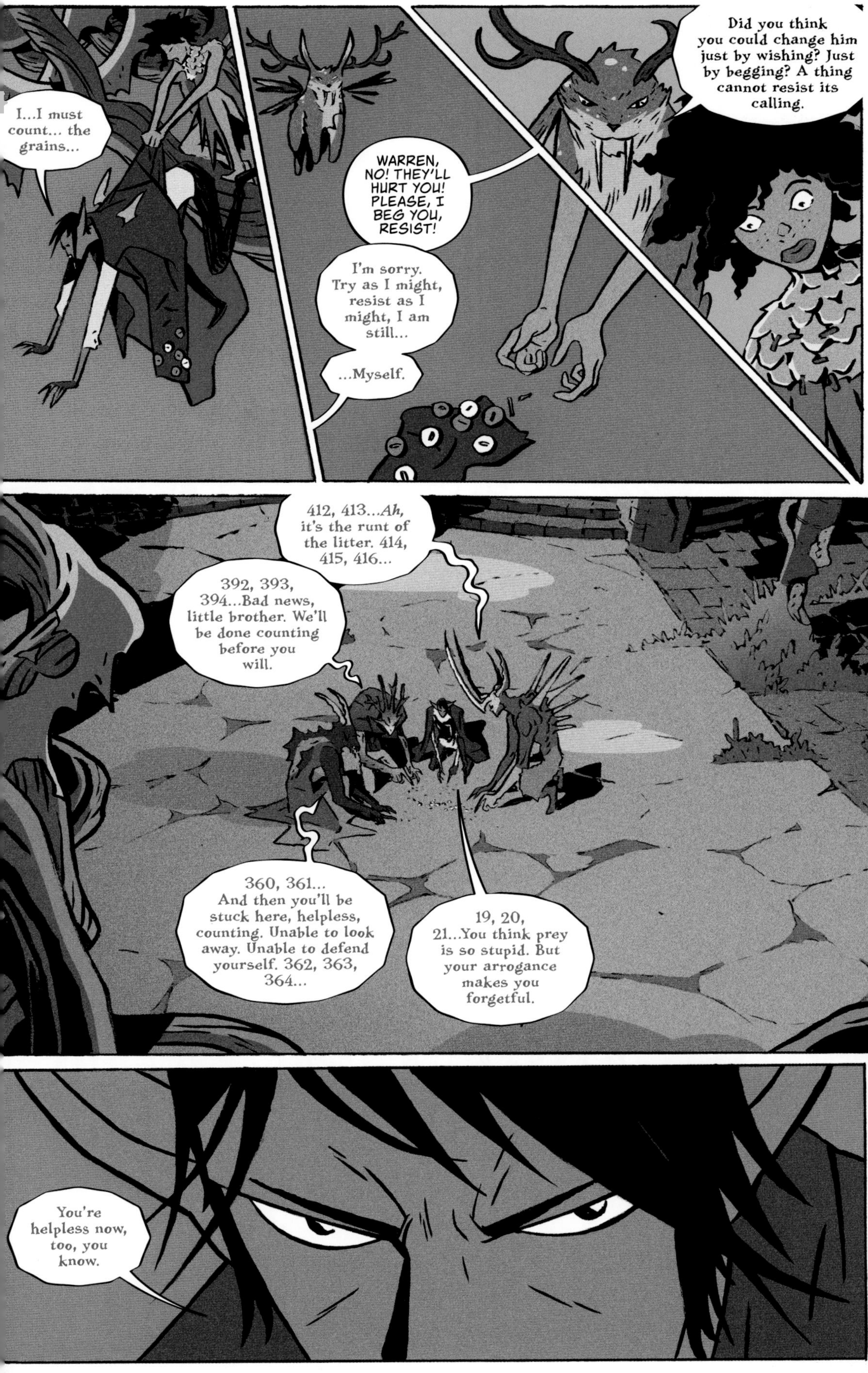
I...I must count... the grains...
WARREN, NO! THEY'LL HURT YOU! PLEASE, I BEG YOU, RESIST!
I'm sorry. Try as I might, resist as I might, I am still...
...Myself.
Did you think you could change him just by wishing? Just by begging? A thing cannot resist its calling.
412, 413...*Ah,* it's the runt of the litter. 414, 415, 416...
392, 393, 394...Bad news, little brother. We'll be done counting before you will.
360, 361... And then you'll be stuck here, helpless, counting. Unable to look away. Unable to defend yourself. 362, 363, 364...
19, 20, 21...You think prey is so stupid. But your arrogance makes you forgetful.
You're helpless now, too, you know.

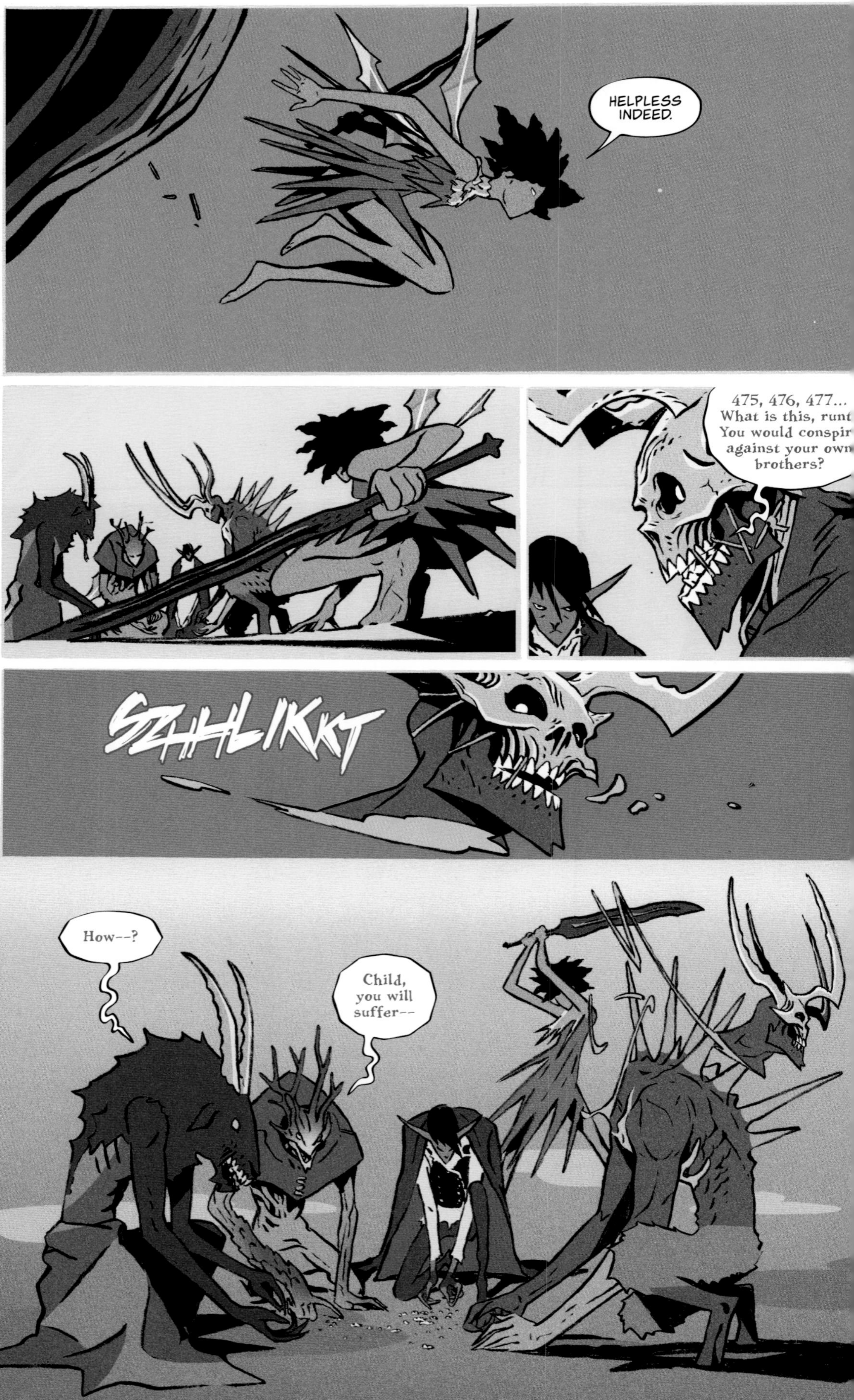
HELPLESS INDEED.
475, 476, 477... What is this, runt You would conspir against your own brothers?
SZHHLIKKT
How--?
Child, you will suffer--

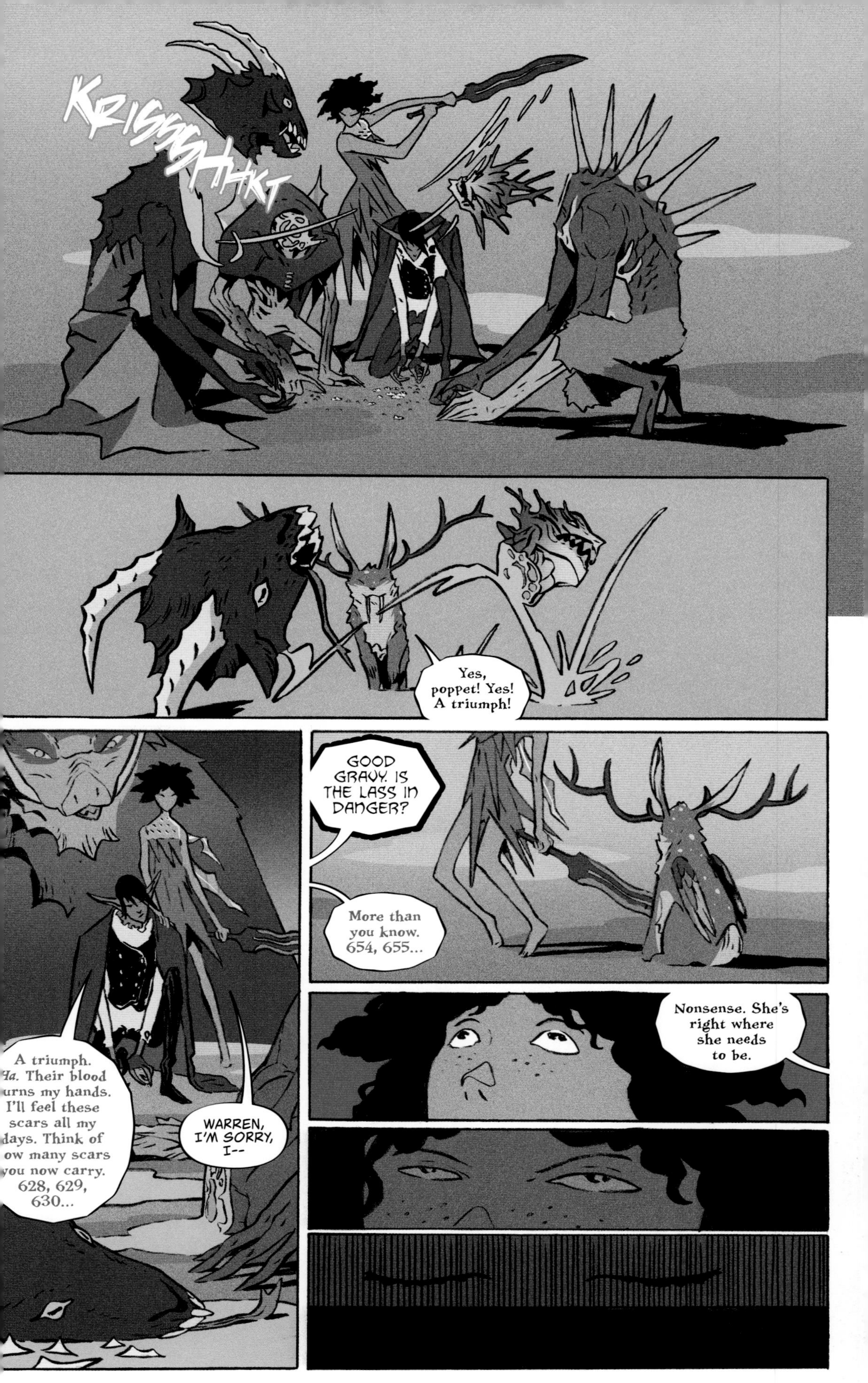

Yes, poppet! Yes! A triumph!
GOOD GRAVY. IS THE LASS IN DANGER?
More than you know. 654, 655...
A triumph. *Ha.* Their blood urns my hands. I'll feel these scars all my days. Think of ow many scars you now carry. 628, 629, 630...
WARREN, I'M SORRY, I--
Nonsense. She's right where she needs to be.

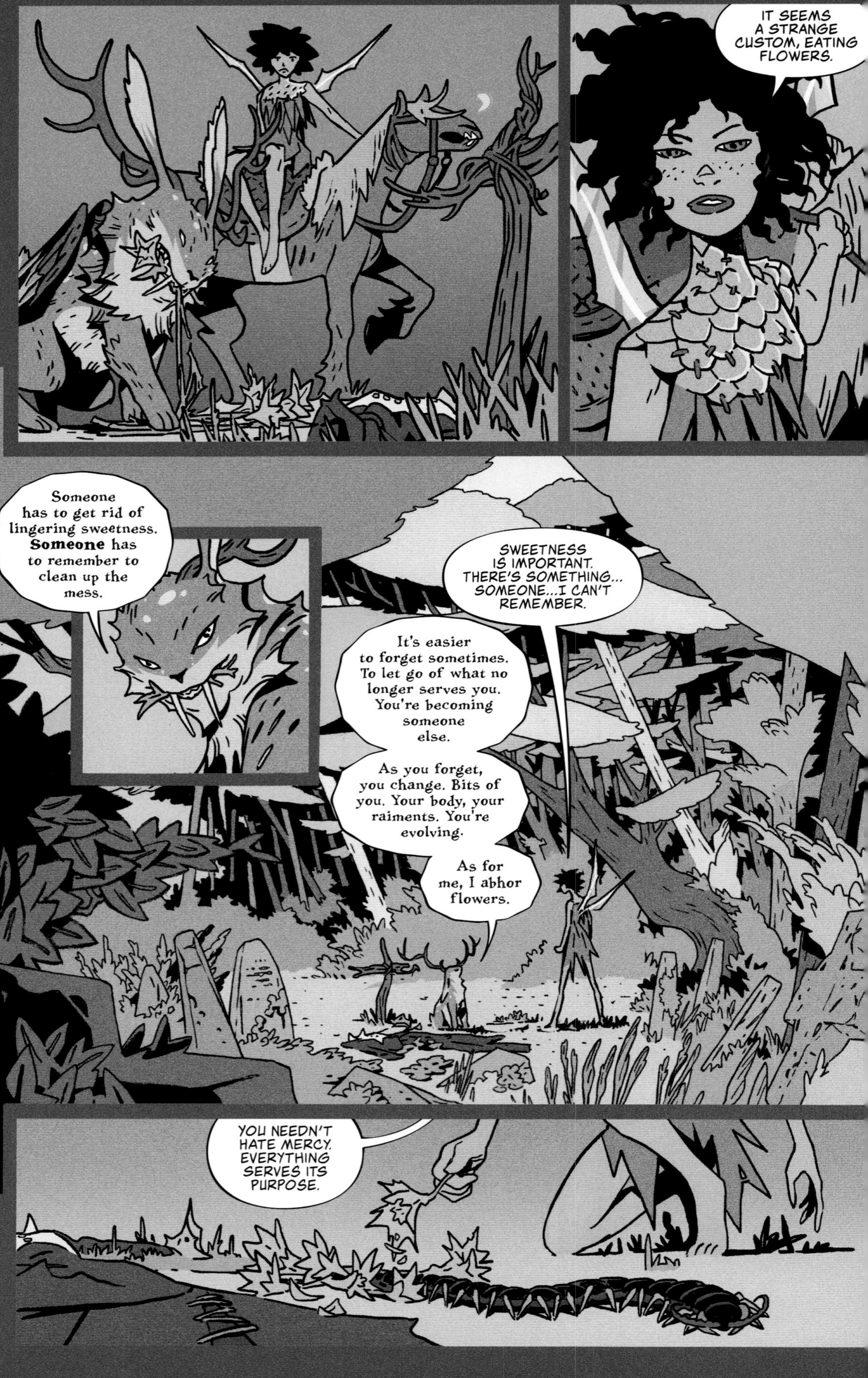
IT SEEMS A STRANGE CUSTOM, EATING FLOWERS.
Someone has to get rid of lingering sweetness. **Someone** has to remember to clean up the mess.
SWEETNESS IS IMPORTANT. THERE'S SOMETHING... SOMEONE...I CAN'T REMEMBER.
It's easier to forget sometimes. To let go of what no longer serves you. You're becoming someone else.
As you forget, you change. Bits of you. Your body, your raiments. You're evolving.
As for me, I abhor flowers.
YOU NEEDN'T HATE MERCY. EVERYTHING SERVES ITS PURPOSE.

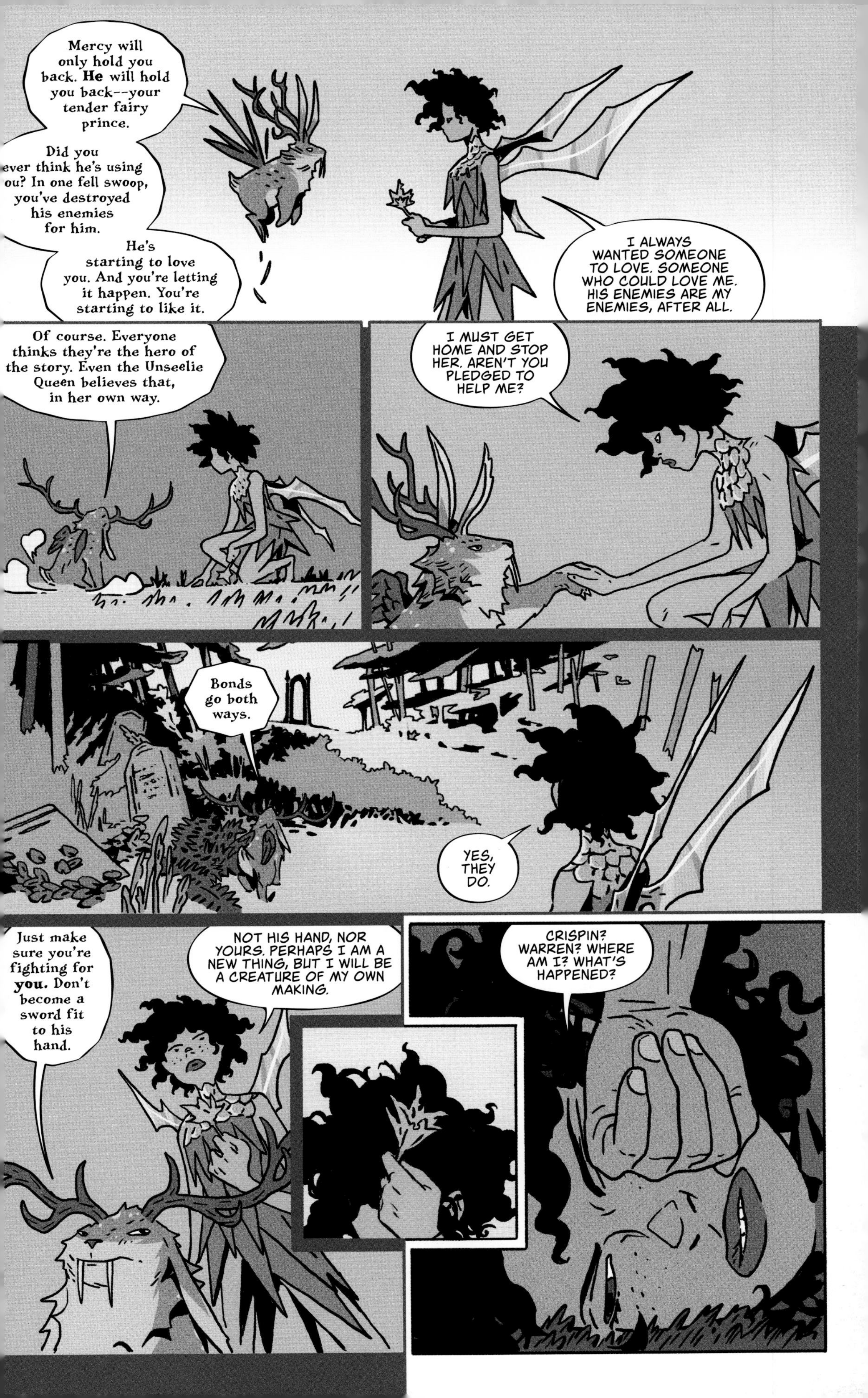

Mercy will only hold you back. **He** will hold you back--your tender fairy prince.
Did you ever think he's using ou? In one fell swoop, you've destroyed his enemies for him.
He's starting to love you. And you're letting it happen. You're starting to like it.
I ALWAYS WANTED SOMEONE TO LOVE. SOMEONE WHO COULD LOVE ME. HIS ENEMIES ARE MY ENEMIES, AFTER ALL.
Of course. Everyone thinks they're the hero of the story. Even the Unseelie Queen believes that, in her own way.
I MUST GET HOME AND STOP HER. AREN'T YOU PLEDGED TO HELP ME?
Bonds go both ways.
YES, THEY DO.
Just make sure you're fighting for **you.** Don't become a sword fit to his hand.
NOT HIS HAND, NOR YOURS. PERHAPS I AM A NEW THING, BUT I WILL BE A CREATURE OF MY OWN MAKING.
CRISPIN? WARREN? WHERE AM I? WHAT'S HAPPENED?

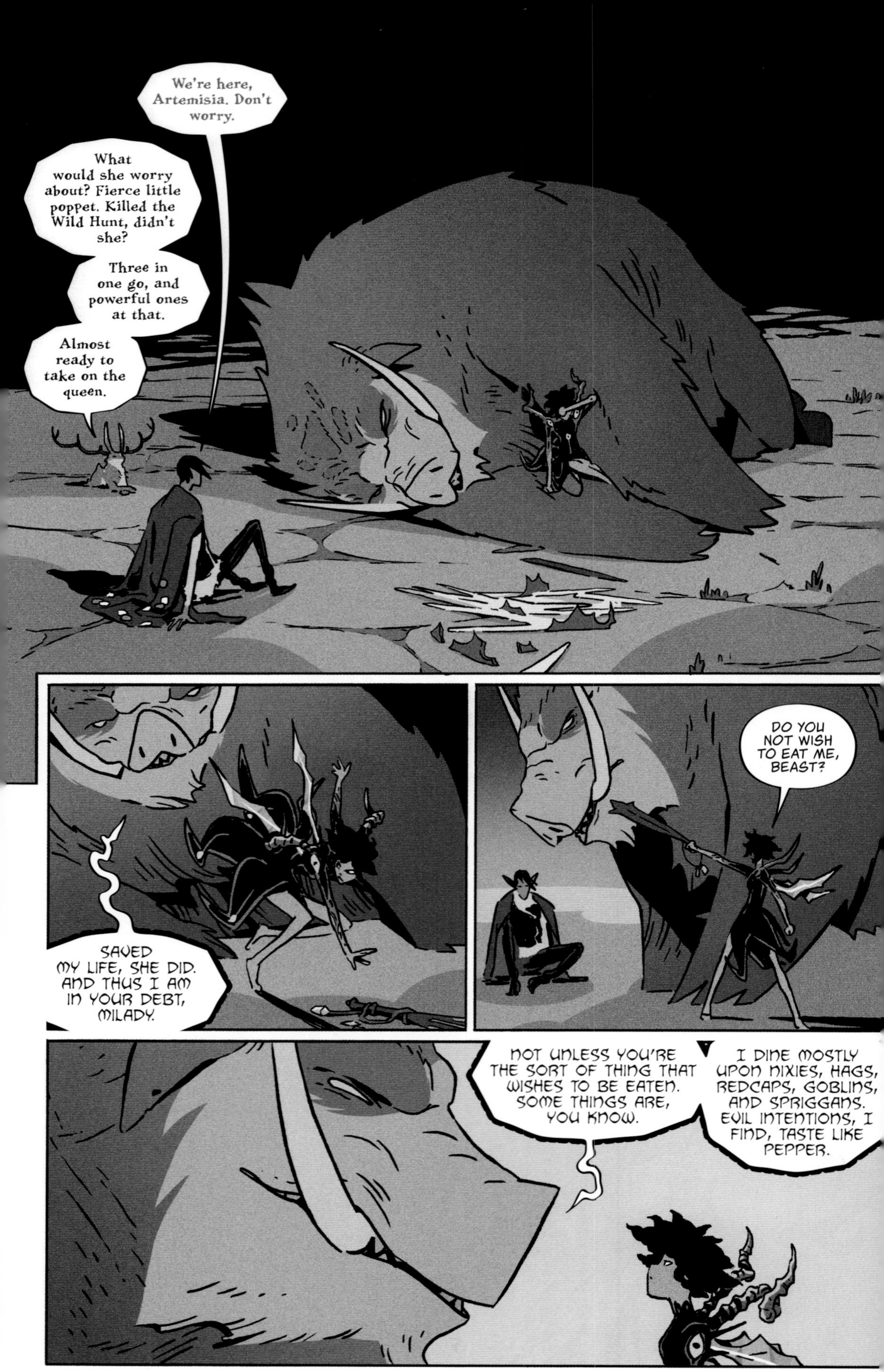
What would she worry about? Fierce little poppet. Killed the Wild Hunt, didn't she?
Three in one go, and powerful ones at that.
Almost ready to take on the queen.
We're here, Artemisia. Don't worry.
SAVED MY LIFE, SHE DID. AND THUS I AM IN YOUR DEBT, MILADY.
DO YOU NOT WISH TO EAT ME, BEAST?
NOT UNLESS YOU'RE THE SORT OF THING THAT WISHES TO BE EATEN. SOME THINGS ARE, YOU KNOW.
I DINE MOSTLY UPON NIXIES, HAGS, REDCAPS, GOBLINS, AND SPRIGGANS. EVIL INTENTIONS, I FIND, TASTE LIKE PEPPER.

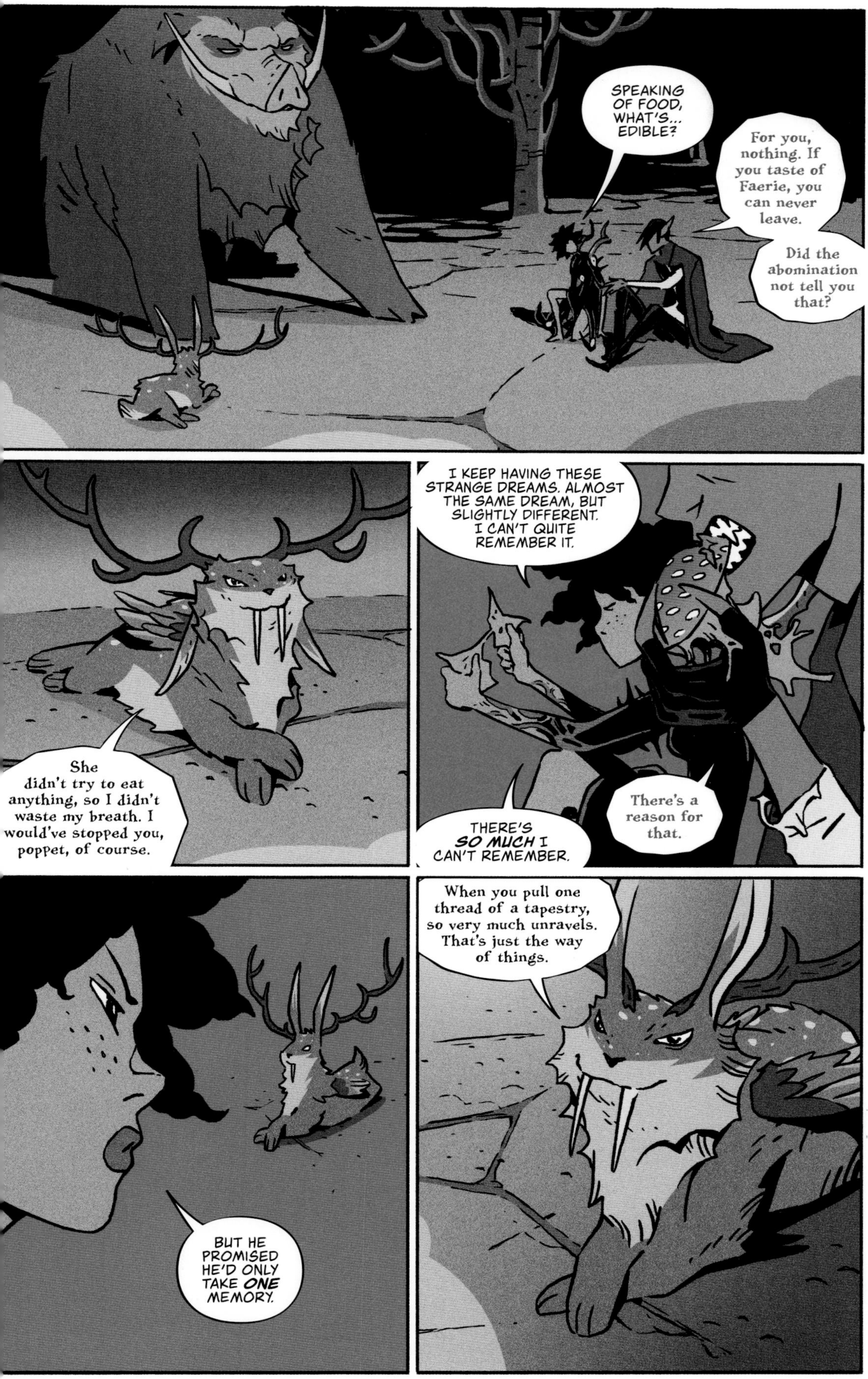
SPEAKING OF FOOD, WHAT'S... EDIBLE?
For you, nothing. If you taste of Faerie, you can never leave.
Did the abomination not tell you that?
She didn't try to eat anything, so I didn't waste my breath. I would've stopped you, poppet, of course.
I KEEP HAVING THESE STRANGE DREAMS. ALMOST THE SAME DREAM, BUT SLIGHTLY DIFFERENT. I CAN'T QUITE REMEMBER IT.
THERE'S *SO MUCH* I CAN'T REMEMBER.
There's a reason for that.
BUT HE PROMISED HE'D ONLY TAKE *ONE* MEMORY.
When you pull one thread of a tapestry, so very much unravels. That's just the way of things.

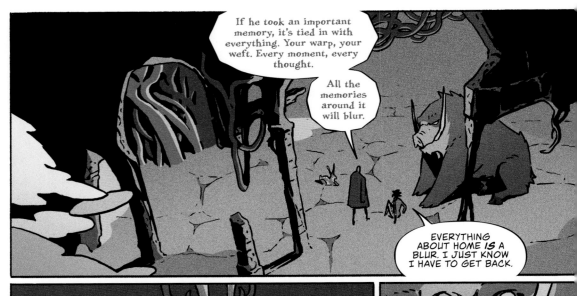

If he took an important memory, it's tied in with everything. Your warp, your weft. Every moment, every thought.

All the memories around it will blur.

EVERYTHING ABOUT HOME *IS* A BLUR. I JUST KNOW I HAVE TO GET BACK.

Like most things, the mirror will appear when you're ready.

The Wild Hunt brought you much glamour and power, but not enough. Now that you're strong, we should head toward the castle.

Many things to kill, over that way.

Ugh! Not the castle!

UGH! NOT THE CASTLE!

WHAT'S WRONG WITH THE CASTLE?

It's the seat of my mother's power. Everything around it is poisoned.

This thing is the least of her abominations.

Somebody has some issues with mummy!

I don't like you. Why would I want to be around things that are **worse** than you?

This is a bad idea.

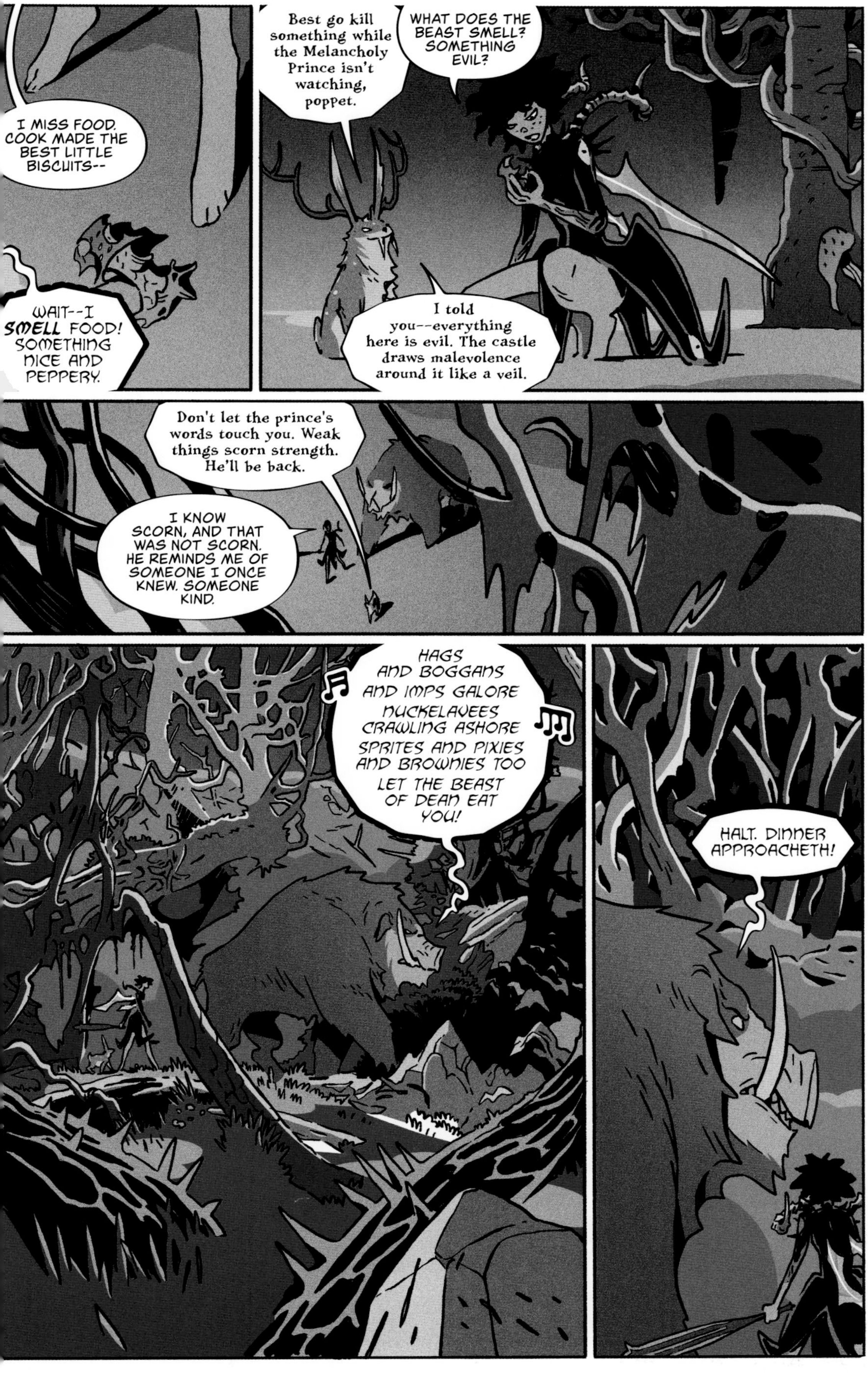
I MISS FOOD. COOK MADE THE BEST LITTLE BISCUITS--
WAIT--I SMELL FOOD! SOMETHING NICE AND PEPPERY.
Best go kill something while the Melancholy Prince isn't watching, poppet.
WHAT DOES THE BEAST SMELL? SOMETHING EVIL?
I told you--everything here is evil. The castle draws malevolence around it like a veil.
Don't let the prince's words touch you. Weak things scorn strength. He'll be back.
I KNOW SCORN, AND THAT WAS NOT SCORN. HE REMINDS ME OF SOMEONE I ONCE KNEW. SOMEONE KIND.
HAGS AND BOGGANS AND IMPS GALORE NUCKELAVEES CRAWLING ASHORE SPRITES AND PIXIES AND BROWNIES TOO LET THE BEAST OF DEAN EAT YOU!
HALT. DINNER APPROACHETH!

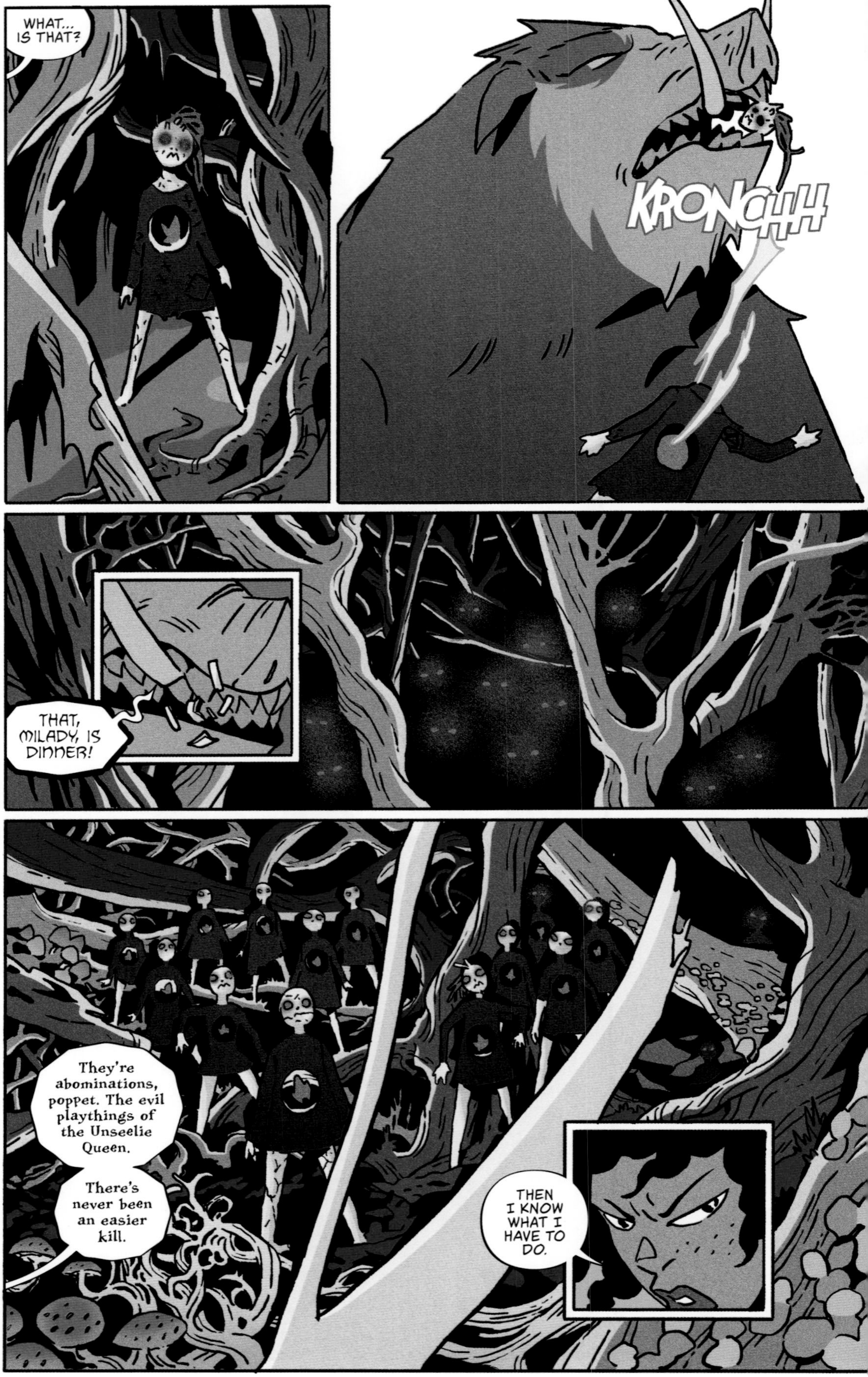
WHAT... IS THAT?
KRONCHH
THAT, MILADY, IS DINNER!
They're abominations, poppet. The evil playthings of the Unseelie Queen.
There's never been an easier kill.
THEN I KNOW WHAT I HAVE TO DO.

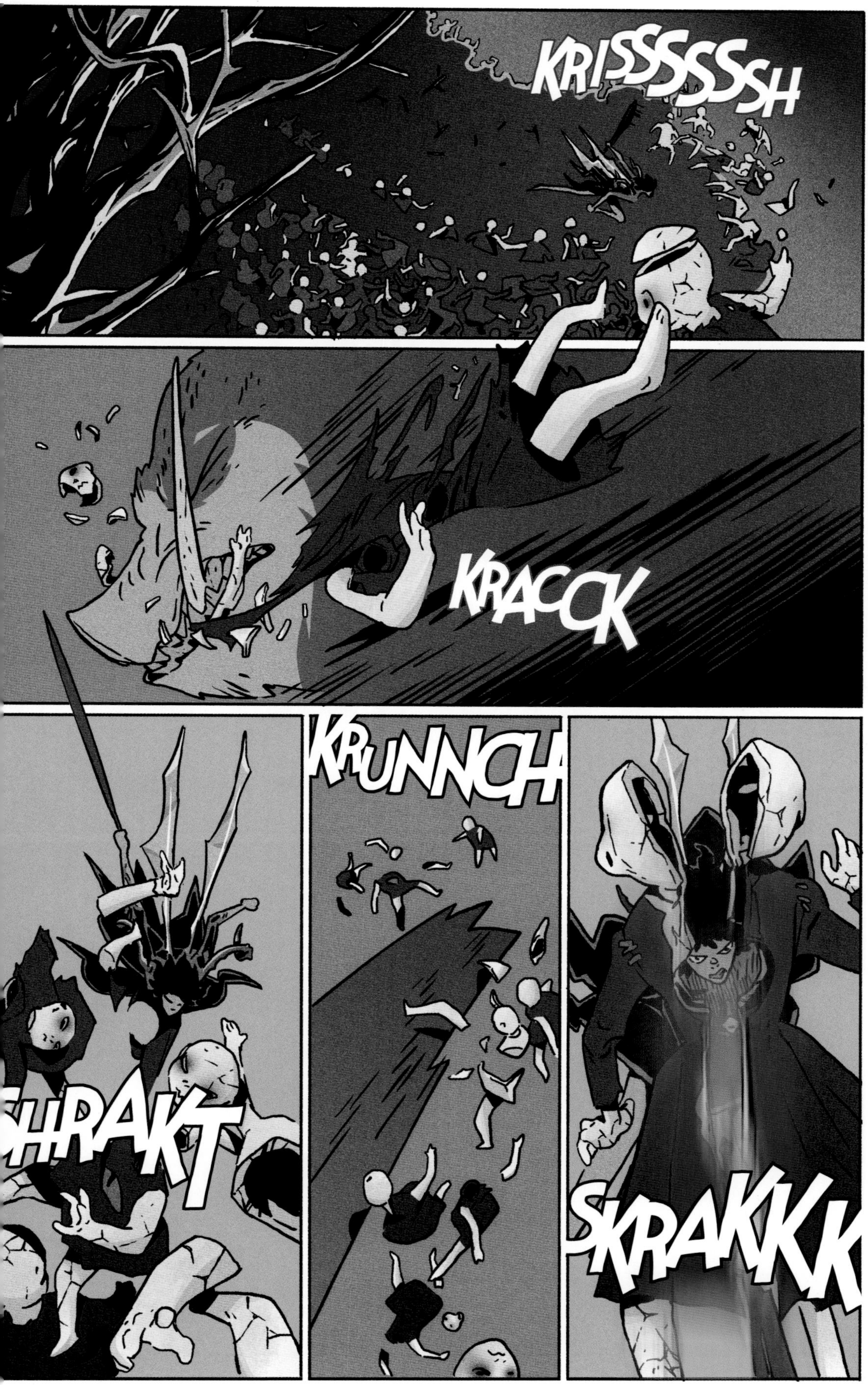
KRISSSSSSH
KRACCK
SHRAKT
KRUNNCH
SKRAKKK

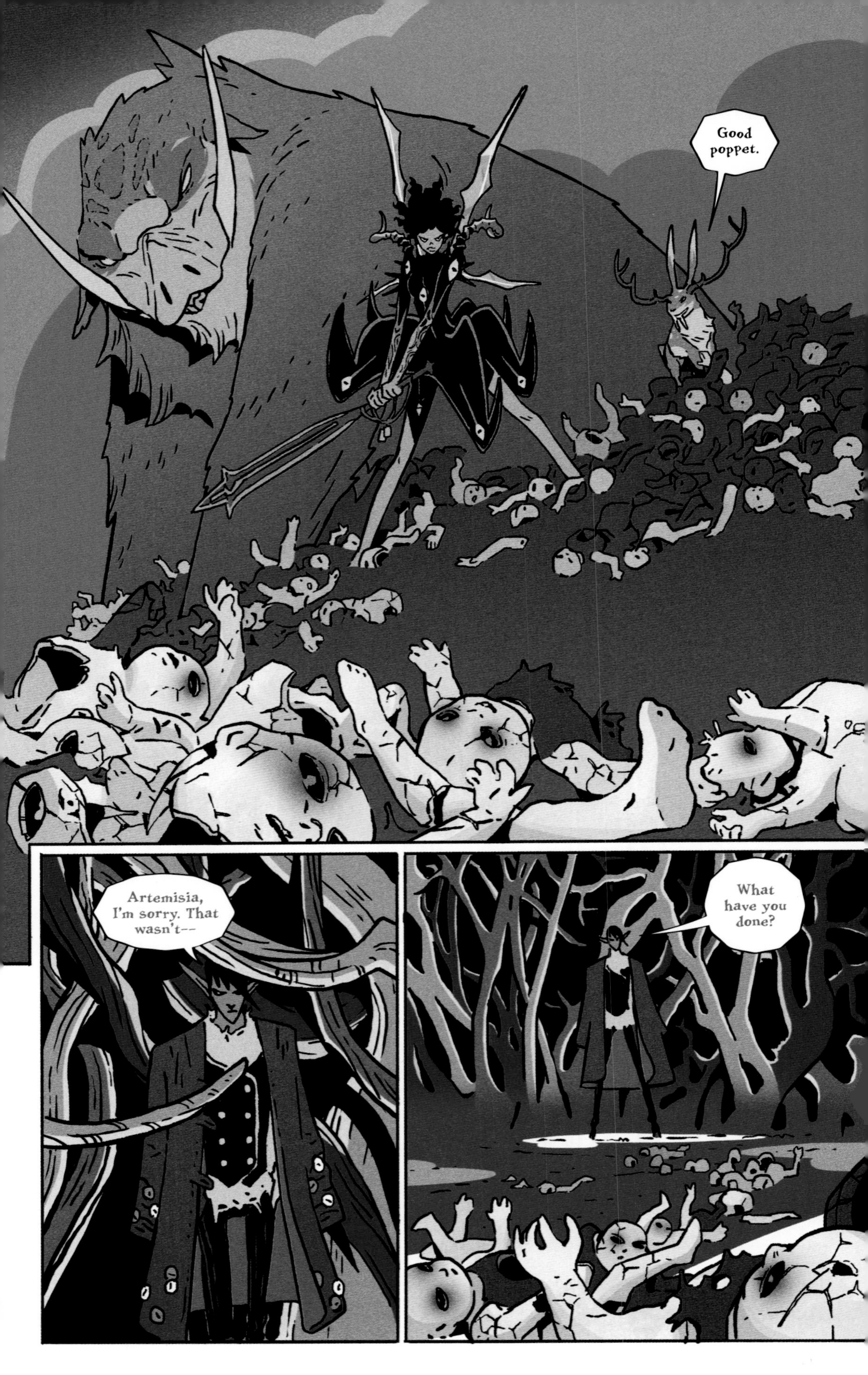
Good poppet.
Artemisia, I'm sorry. That wasn't--
What have you done?

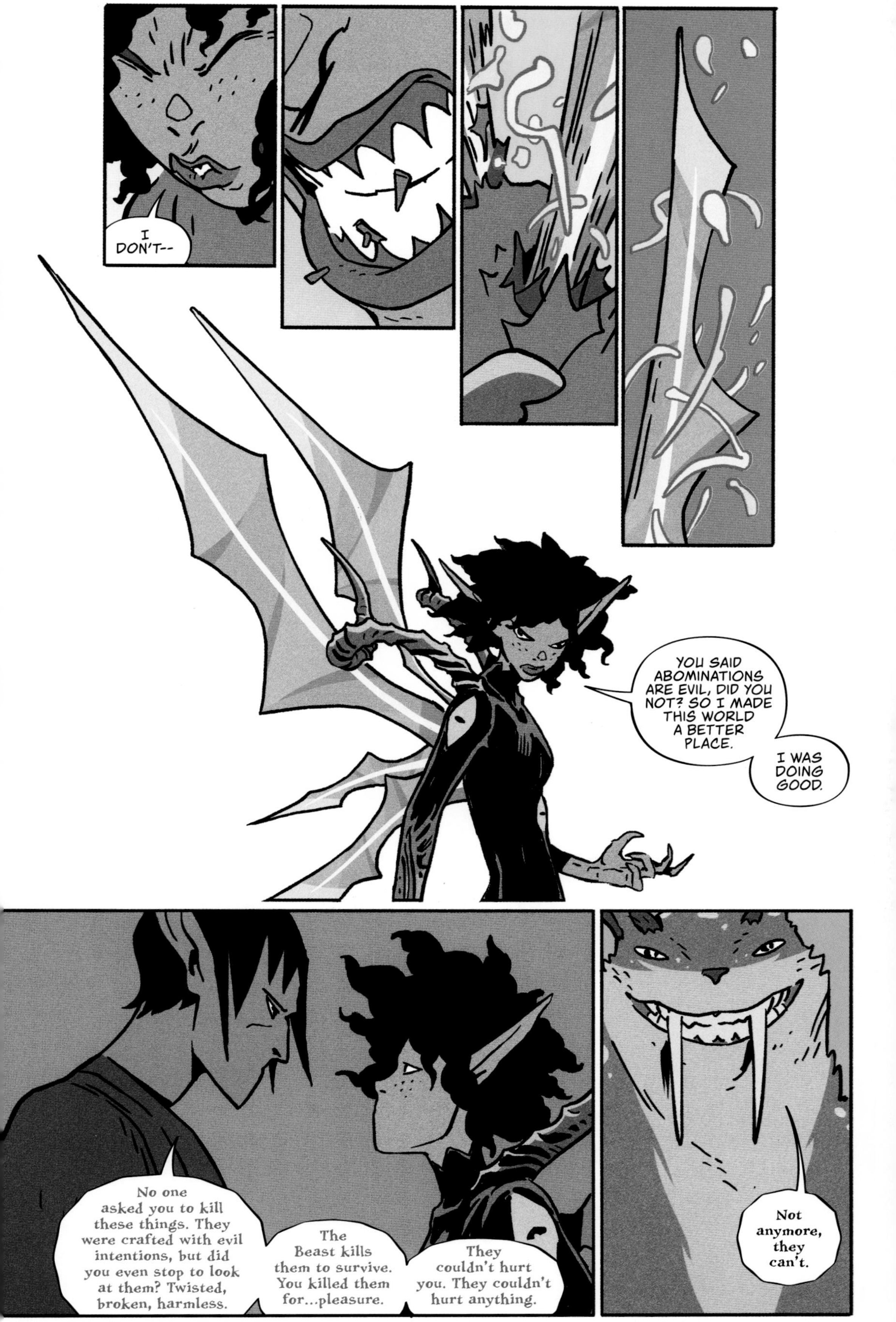
I DON'T--
YOU SAID ABOMINATIONS ARE EVIL, DID YOU NOT? SO I MADE THIS WORLD A BETTER PLACE.
I WAS DOING GOOD.
No one asked you to kill these things. They were crafted with evil intentions, but did you even stop to look at them? Twisted, broken, harmless.
The Beast kills them to survive. You killed them for...pleasure.
They couldn't hurt you. They couldn't hurt anything.
Not anymore, they can't.

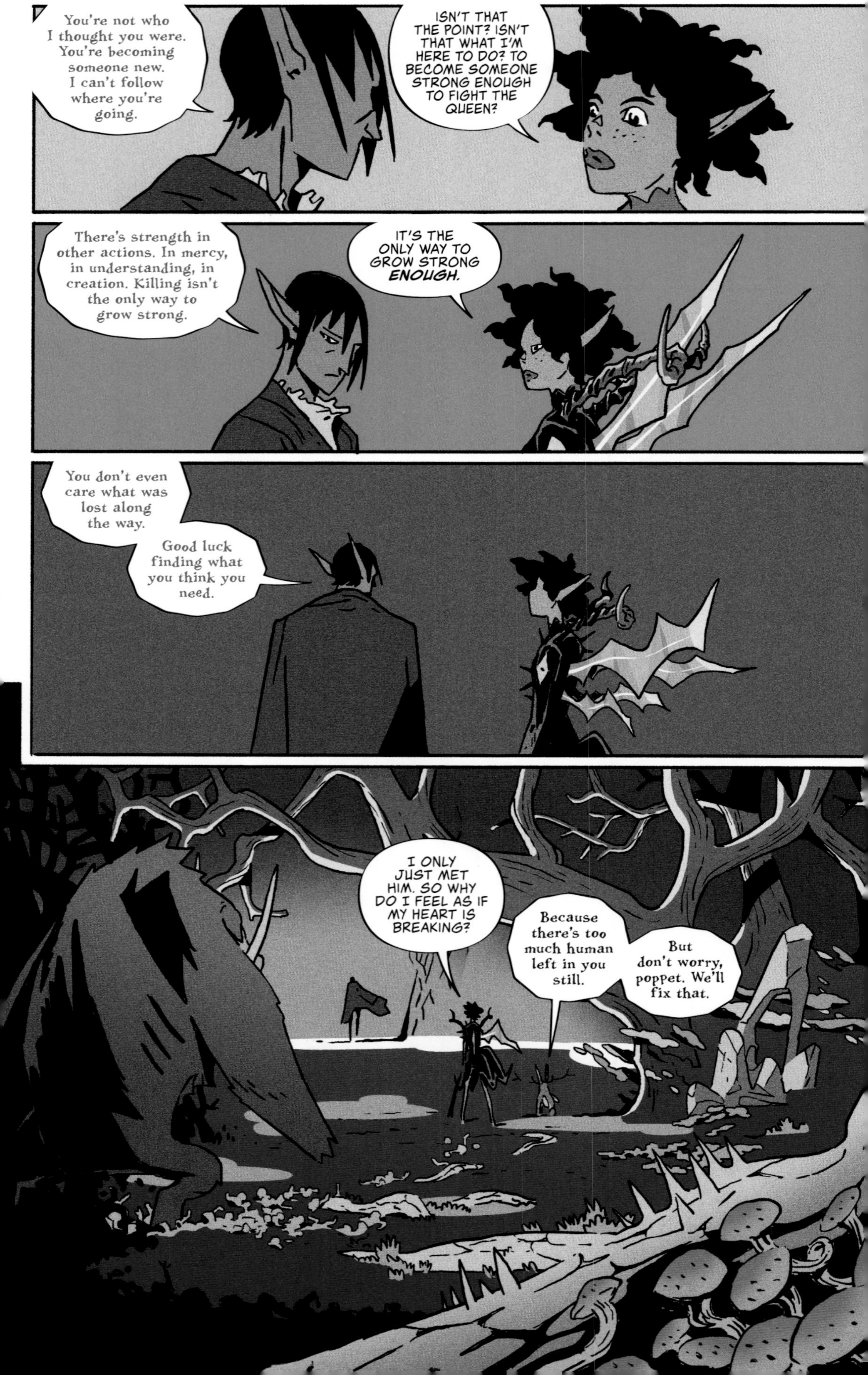

You're not who I thought you were. You're becoming someone new. I can't follow where you're going.
ISN'T THAT THE POINT? ISN'T THAT WHAT I'M HERE TO DO? TO BECOME SOMEONE STRONG ENOUGH TO FIGHT THE QUEEN?
There's strength in other actions. In mercy, in understanding, in creation. Killing isn't the only way to grow strong.
IT'S THE ONLY WAY TO GROW STRONG ENOUGH.
You don't even care what was lost along the way.
Good luck finding what you think you need.
I ONLY JUST MET HIM. SO WHY DO I FEEL AS IF MY HEART IS BREAKING?
Because there's too much human left in you still.
But don't worry, poppet. We'll fix that.

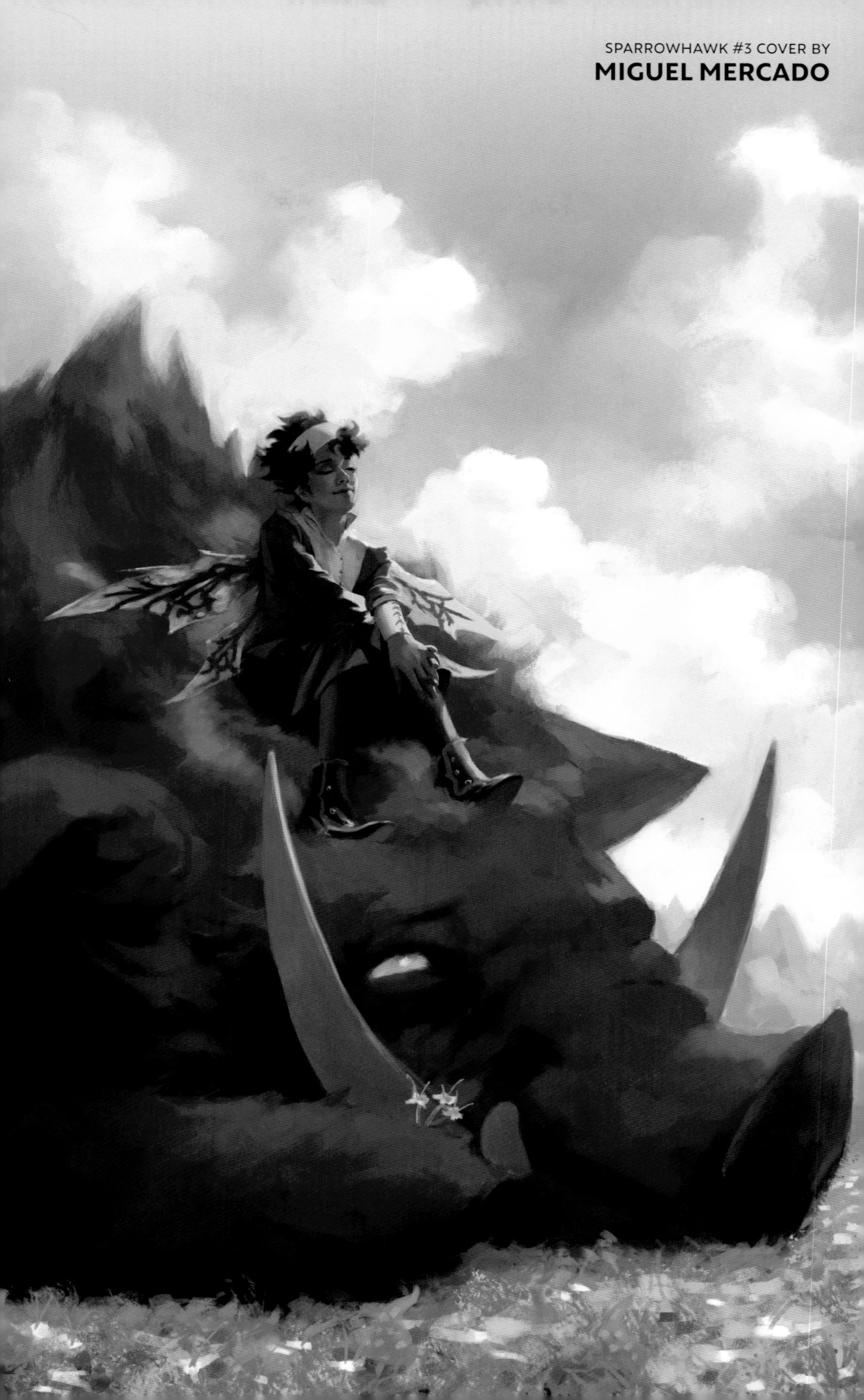

SPARROWHAWK #3 COVER BY
MIGUEL MERCADO

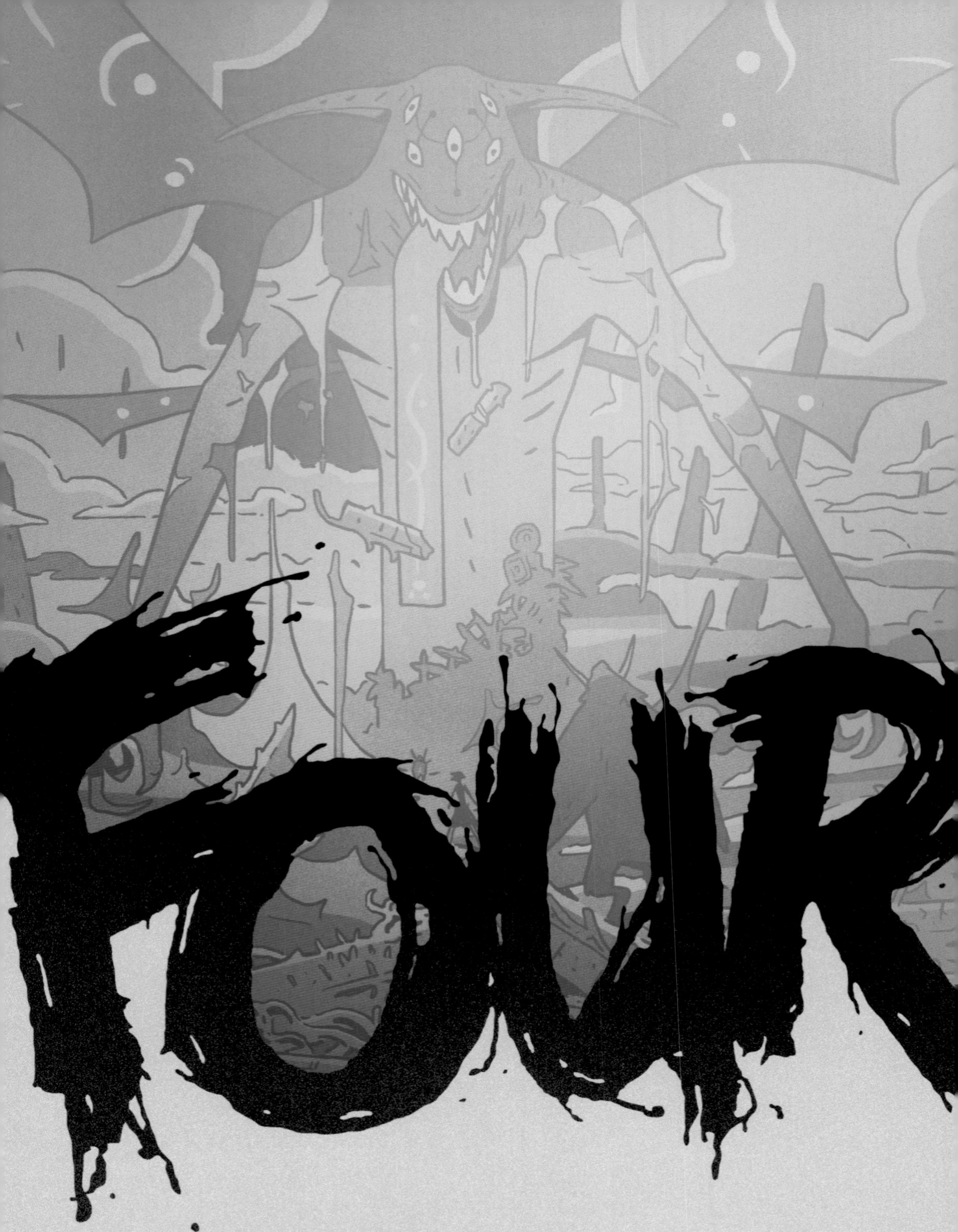

FOUR

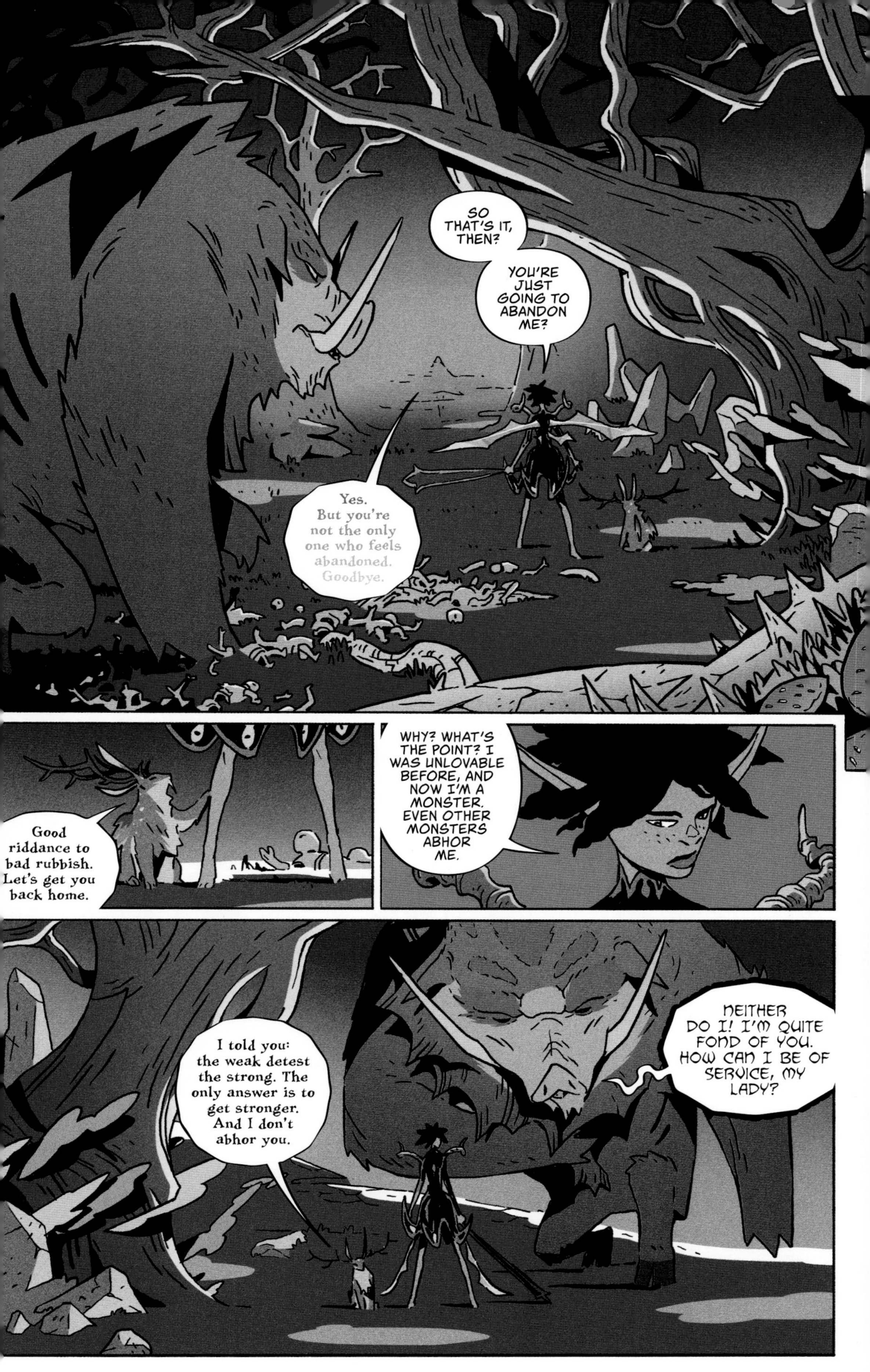
SO THAT'S IT, THEN?
YOU'RE JUST GOING TO ABANDON ME?
Yes. But you're not the only one who feels abandoned. Goodbye.
Good riddance to bad rubbish. Let's get you back home.
WHY? WHAT'S THE POINT? I WAS UNLOVABLE BEFORE, AND NOW I'M A MONSTER. EVEN OTHER MONSTERS ABHOR ME.
I told you: the weak detest the strong. The only answer is to get stronger. And I don't abhor you.
NEITHER DO I! I'M QUITE FOND OF YOU. HOW CAN I BE OF SERVICE, MY LADY?

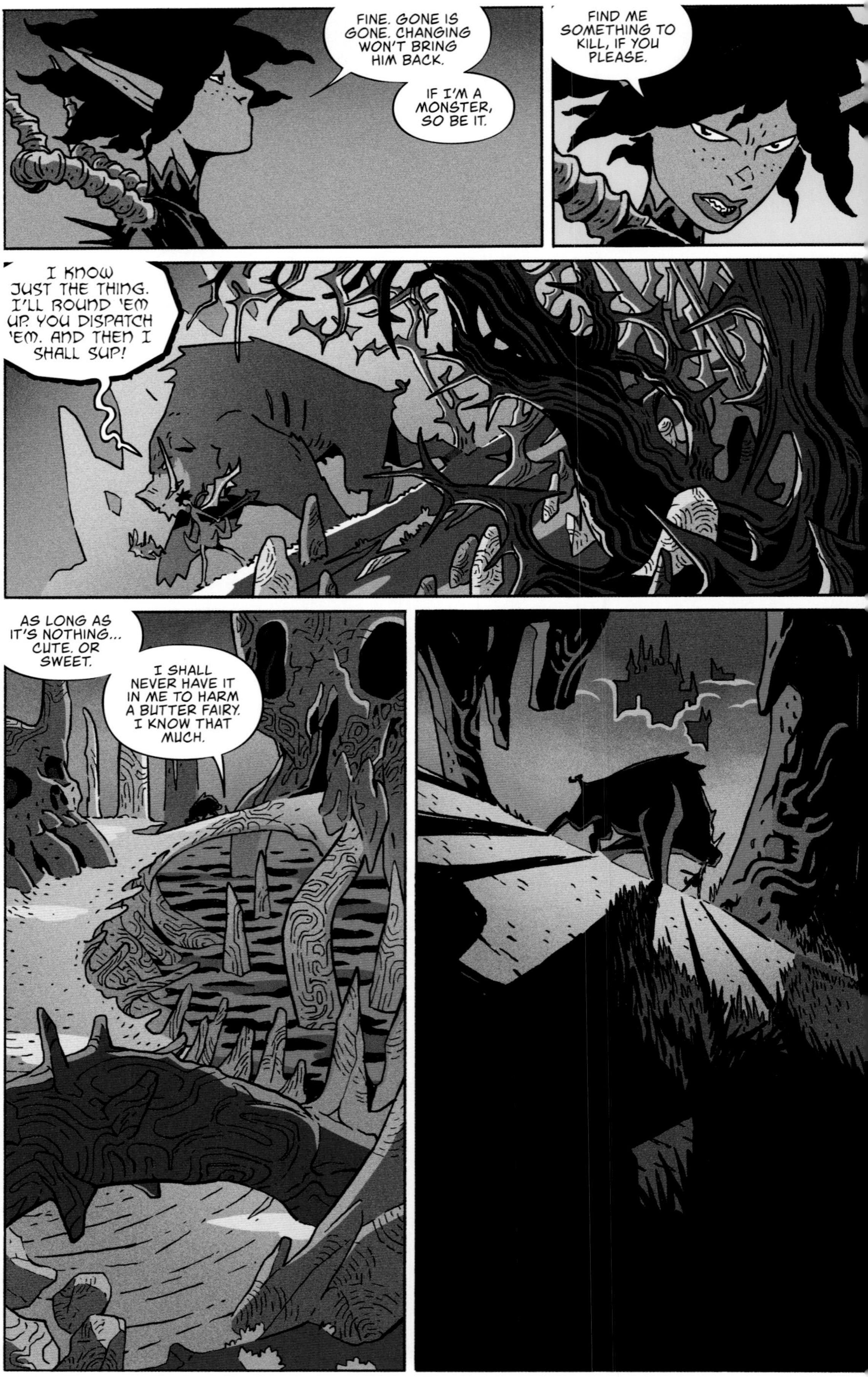
FINE. GONE IS GONE. CHANGING WON'T BRING HIM BACK.
IF I'M A MONSTER, SO BE IT.
FIND ME SOMETHING TO KILL, IF YOU PLEASE.
I KNOW JUST THE THING. I'LL ROUND 'EM UP. YOU DISPATCH 'EM. AND THEN I SHALL SUP!
AS LONG AS IT'S NOTHING... CUTE. OR SWEET.
I SHALL NEVER HAVE IT IN ME TO HARM A BUTTER FAIRY. I KNOW THAT MUCH.

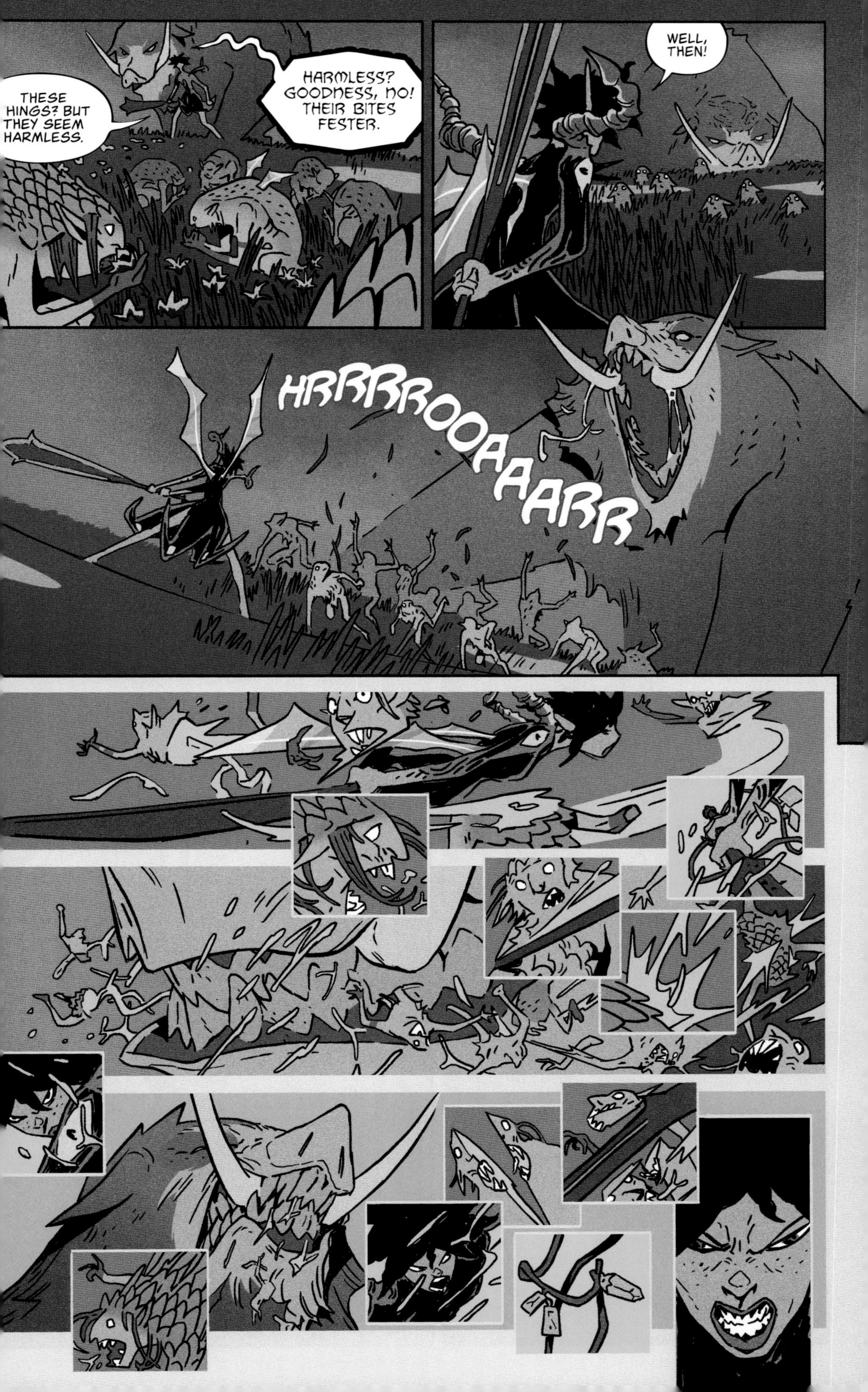
THESE HINGS? BUT THEY SEEM HARMLESS.
HARMLESS? GOODNESS, NO! THEIR BITES FESTER.
WELL, THEN!
HRRRROOAAARR

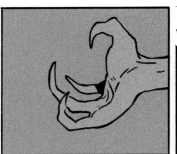

TO THINK: I ALMOST WELCOME THIS NOW...

I recall a nasty sort of fellow out this way. Follow me.

WHERE DO YOU THINK WARREN WENT?

THIS CARNAGE DOESN'T FEEL LIKE MUCH OF A VICTORY.

That's because you need to kill something bigger.

These wee things are just drops in a bucket.

Who cares? He's gone. That's all that matters.

HE CAME BACK ONCE. MIGHT HE RETURN AGAIN? IS HE THE FORGIVING SORT, DO YOU THINK?

Poppet, you can't let doubt and a soft heart slow you down.

You are on a mission. Do you want to save your world or not?

FOR WHAT IT'S WORTH, I DO BELIEVE HE HAS A NOBLE HEART.

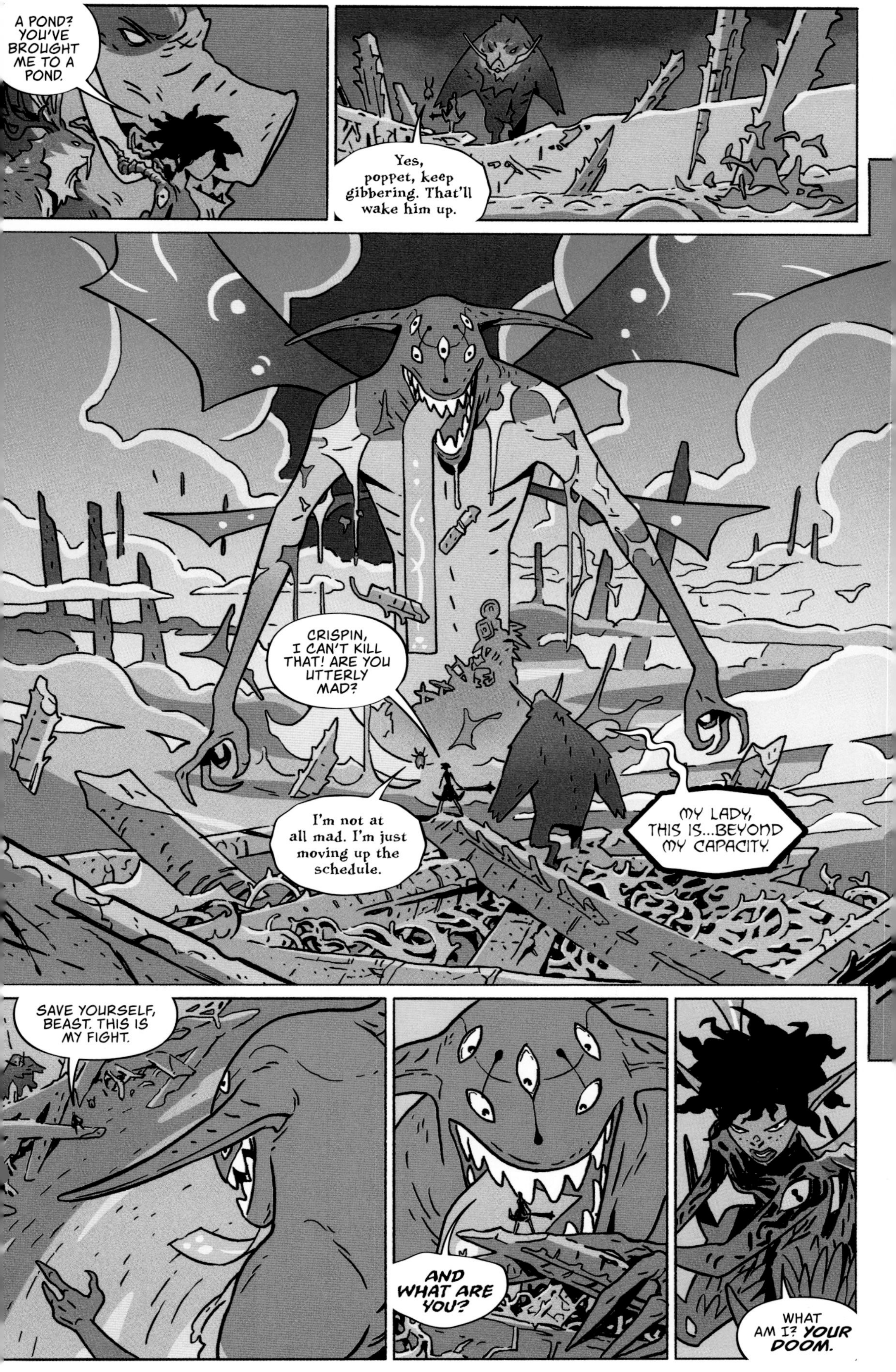
A POND? YOU'VE BROUGHT ME TO A POND.
Yes, poppet, keep gibbering. That'll wake him up.
CRISPIN, I CAN'T KILL THAT! ARE YOU UTTERLY MAD?
I'm not at all mad. I'm just moving up the schedule.
MY LADY, THIS IS...BEYOND MY CAPACITY.
SAVE YOURSELF, BEAST. THIS IS MY FIGHT.
AND WHAT ARE YOU?
WHAT AM I? YOUR DOOM.

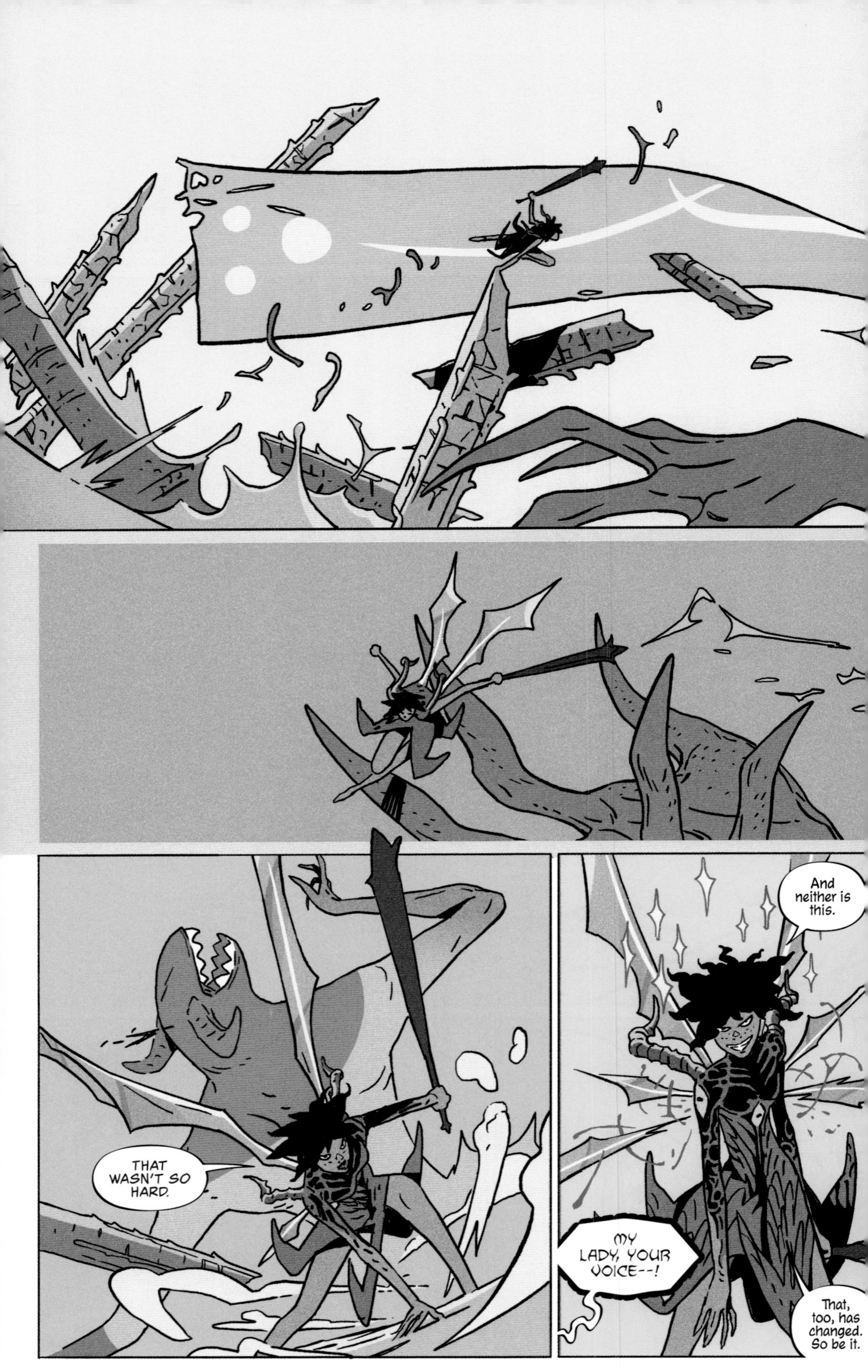
THAT WASN'T SO HARD.
And neither is this.
MY LADY, YOUR VOICE--!
That, too, has changed. So be it.

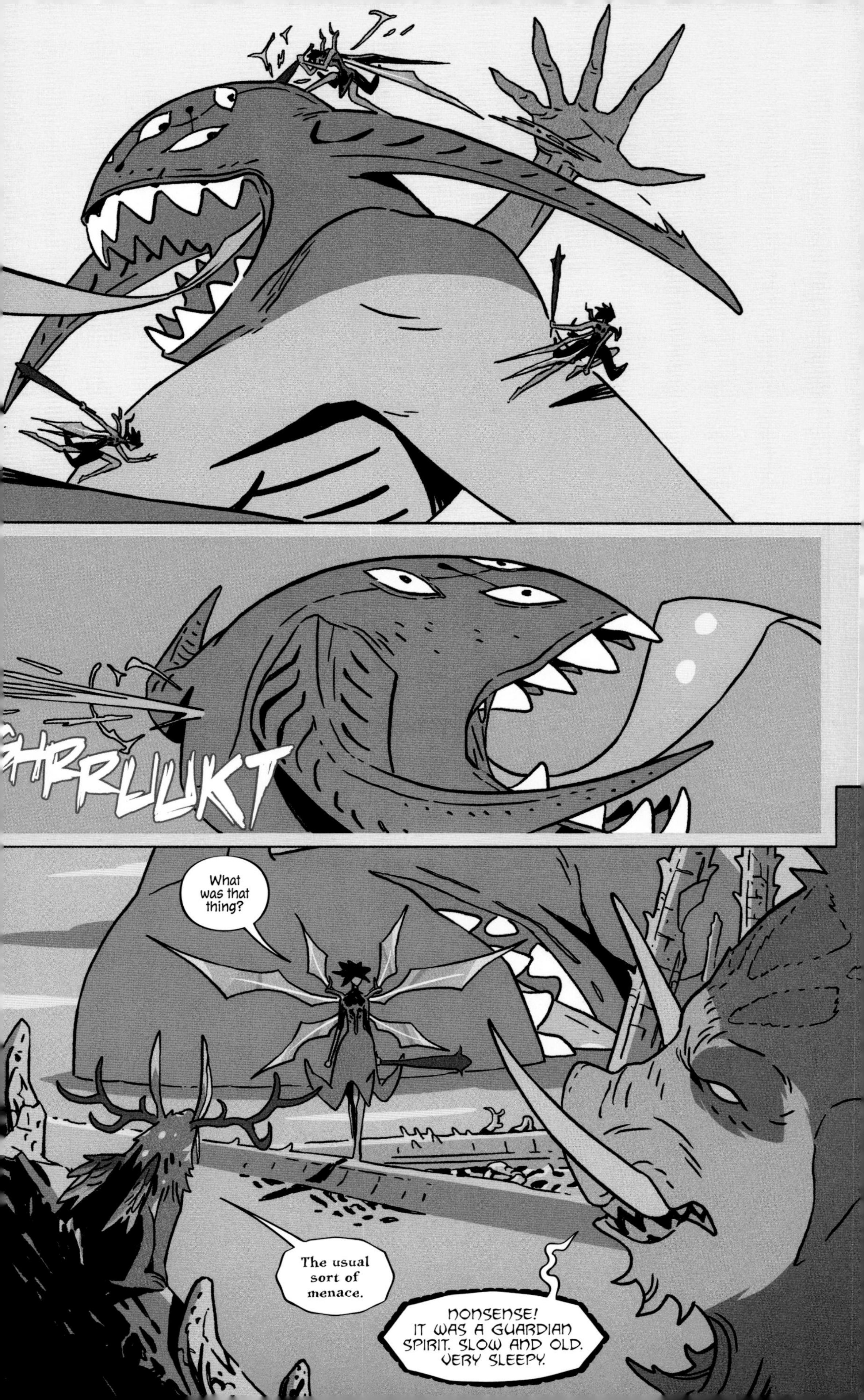
HRRUUKT
What was that thing?
The usual sort of menace.
NONSENSE! IT WAS A GUARDIAN SPIRIT. SLOW AND OLD. VERY SLEEPY.

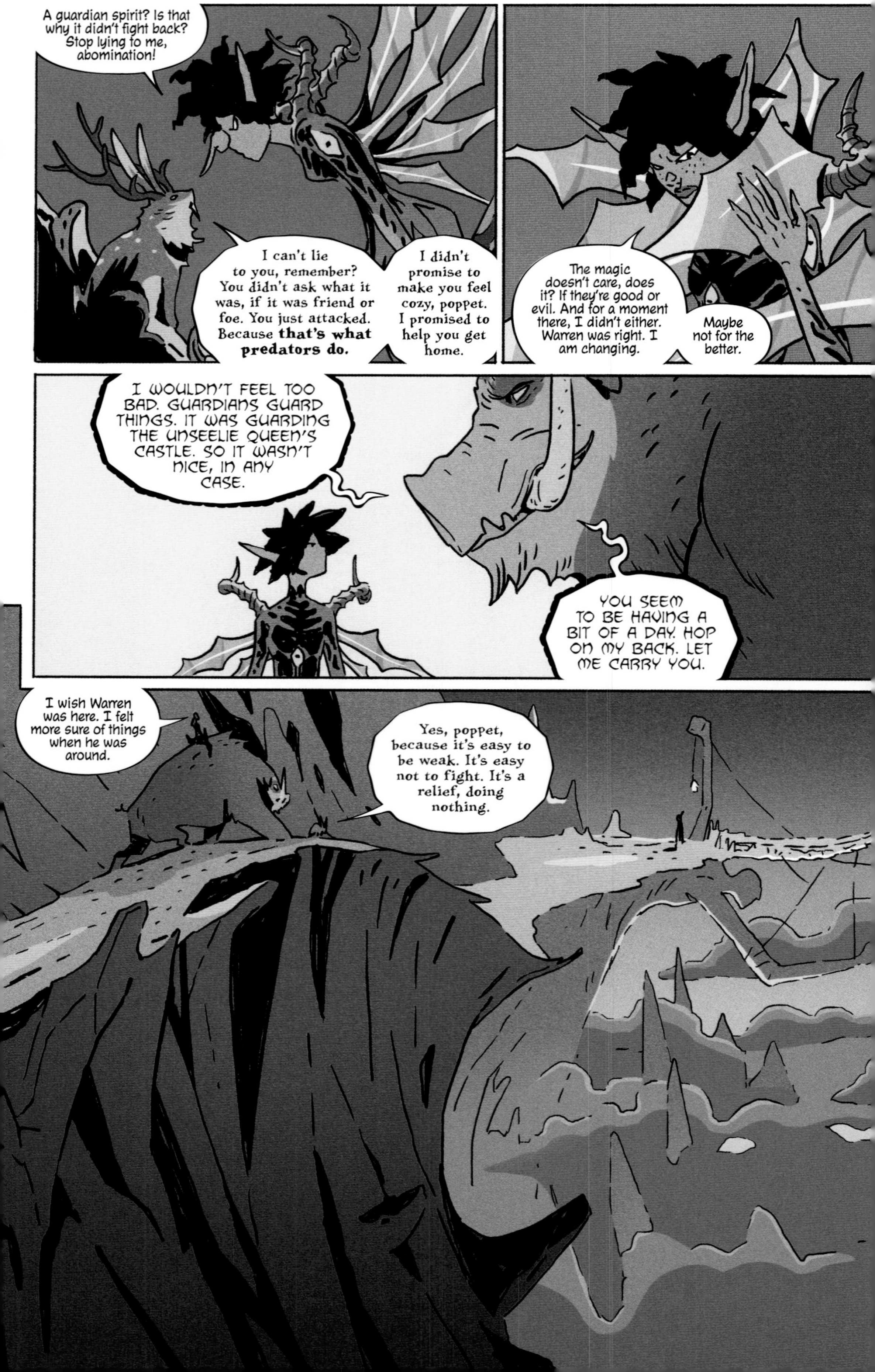
A guardian spirit? Is that why it didn't fight back? Stop lying to me, abomination!
I can't lie to you, remember? You didn't ask what it was, if it was friend or foe. You just attacked. Because **that's what predators do.**
I didn't promise to make you feel cozy, poppet. I promised to help you get home.
The magic doesn't care, does it? If they're good or evil. And for a moment there, I didn't either. Warren was right. I am changing.
Maybe not for the better.
I WOULDN'T FEEL TOO BAD. GUARDIANS GUARD THINGS. IT WAS GUARDING THE UNSEELIE QUEEN'S CASTLE. SO IT WASN'T NICE, IN ANY CASE.
YOU SEEM TO BE HAVING A BIT OF A DAY. HOP ON MY BACK. LET ME CARRY YOU.
I wish Warren was here. I felt more sure of things when he was around.
Yes, poppet, because it's easy to be weak. It's easy not to fight. It's a relief, doing nothing.

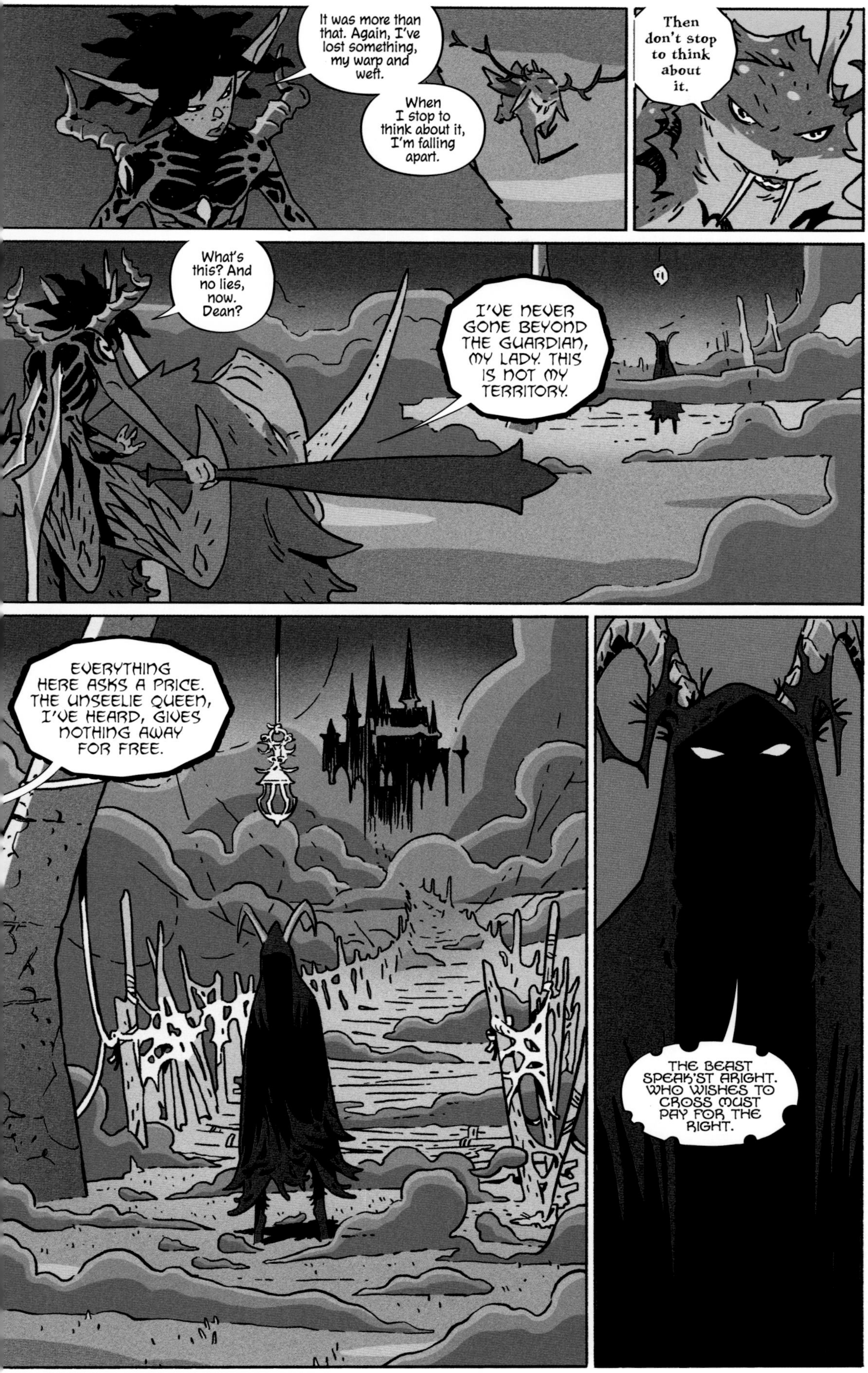
It was more than that. Again, I've lost something, my warp and weft.
When I stop to think about it, I'm falling apart.
Then don't stop to think about it.
What's this? And no lies, now. Dean?
I'VE NEVER GONE BEYOND THE GUARDIAN, MY LADY. THIS IS NOT MY TERRITORY.
EVERYTHING HERE ASKS A PRICE. THE UNSEELIE QUEEN, I'VE HEARD, GIVES NOTHING AWAY FOR FREE.
THE BEAST SPEAK'ST ARIGHT. WHO WISHES TO CROSS MUST PAY FOR THE RIGHT.

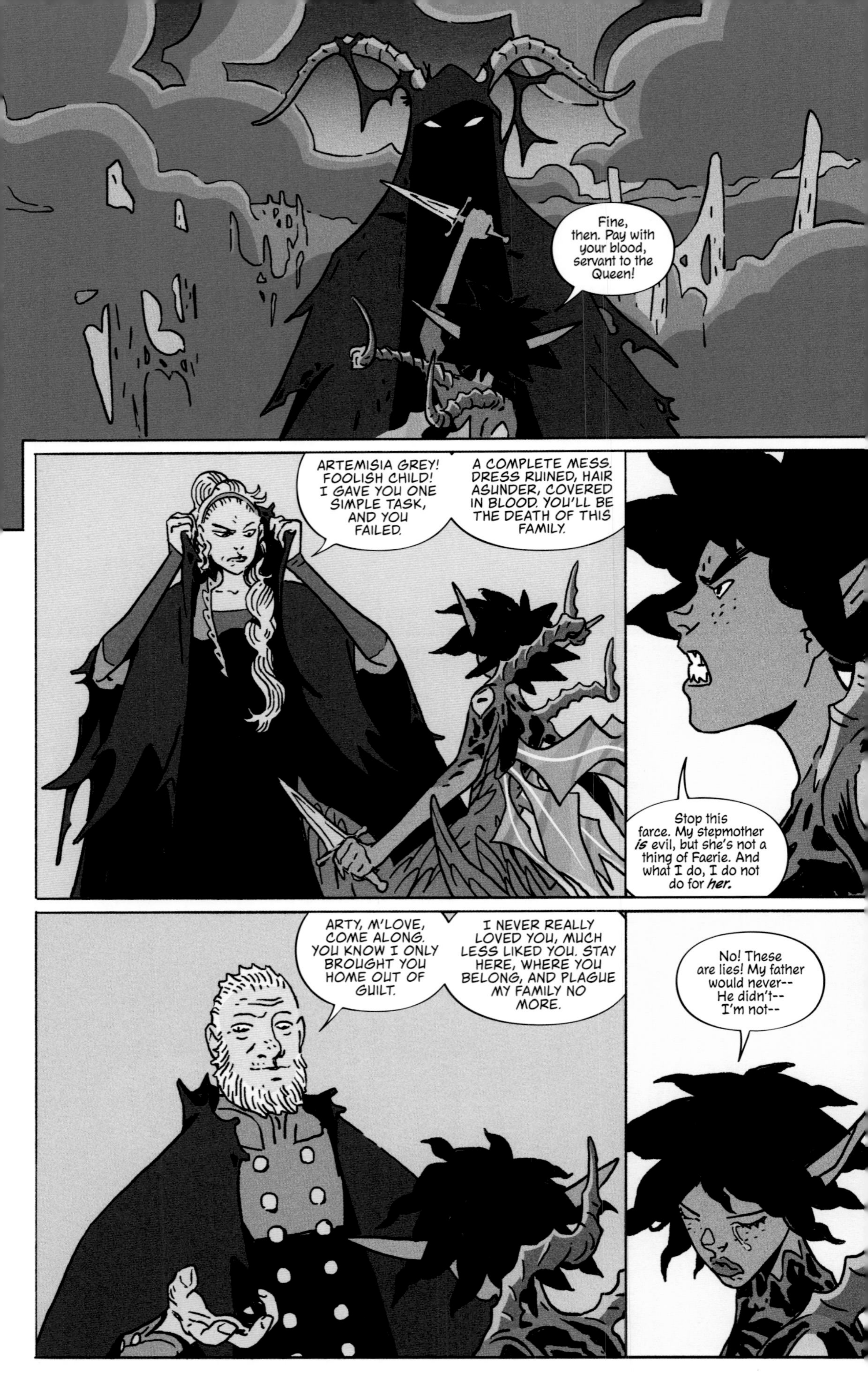
Fine, then. Pay with your blood, servant to the Queen!
ARTEMISIA GREY! FOOLISH CHILD! I GAVE YOU ONE SIMPLE TASK, AND YOU FAILED.
A COMPLETE MESS. DRESS RUINED, HAIR ASUNDER, COVERED IN BLOOD. YOU'LL BE THE DEATH OF THIS FAMILY.
Stop this farce. My stepmother *is* evil, but she's not a thing of Faerie. And what I do, I do not do for *her.*
ARTY, M'LOVE, COME ALONG. YOU KNOW I ONLY BROUGHT YOU HOME OUT OF GUILT.
I NEVER REALLY LOVED YOU, MUCH LESS LIKED YOU. STAY HERE, WHERE YOU BELONG, AND PLAGUE MY FAMILY NO MORE.
No! These are lies! My father would never-- He didn't-- I'm not--

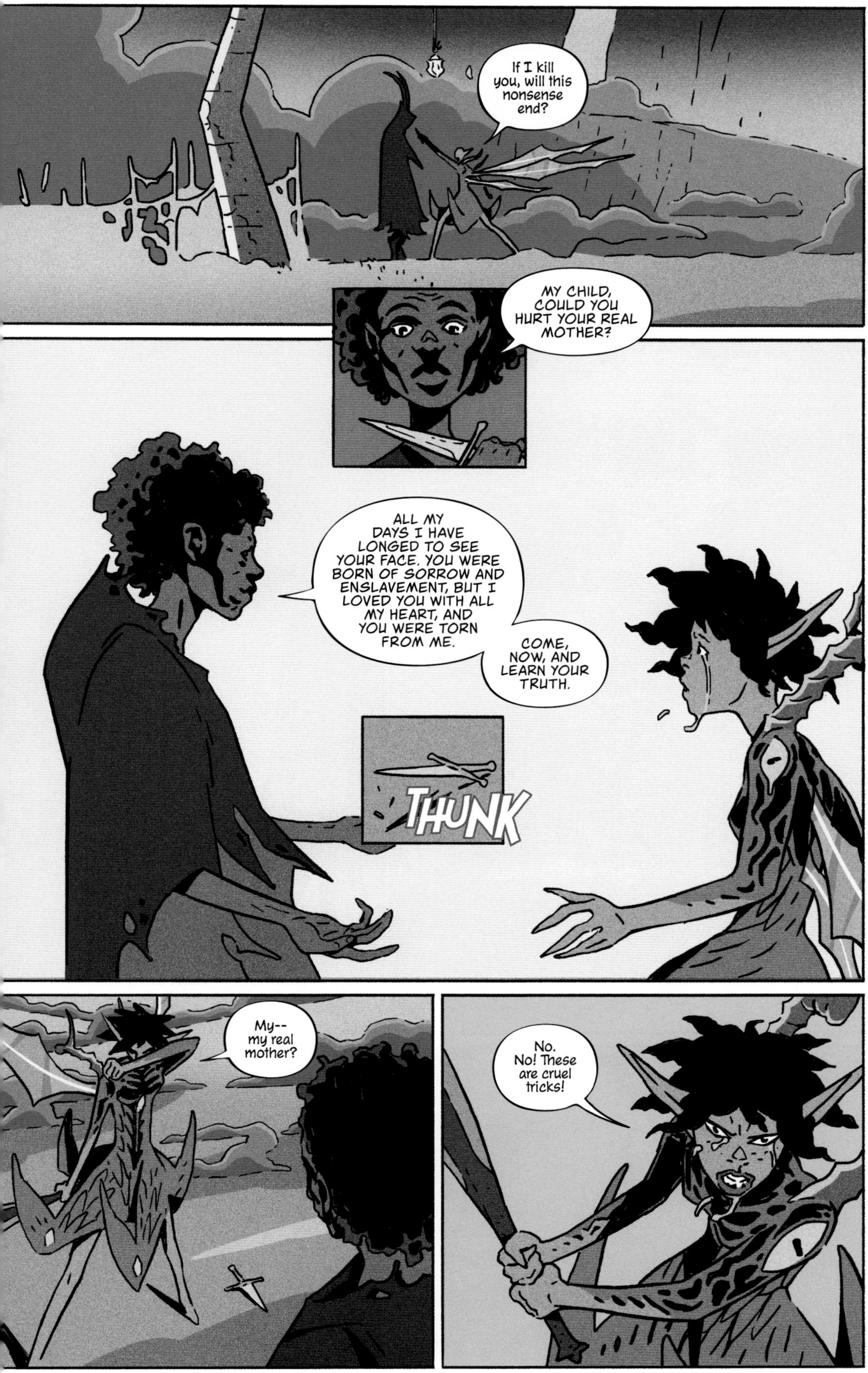
If I kill you, will this nonsense end?
MY CHILD, COULD YOU HURT YOUR REAL MOTHER?
ALL MY DAYS I HAVE LONGED TO SEE YOUR FACE. YOU WERE BORN OF SORROW AND ENSLAVEMENT, BUT I LOVED YOU WITH ALL MY HEART, AND YOU WERE TORN FROM ME.
COME, NOW, AND LEARN YOUR TRUTH.
THUNK
My-- my real mother?
No. No! These are cruel tricks!

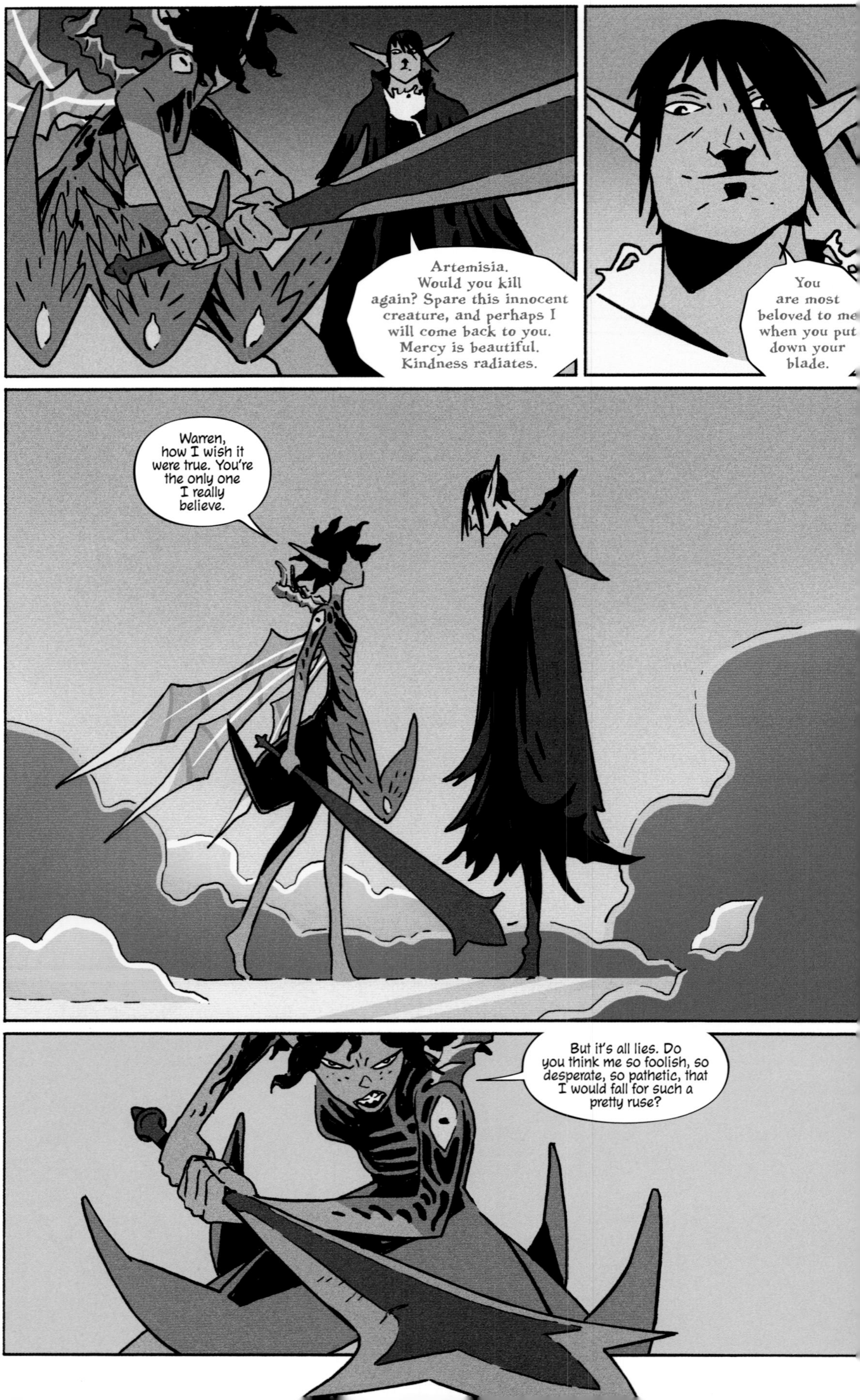
Artemisia. Would you kill again? Spare this innocent creature, and perhaps I will come back to you. Mercy is beautiful. Kindness radiates.
You are most beloved to me when you put down your blade.
Warren, how I wish it were true. You're the only one I really believe.
But it's all lies. Do you think me so foolish, so desperate, so pathetic, that I would fall for such a pretty ruse?

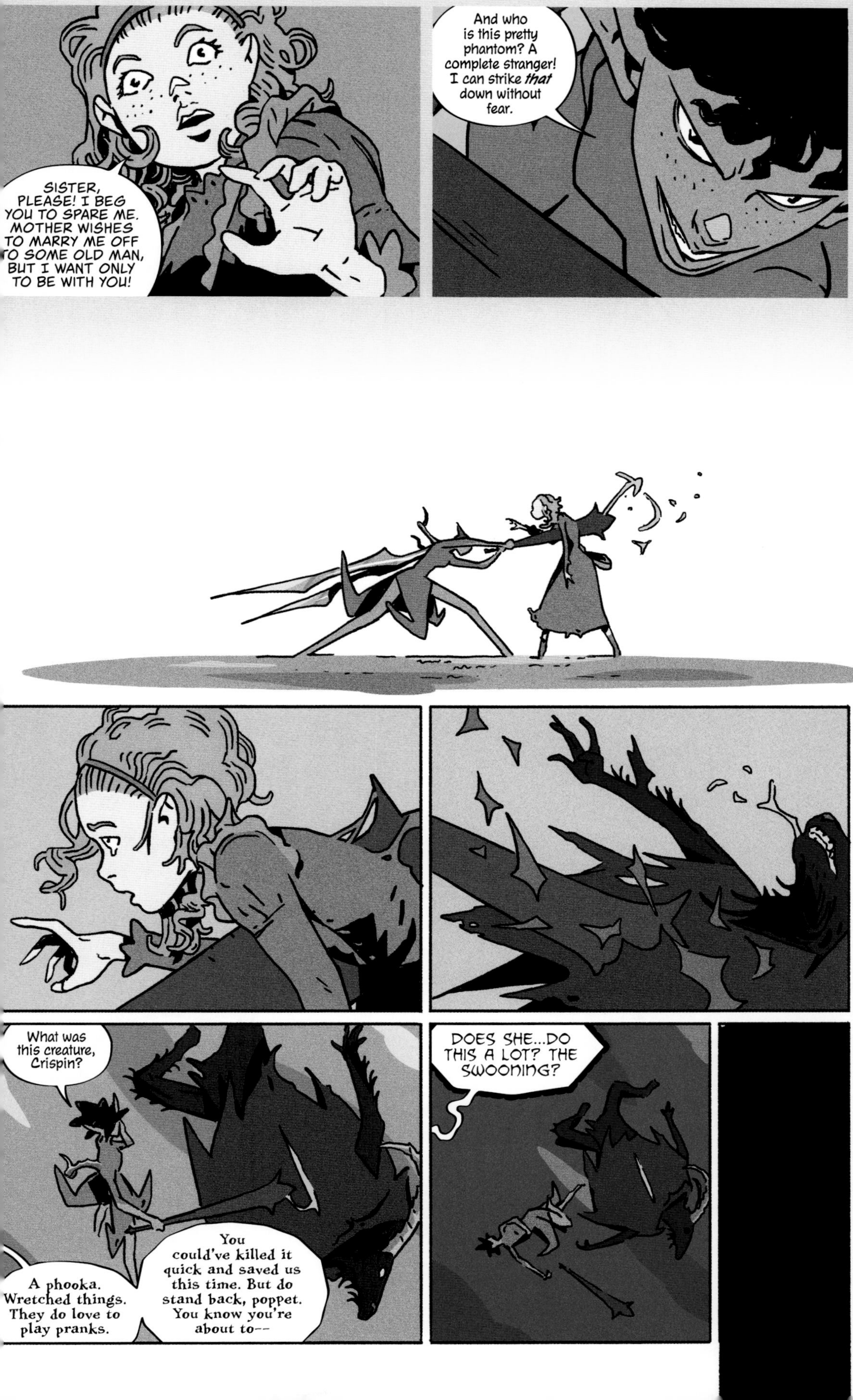
SISTER, PLEASE! I BEG YOU TO SPARE ME. MOTHER WISHES TO MARRY ME OFF TO SOME OLD MAN, BUT I WANT ONLY TO BE WITH YOU!
And who is this pretty phantom? A complete stranger! I can strike *that* down without fear.
What was this creature, Crispin?
A phooka. Wretched things. They do love to play pranks.
You could've killed it quick and saved us this time. But do stand back, poppet. You know you're about to--
DOES SHE...DO THIS A LOT? THE SWOONING?

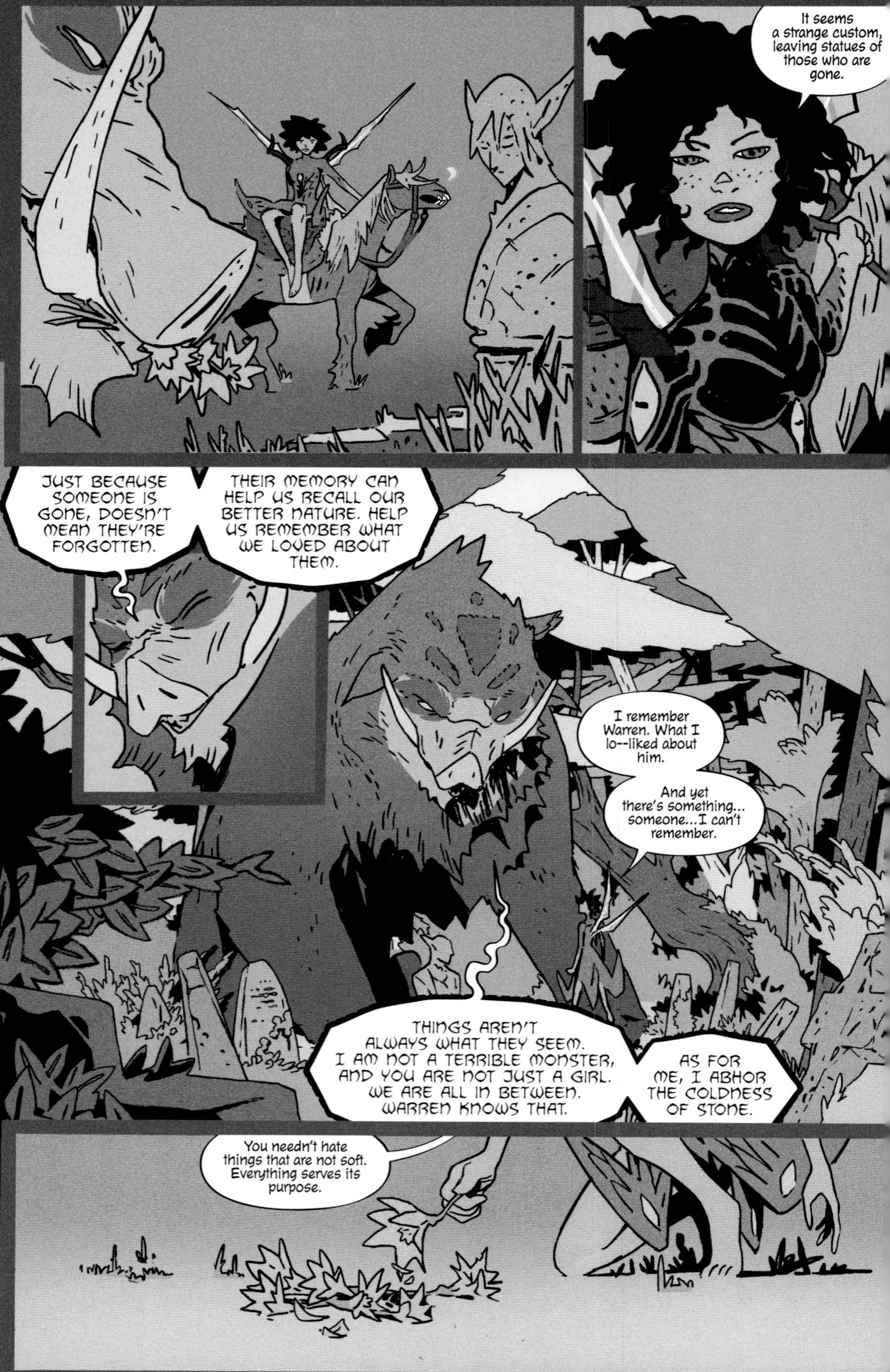
It seems a strange custom, leaving statues of those who are gone.
JUST BECAUSE SOMEONE IS GONE, DOESN'T MEAN THEY'RE FORGOTTEN.
THEIR MEMORY CAN HELP US RECALL OUR BETTER NATURE. HELP US REMEMBER WHAT WE LOVED ABOUT THEM.
I remember Warren. What I lo--liked about him.
And yet there's something... someone...I can't remember.
THINGS AREN'T ALWAYS WHAT THEY SEEM. I AM NOT A TERRIBLE MONSTER, AND YOU ARE NOT JUST A GIRL. WE ARE ALL IN BETWEEN. WARREN KNOWS THAT.
AS FOR ME, I ABHOR THE COLDNESS OF STONE.
You needn't hate things that are not soft. Everything serves its purpose.

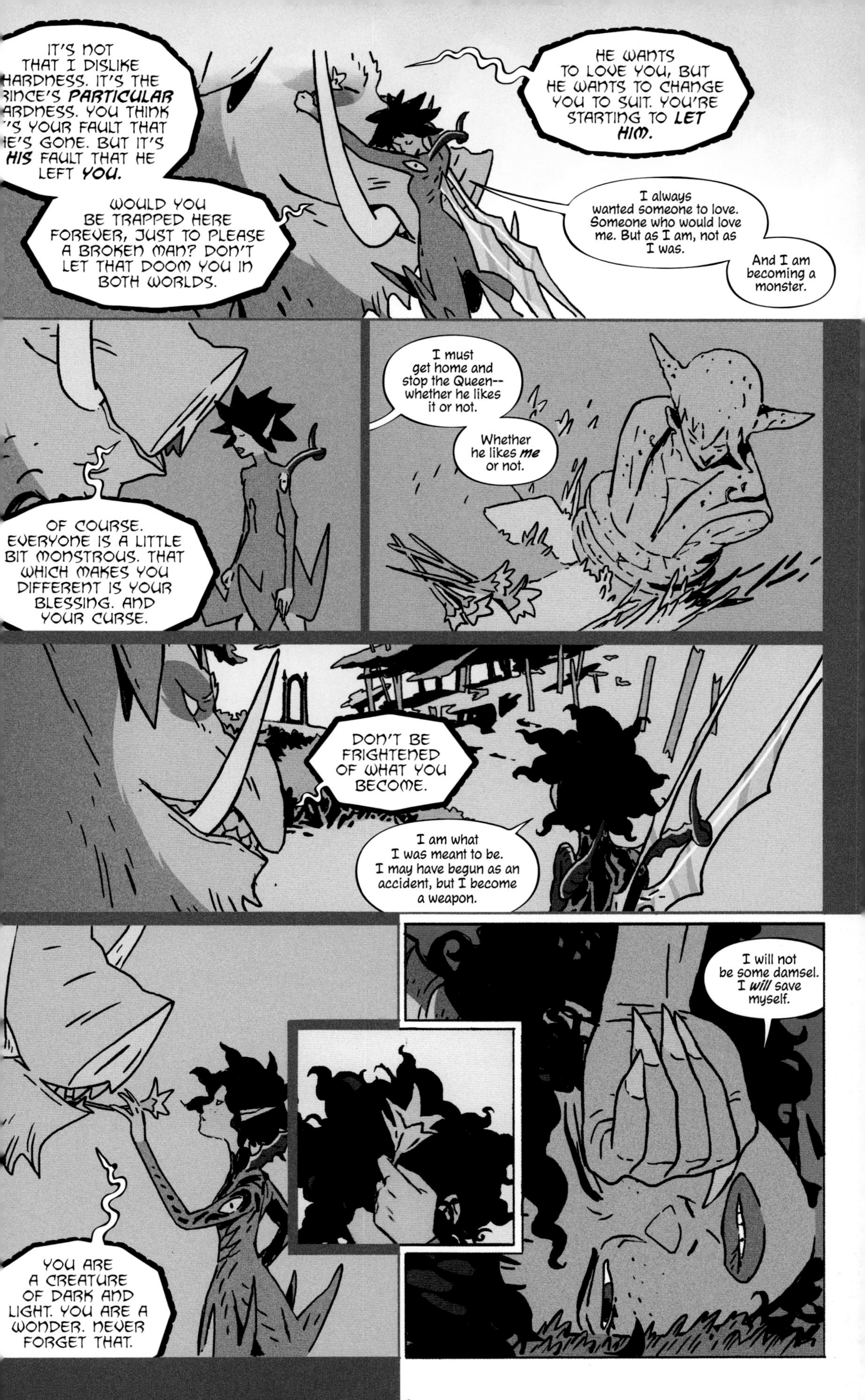
IT'S NOT THAT I DISLIKE HARDNESS. IT'S THE PRINCE'S PARTICULAR HARDNESS. YOU THINK IT'S YOUR FAULT THAT HE'S GONE. BUT IT'S HIS FAULT THAT HE LEFT YOU.
HE WANTS TO LOVE YOU, BUT HE WANTS TO CHANGE YOU TO SUIT. YOU'RE STARTING TO LET HIM.
WOULD YOU BE TRAPPED HERE FOREVER, JUST TO PLEASE A BROKEN MAN? DON'T LET THAT DOOM YOU IN BOTH WORLDS.
I always wanted someone to love. Someone who would love me. But as I am, not as I was.
And I am becoming a monster.
OF COURSE. EVERYONE IS A LITTLE BIT MONSTROUS. THAT WHICH MAKES YOU DIFFERENT IS YOUR BLESSING. AND YOUR CURSE.
I must get home and stop the Queen-- whether he likes it or not.
Whether he likes me or not.
DON'T BE FRIGHTENED OF WHAT YOU BECOME.
I am what I was meant to be. I may have begun as an accident, but I become a weapon.
YOU ARE A CREATURE OF DARK AND LIGHT. YOU ARE A WONDER. NEVER FORGET THAT.
I will not be some damsel. I will save myself.

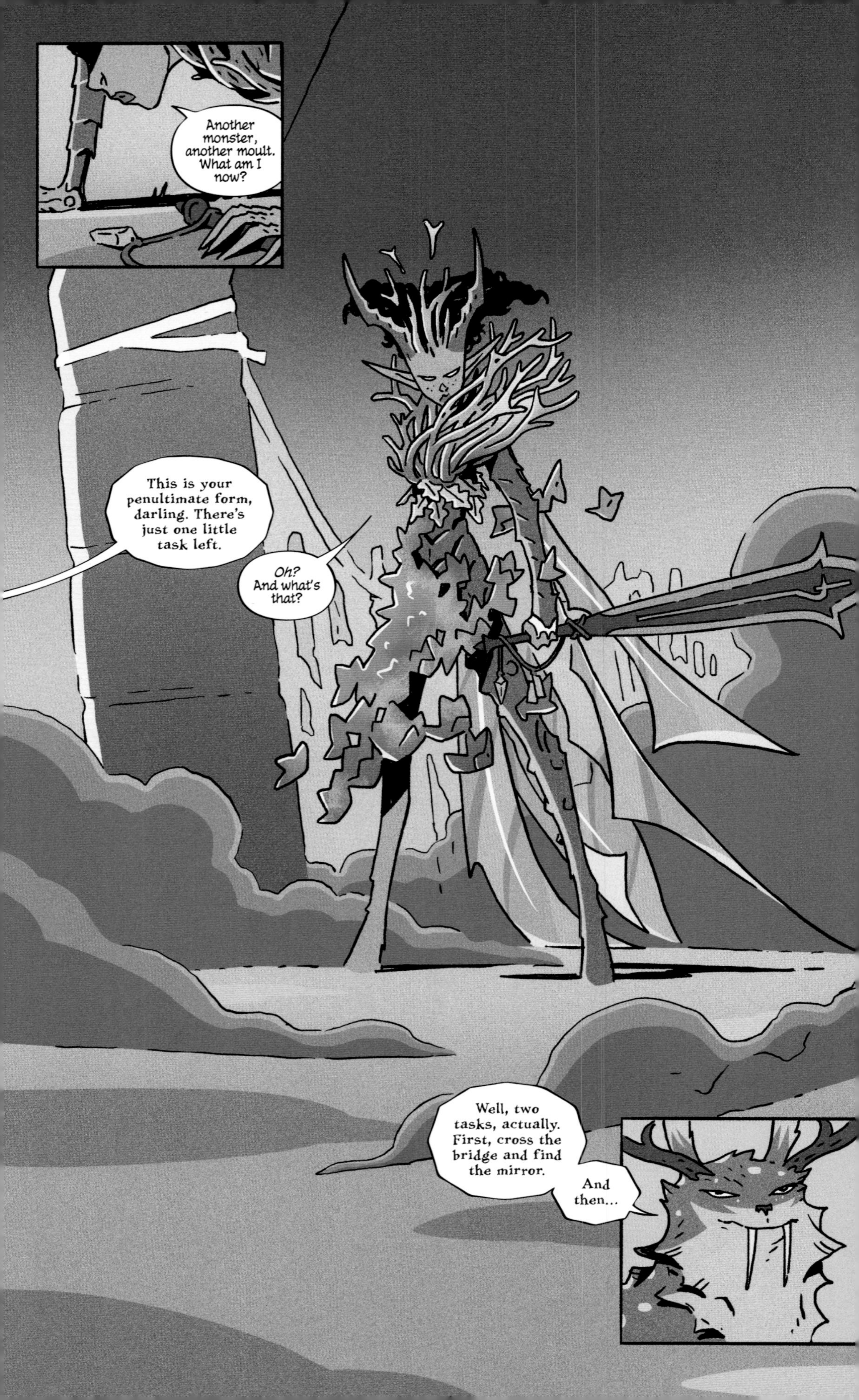
Another monster, another moult. What am I now?
This is your penultimate form, darling. There's just one little task left.
Oh? And what's that?
Well, two tasks, actually. First, cross the bridge and find the mirror.
And then...

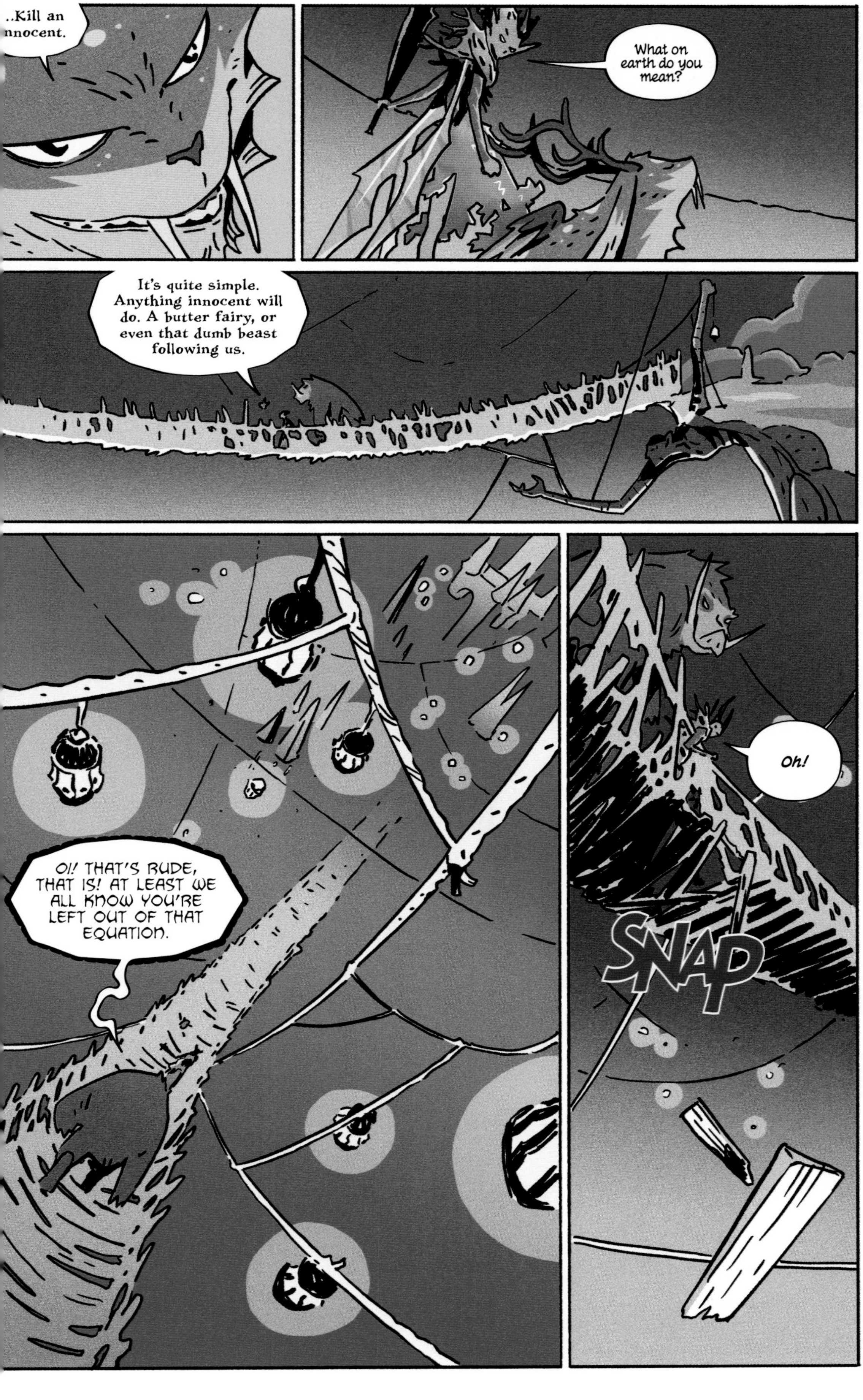
..Kill an
nnocent.
What on earth do you mean?
It's quite simple. Anything innocent will do. A butter fairy, or even that dumb beast following us.
OI! THAT'S RUDE, THAT IS! AT LEAST WE ALL KNOW YOU'RE LEFT OUT OF THAT EQUATION.
Oh!
SNAP

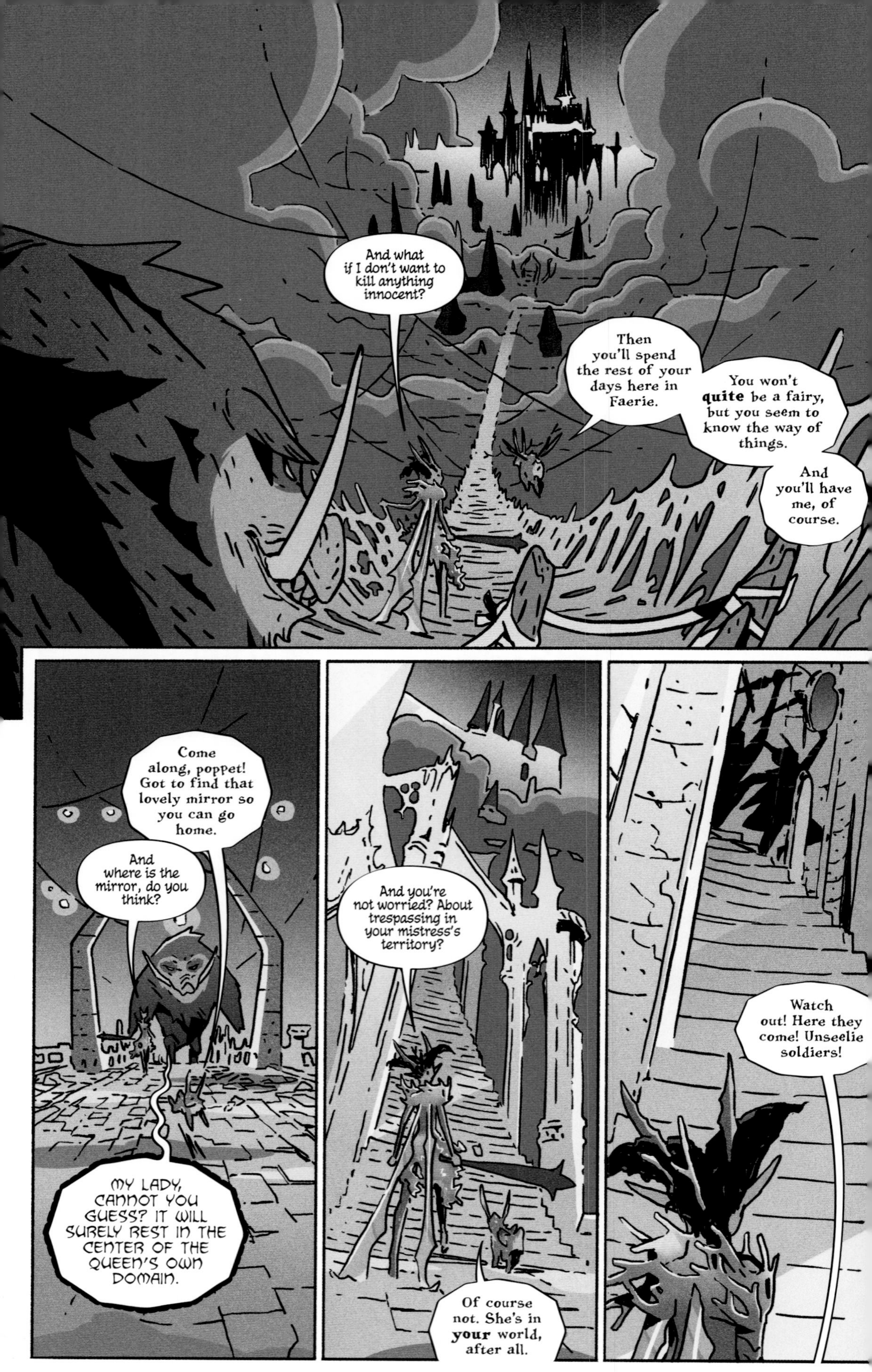
And what if I don't want to kill anything innocent?
Then you'll spend the rest of your days here in Faerie.
You won't **quite** be a fairy, but you seem to know the way of things.
And you'll have me, of course.
Come along, poppet! Got to find that lovely mirror so you can go home.
And where is the mirror, do you think?
MY LADY, CANNOT YOU GUESS? IT WILL SURELY REST IN THE CENTER OF THE QUEEN'S OWN DOMAIN.
And you're not worried? About trespassing in your mistress's territory?
Of course not. She's in **your** world, after all.
Watch out! Here they come! Unseelie soldiers!

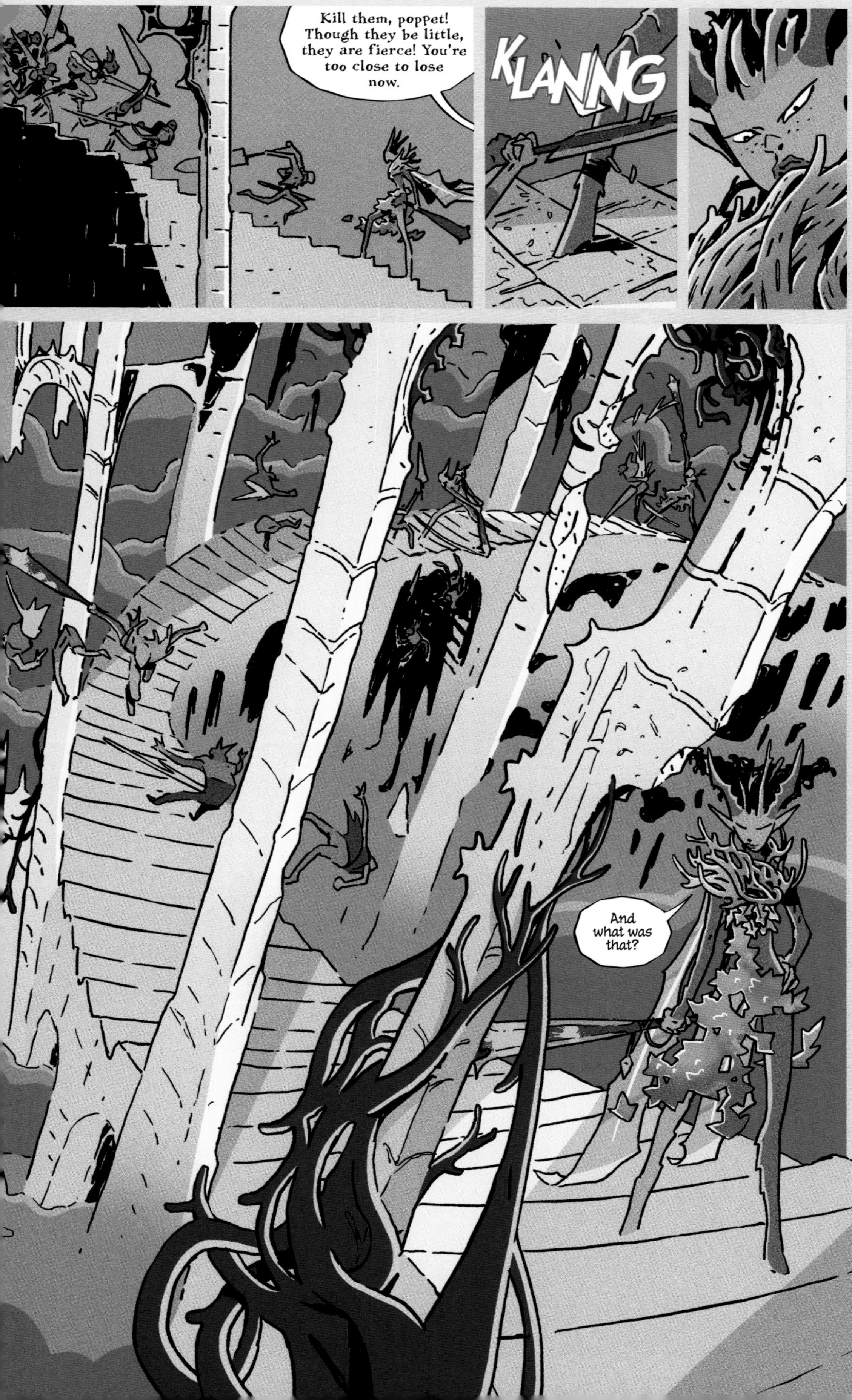
Kill them, poppet! Though they be little, they are fierce! You're too close to lose now.
KLANNG
And what was that?

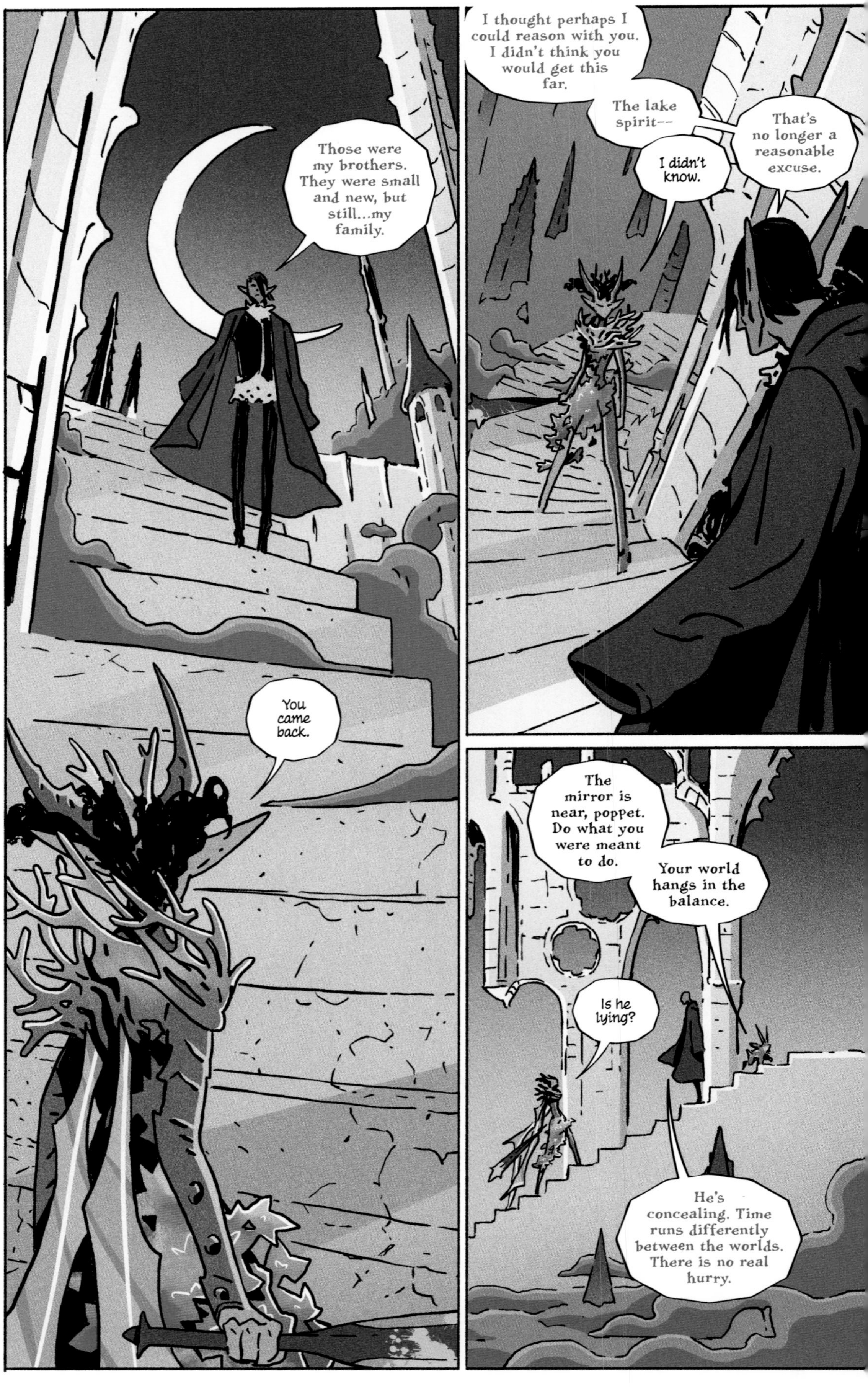
Those were my brothers. They were small and new, but still...my family.
You came back.
I thought perhaps I could reason with you. I didn't think you would get this far.
The lake spirit--
I didn't know.
That's no longer a reasonable excuse.
The mirror is near, poppet. Do what you were meant to do.
Your world hangs in the balance.
Is he lying?
He's concealing. Time runs differently between the worlds. There is no real hurry.

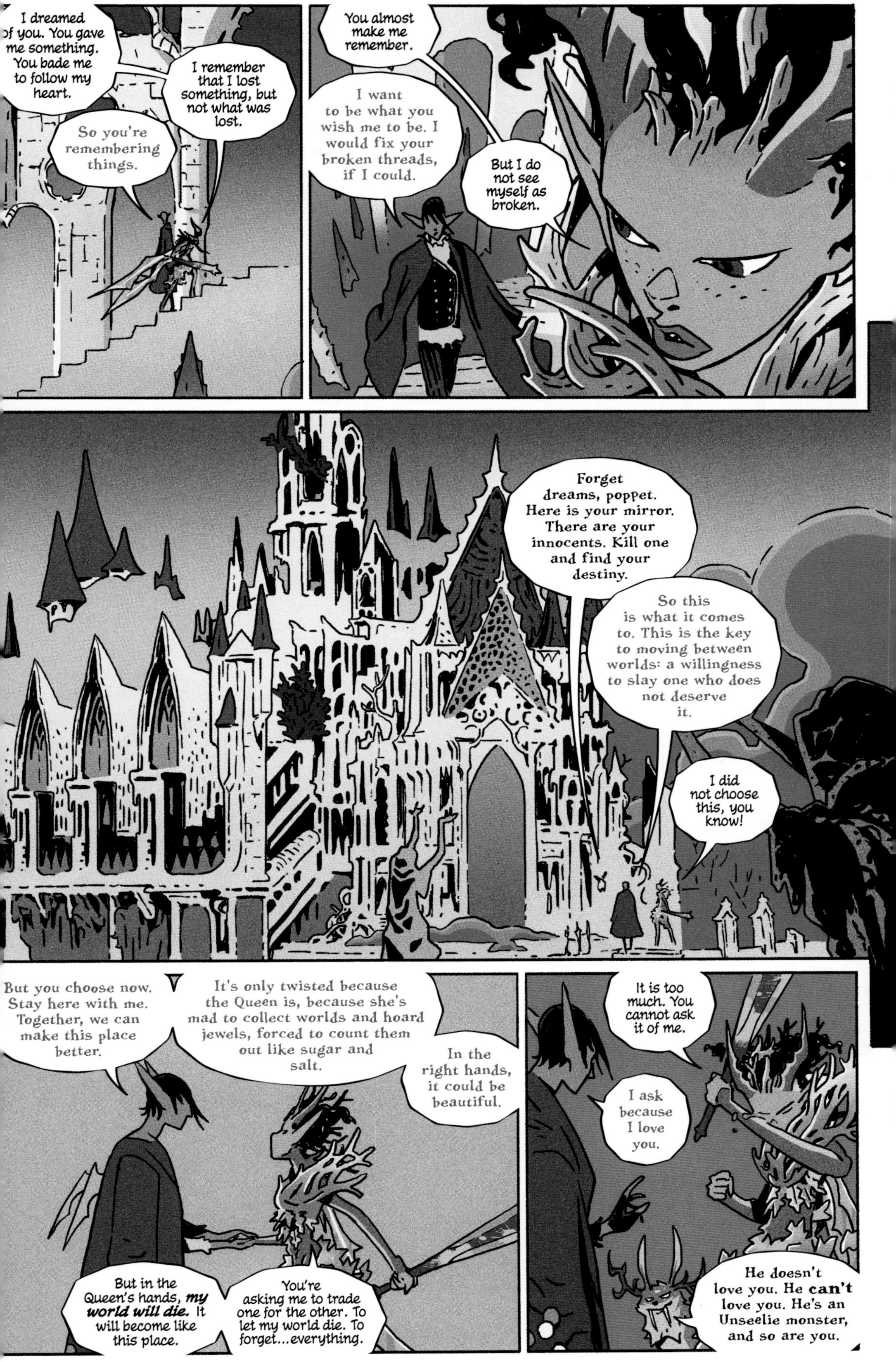
I dreamed of you. You gave me something. You bade me to follow my heart.
So you're remembering things.
I remember that I lost something, but not what was lost.
You almost make me remember.
I want to be what you wish me to be. I would fix your broken threads, if I could.
But I do not see myself as broken.
Forget dreams, poppet. Here is your mirror. There are your innocents. Kill one and find your destiny.
So this is what it comes to. This is the key to moving between worlds: a willingness to slay one who does not deserve it.
I did not choose this, you know!
But you choose now. Stay here with me. Together, we can make this place better.
It's only twisted because the Queen is, because she's mad to collect worlds and hoard jewels, forced to count them out like sugar and salt.
In the right hands, it could be beautiful.
But in the Queen's hands, ***my world will die.*** It will become like this place.
You're asking me to trade one for the other. To let my world die. To forget...everything.
It is too much. You cannot ask it of me.
I ask because I love you.
He doesn't love you. He **can't** love you. He's an Unseelie monster, and so are you.

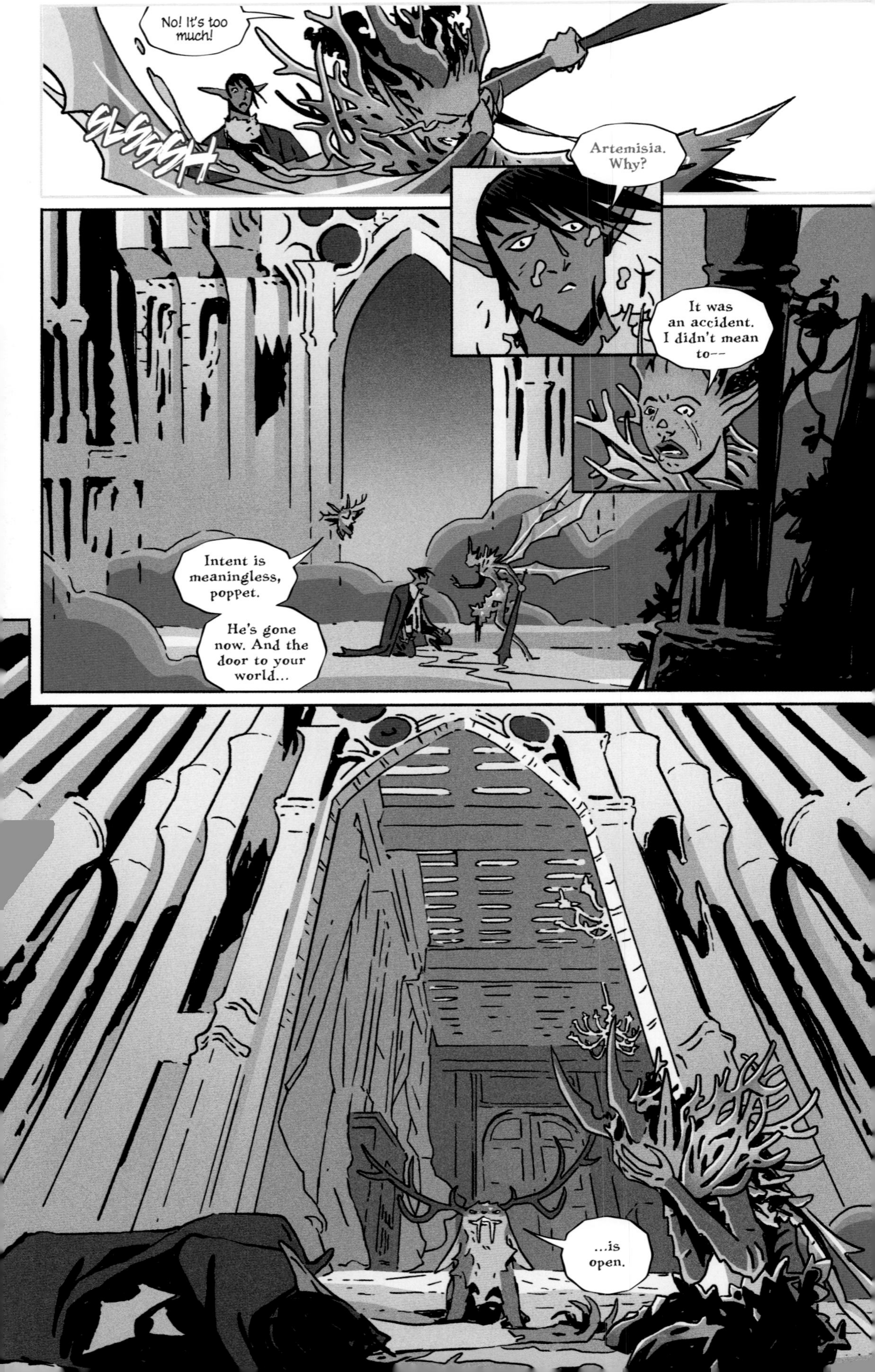
No! It's too much!
SLSSSSH
Artemisia. Why?
It was an accident. I didn't mean to--
Intent is meaningless, poppet.
He's gone now. And the door to your world...
...is open.

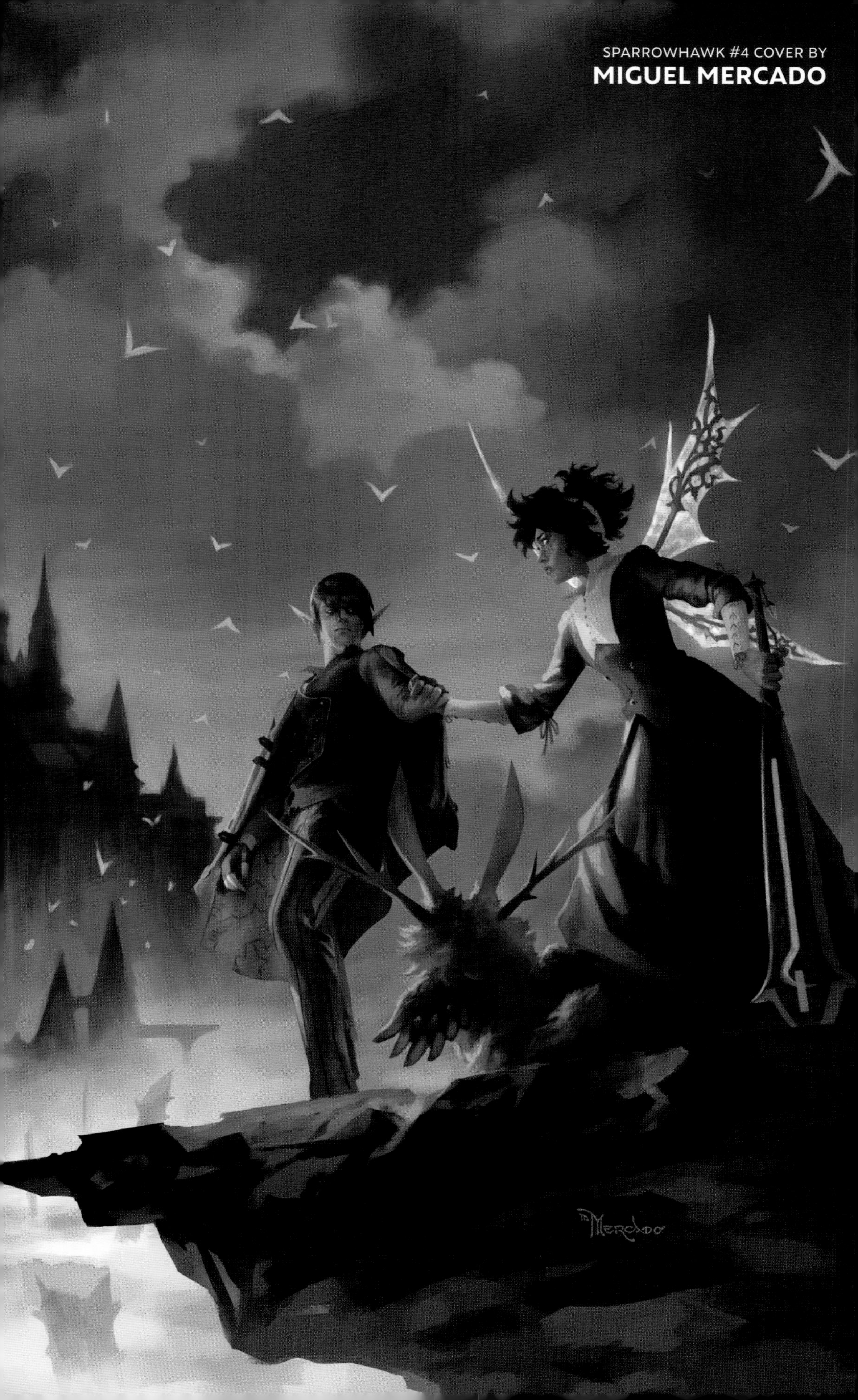

SPARROWHAWK #4 COVER BY
MIGUEL MERCADO

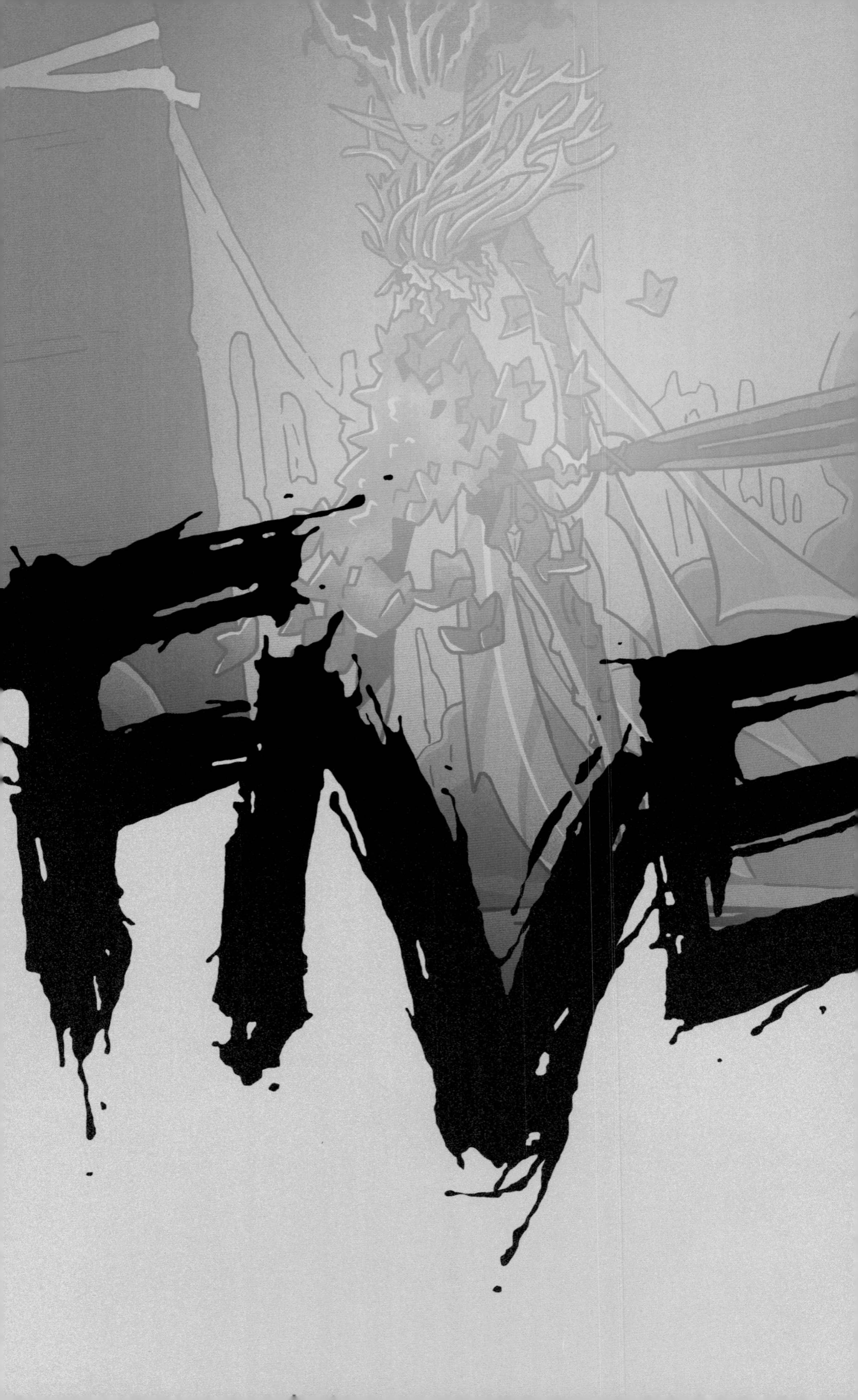
FIVE

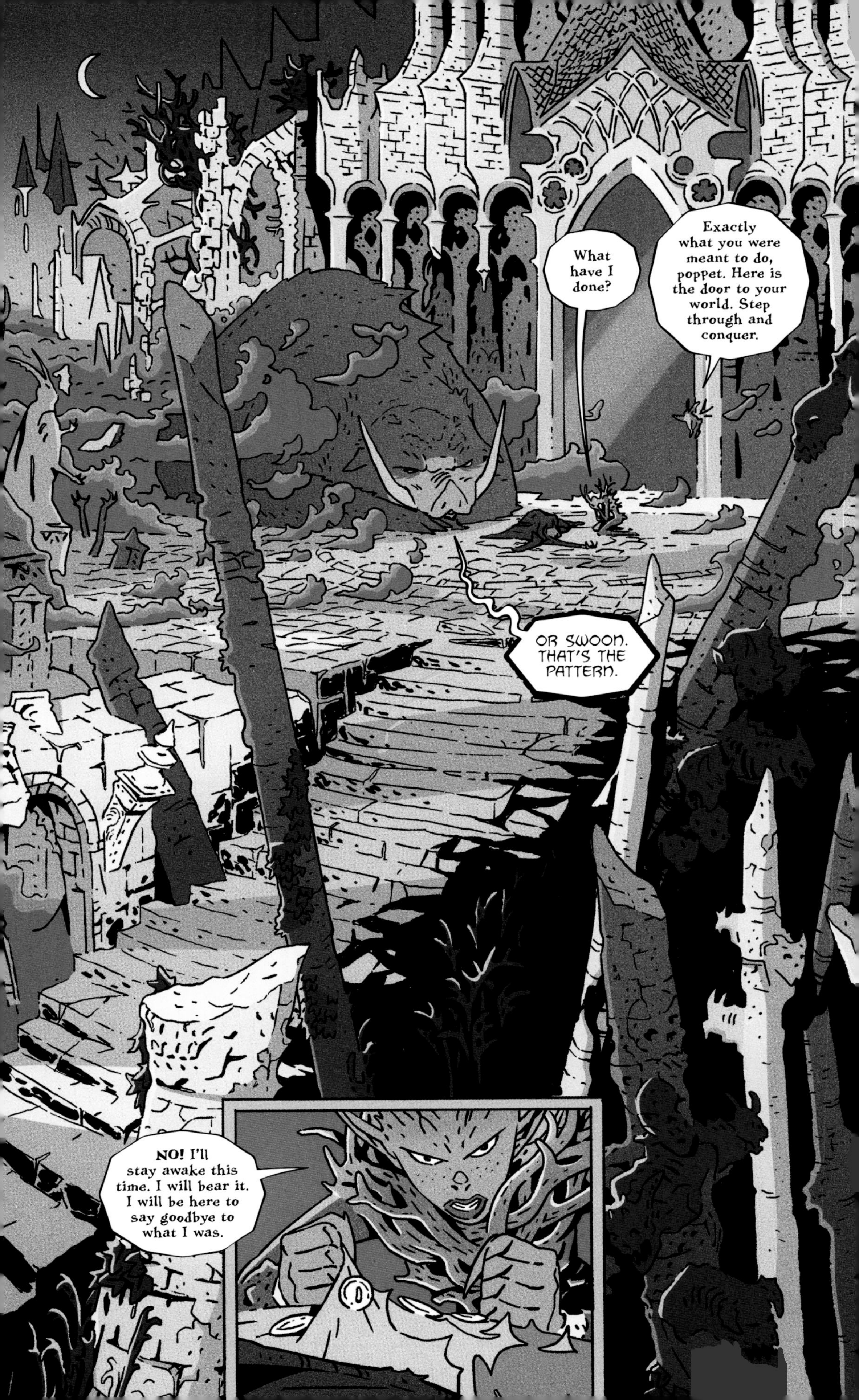
What have I done?
Exactly what you were meant to do, poppet. Here is the door to your world. Step through and conquer.
OR SWOON. THAT'S THE PATTERN.
NO! I'll stay awake this time. I will bear it. I will be here to say goodbye to what I was.

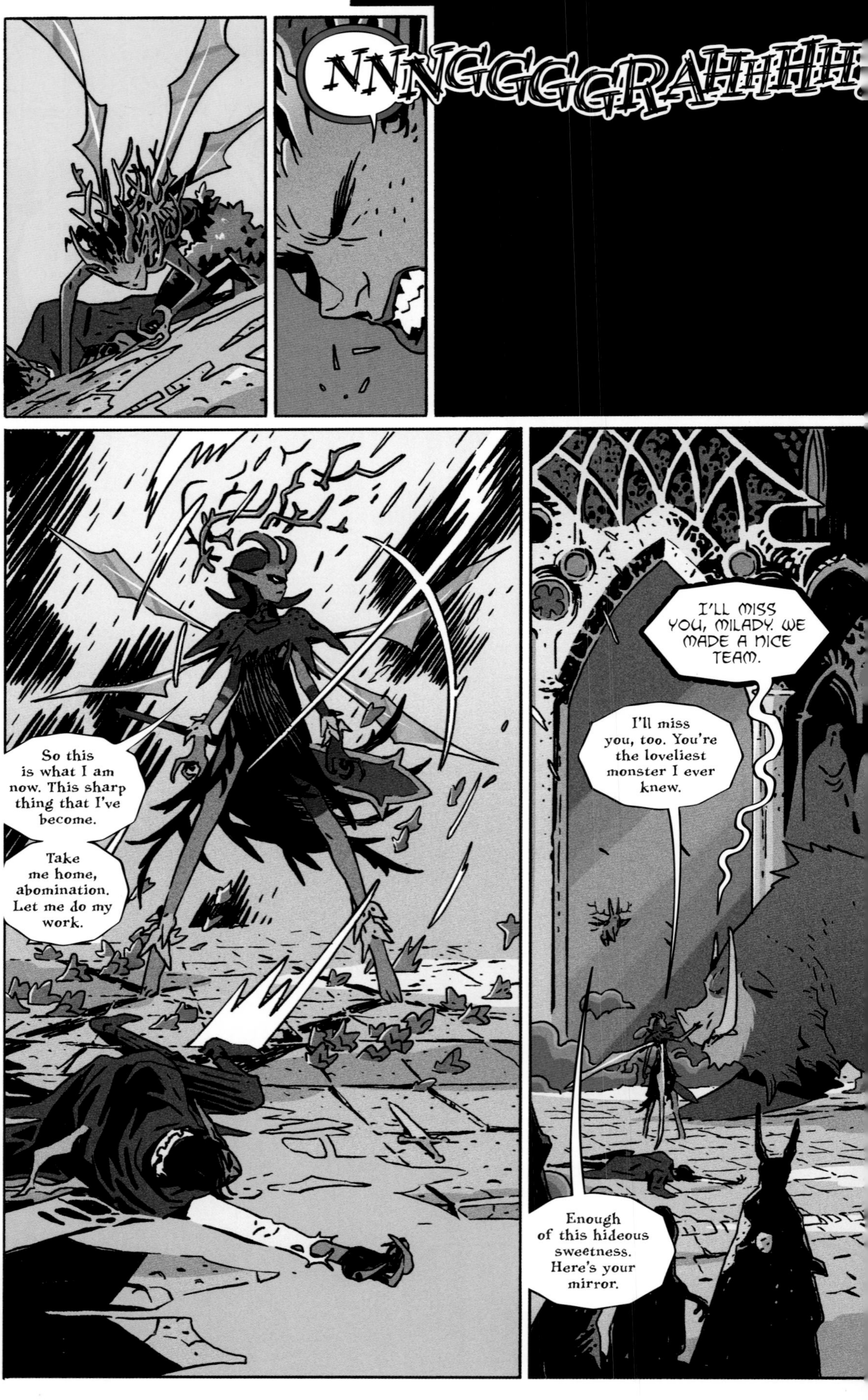
NNNGGGGRAHHHH
So this is what I am now. This sharp thing that I've become.
Take me home, abomination. Let me do my work.
I'LL MISS YOU, MILADY. WE MADE A NICE TEAM.
I'll miss you, too. You're the loveliest monster I ever knew.
Enough of this hideous sweetness. Here's your mirror.

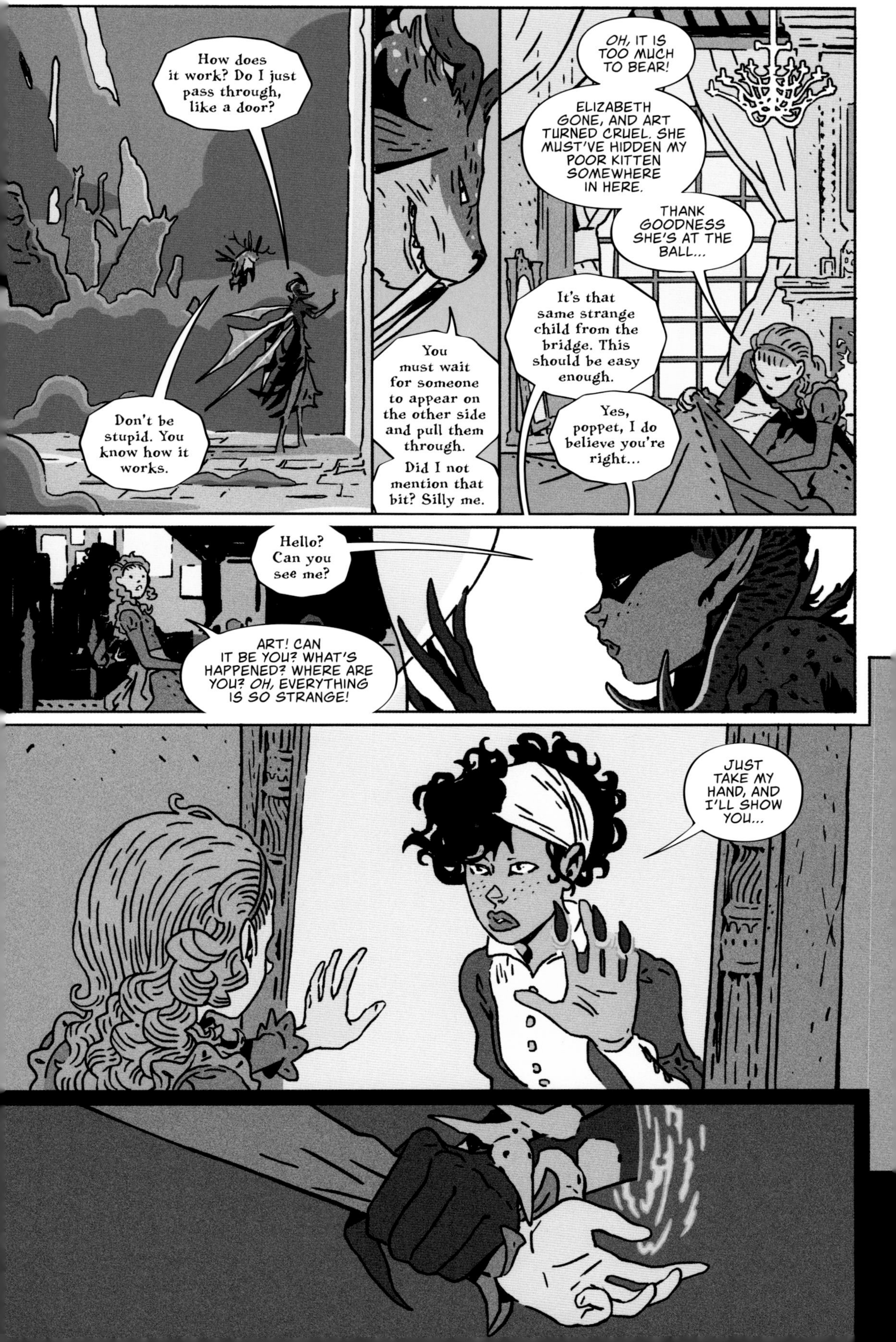
How does it work? Do I just pass through, like a door?
Don't be stupid. You know how it works.
You must wait for someone to appear on the other side and pull them through.
Did I not mention that bit? Silly me.
OH, IT IS TOO MUCH TO BEAR!
ELIZABETH GONE, AND ART TURNED CRUEL. SHE MUST'VE HIDDEN MY POOR KITTEN SOMEWHERE IN HERE.
THANK GOODNESS SHE'S AT THE BALL...
It's that same strange child from the bridge. This should be easy enough.
Yes, poppet, I do believe you're right...
Hello? Can you see me?
ART! CAN IT BE YOU? WHAT'S HAPPENED? WHERE ARE YOU? OH, EVERYTHING IS SO STRANGE!
JUST TAKE MY HAND, AND I'LL SHOW YOU...

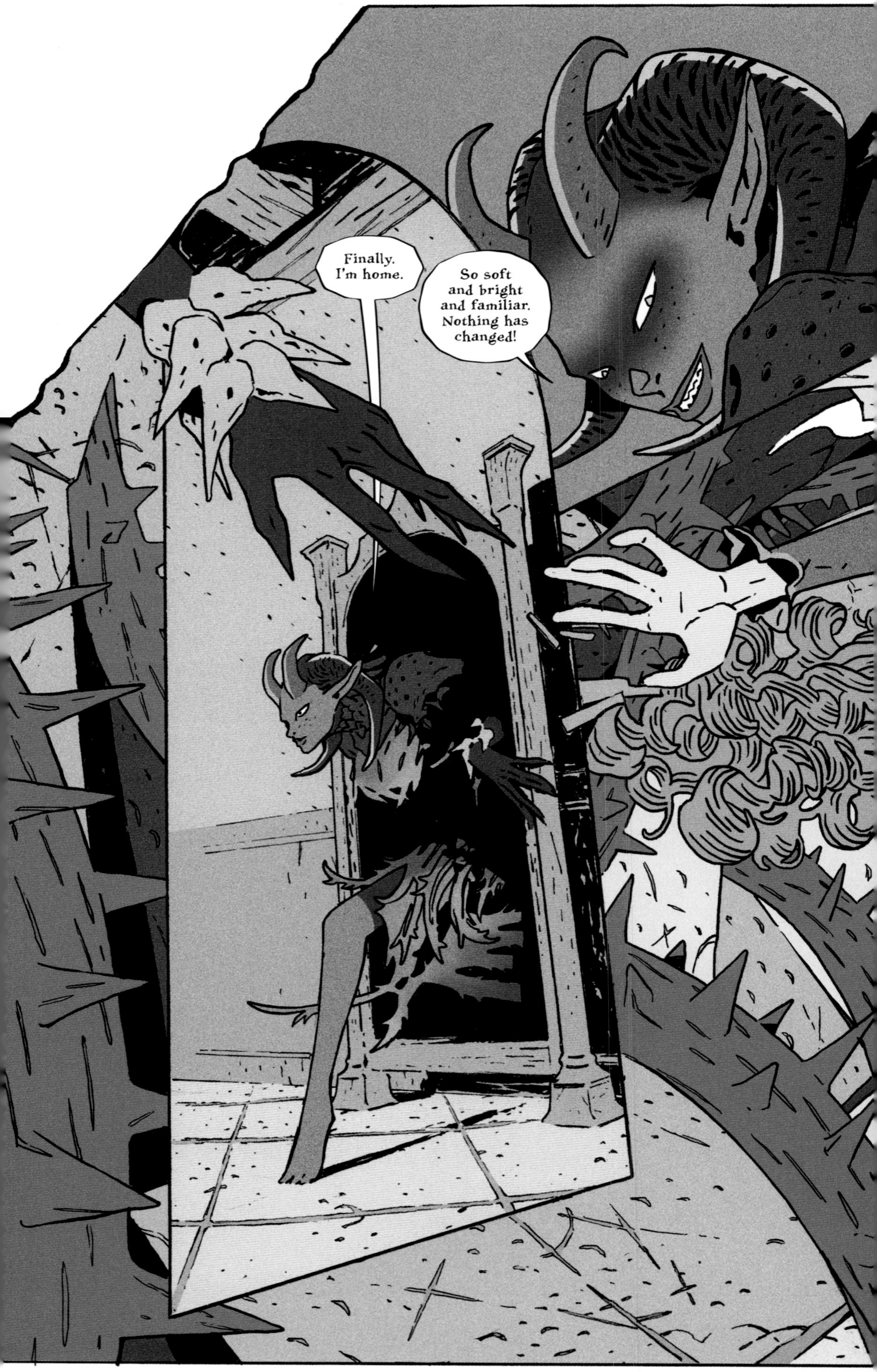
Finally. I'm home.
So soft and bright and familiar. Nothing has changed!

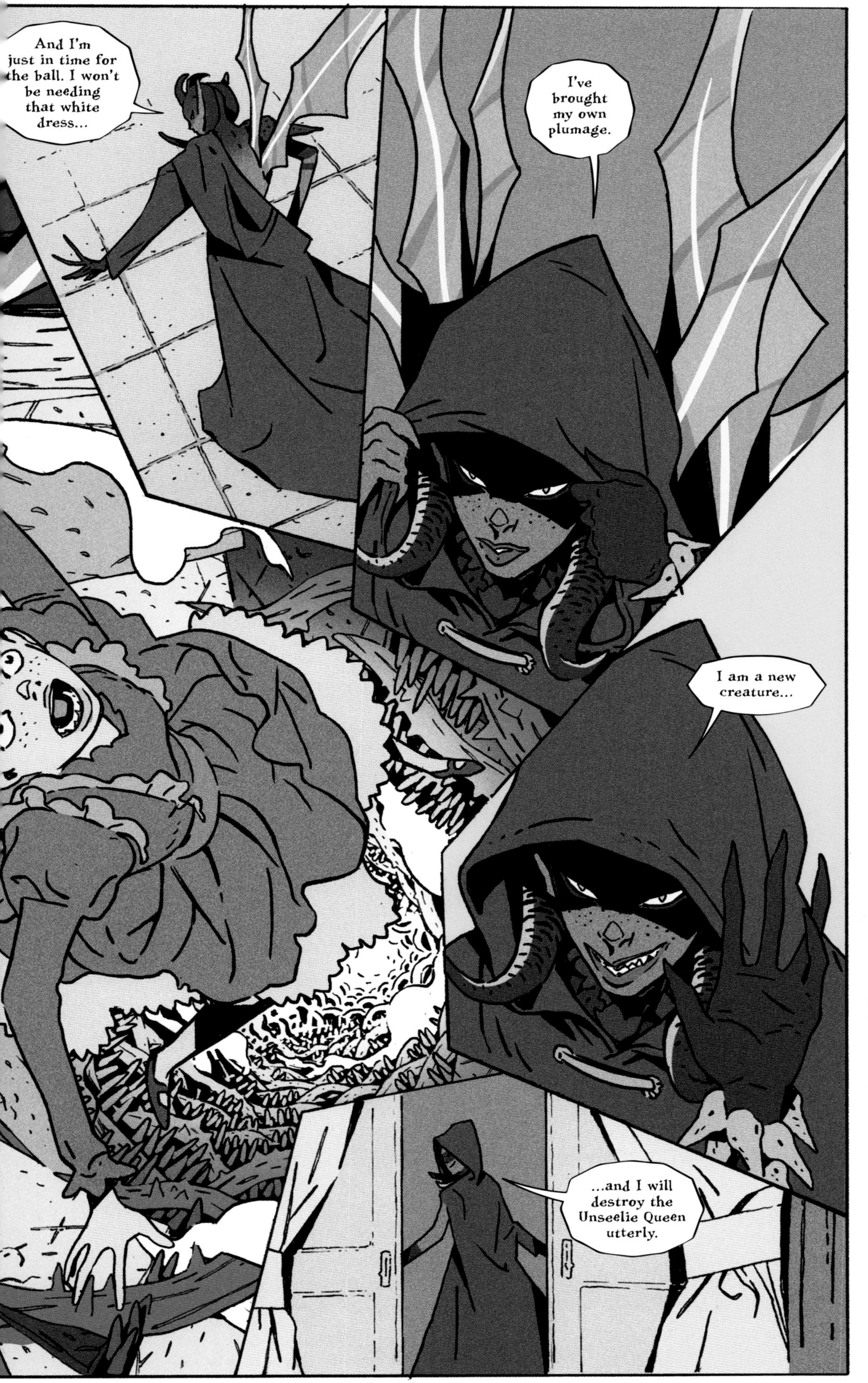
And I'm just in time for the ball. I won't be needing that white dress...
I've brought my own plumage.
I am a new creature...
...and I will destroy the Unseelie Queen utterly.

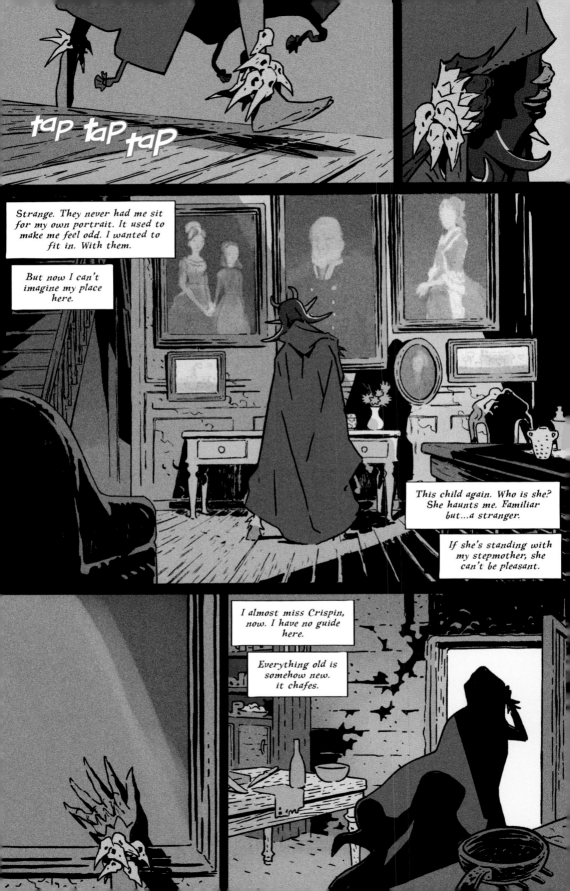

tap tap tap

Strange. They never had me sit for my own portrait. It used to make me feel odd. I wanted to fit in. With them.

But now I can't imagine my place here.

This child again. Who is she? She haunts me. Familiar but...a stranger.

If she's standing with my stepmother, she can't be pleasant.

I almost miss Crispin, now. I have no guide here.

Everything old is somehow new. it chafes.

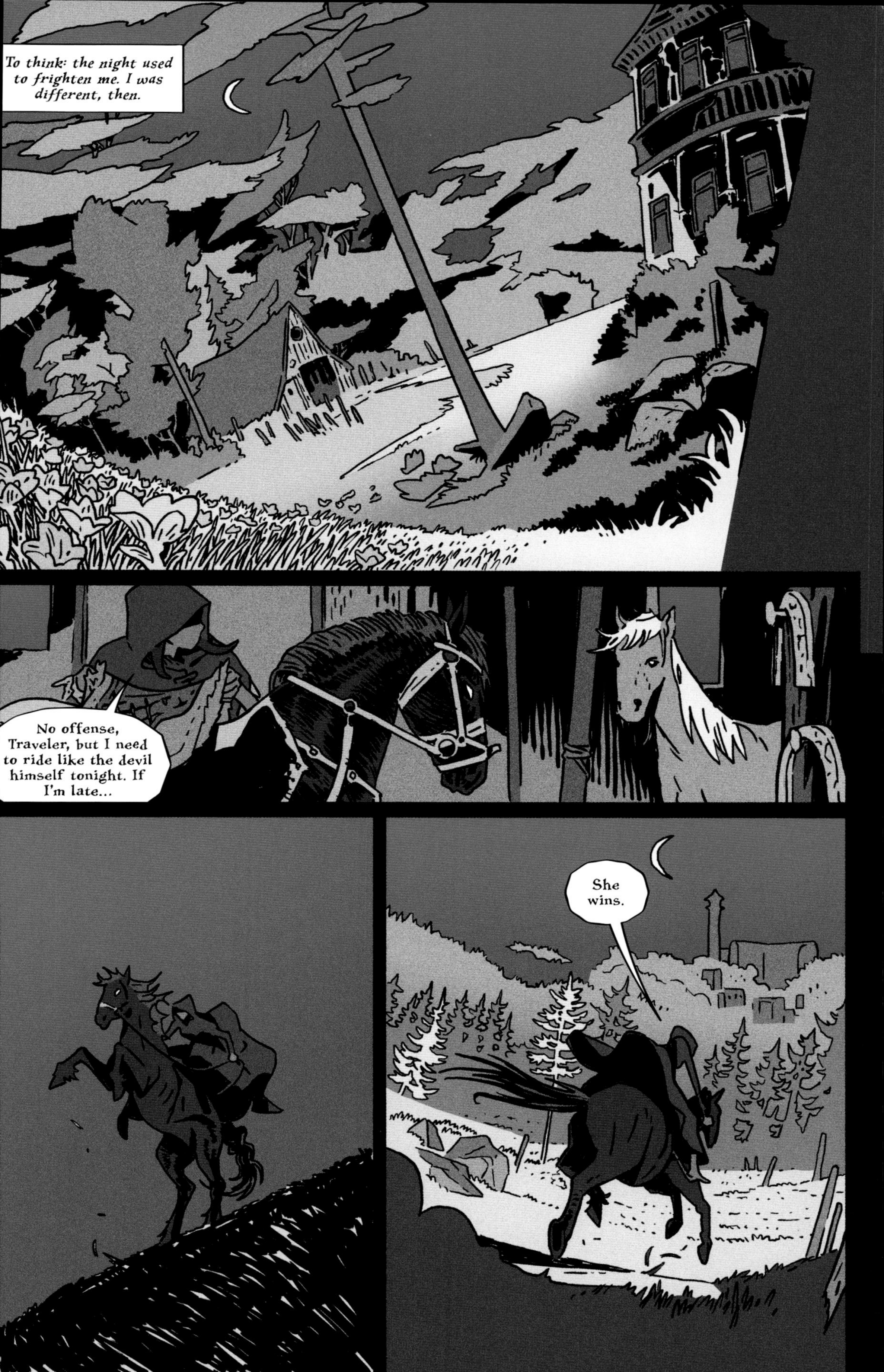
To think: the night used to frighten me. I was different, then.
No offense, Traveler, but I need to ride like the devil himself tonight. If I'm late...
She wins.

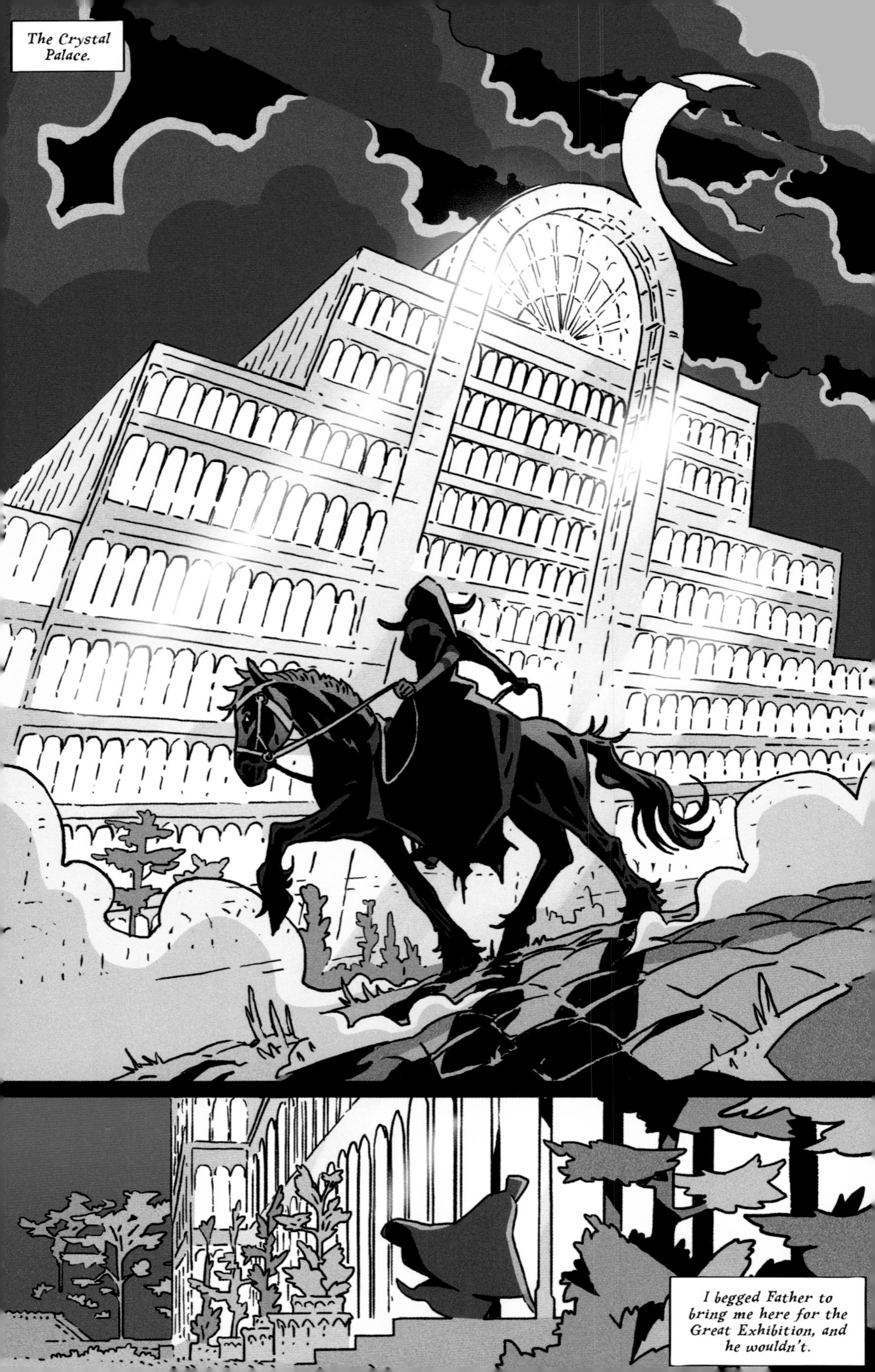
The Crystal Palace.
I begged Father to bring me here for the Great Exhibition, and he wouldn't.

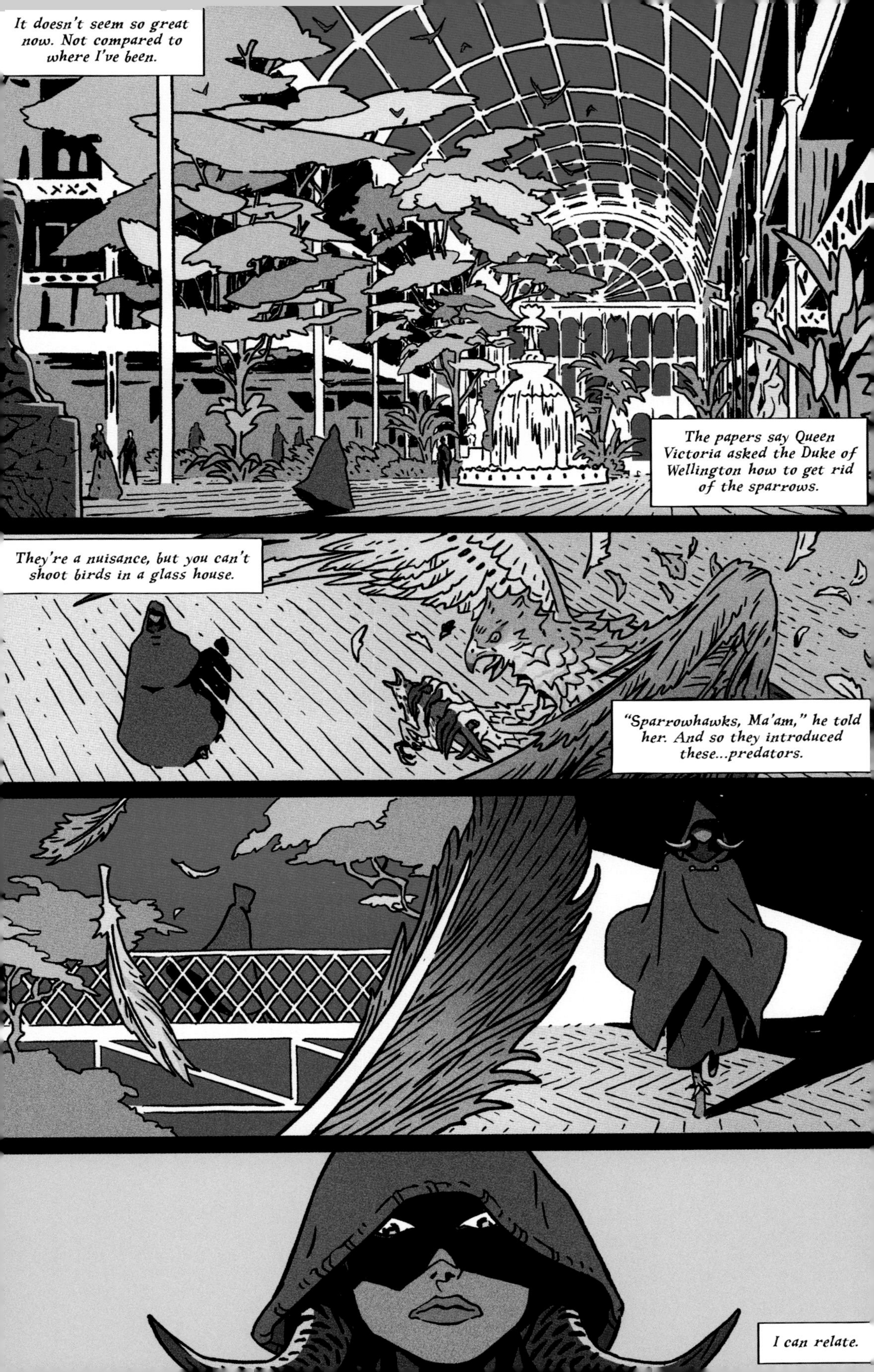
It doesn't seem so great now. Not compared to where I've been.
The papers say Queen Victoria asked the Duke of Wellington how to get rid of the sparrows.
They're a nuisance, but you can't shoot birds in a glass house.
"Sparrowhawks, Ma'am," he told her. And so they introduced these...predators.
I can relate.

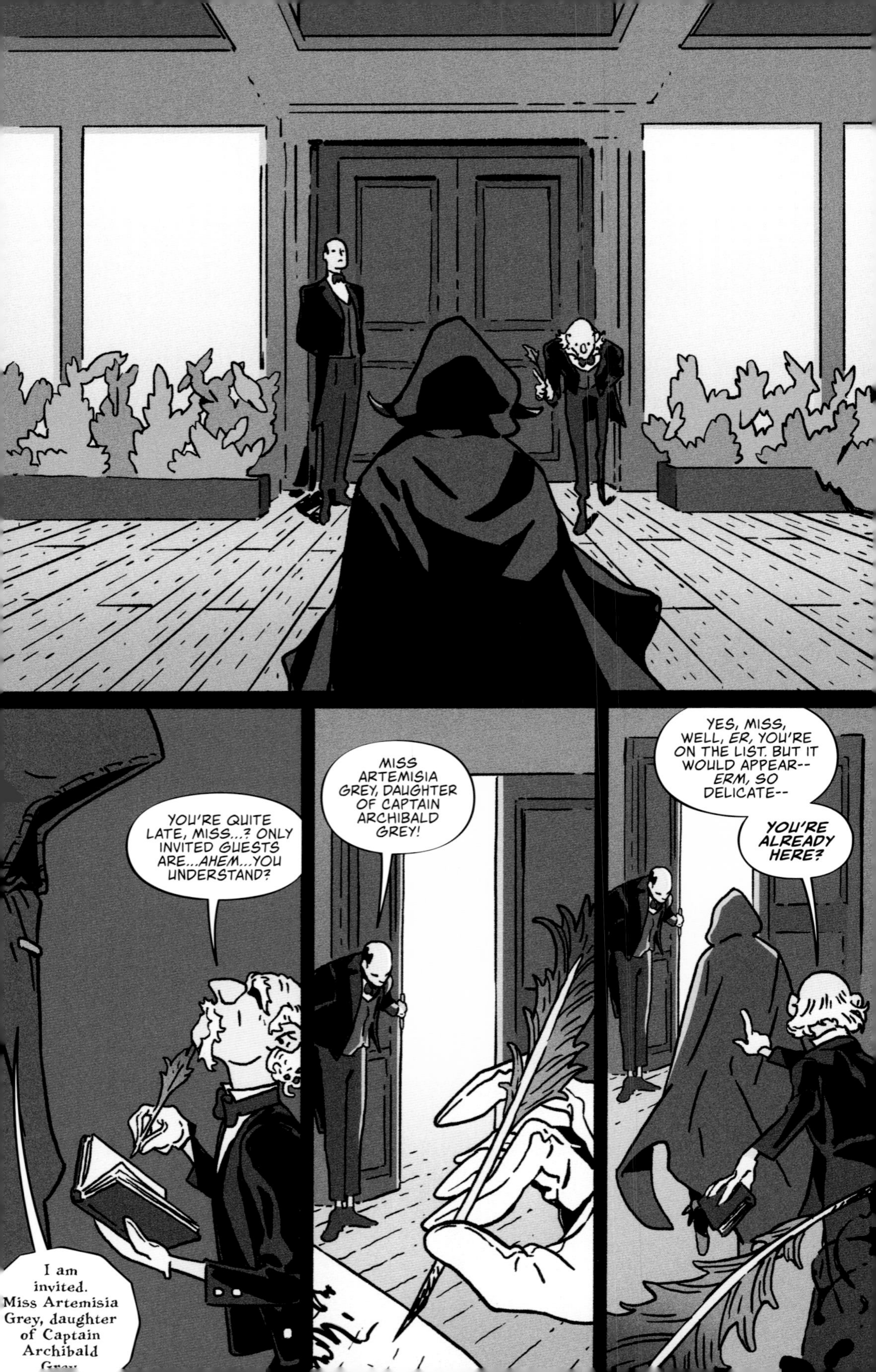
YOU'RE QUITE LATE, MISS...? ONLY INVITED GUESTS ARE...AHEM...YOU UNDERSTAND?
I am invited. Miss Artemisia Grey, daughter of Captain Archibald
MISS ARTEMISIA GREY, DAUGHTER OF CAPTAIN ARCHIBALD GREY!
YES, MISS, WELL, ER, YOU'RE ON THE LIST. BUT IT WOULD APPEAR-- ERM, SO DELICATE--
YOU'RE ALREADY HERE?

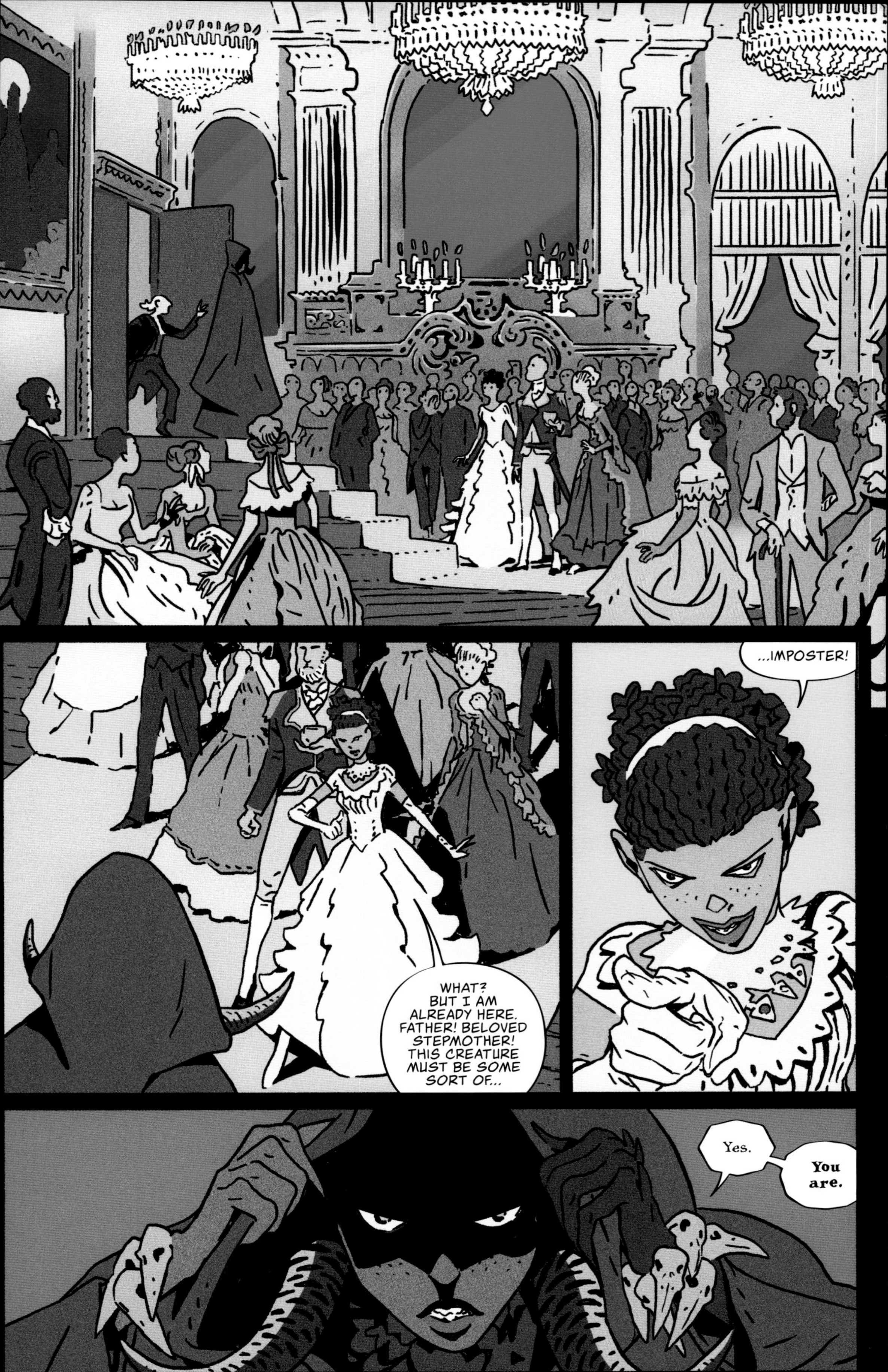
WHAT? BUT I AM ALREADY HERE. FATHER! BELOVED STEPMOTHER! THIS CREATURE MUST BE SOME SORT OF...
...IMPOSTER!
Yes.
You are.

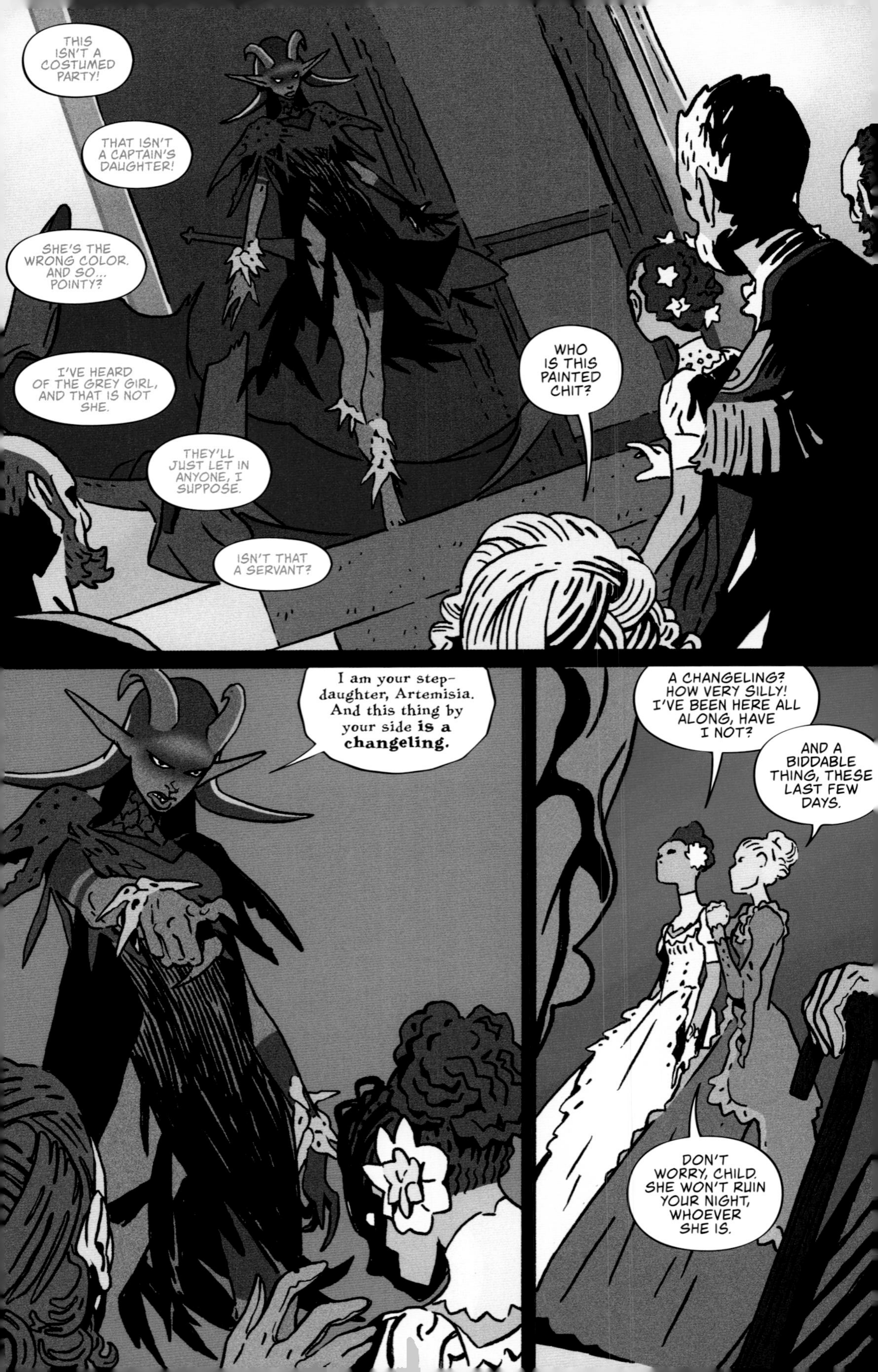
THIS ISN'T A COSTUMED PARTY!
THAT ISN'T A CAPTAIN'S DAUGHTER!
SHE'S THE WRONG COLOR. AND SO... POINTY?
I'VE HEARD OF THE GREY GIRL, AND THAT IS NOT SHE.
THEY'LL JUST LET IN ANYONE, I SUPPOSE.
ISN'T THAT A SERVANT?
WHO IS THIS PAINTED CHIT?
I am your step-daughter, Artemisia. And this thing by your side **is a changeling.**
A CHANGELING? HOW VERY SILLY! I'VE BEEN HERE ALL ALONG, HAVE I NOT?
AND A BIDDABLE THING, THESE LAST FEW DAYS.
DON'T WORRY, CHILD. SHE WON'T RUIN YOUR NIGHT, WHOEVER SHE IS.

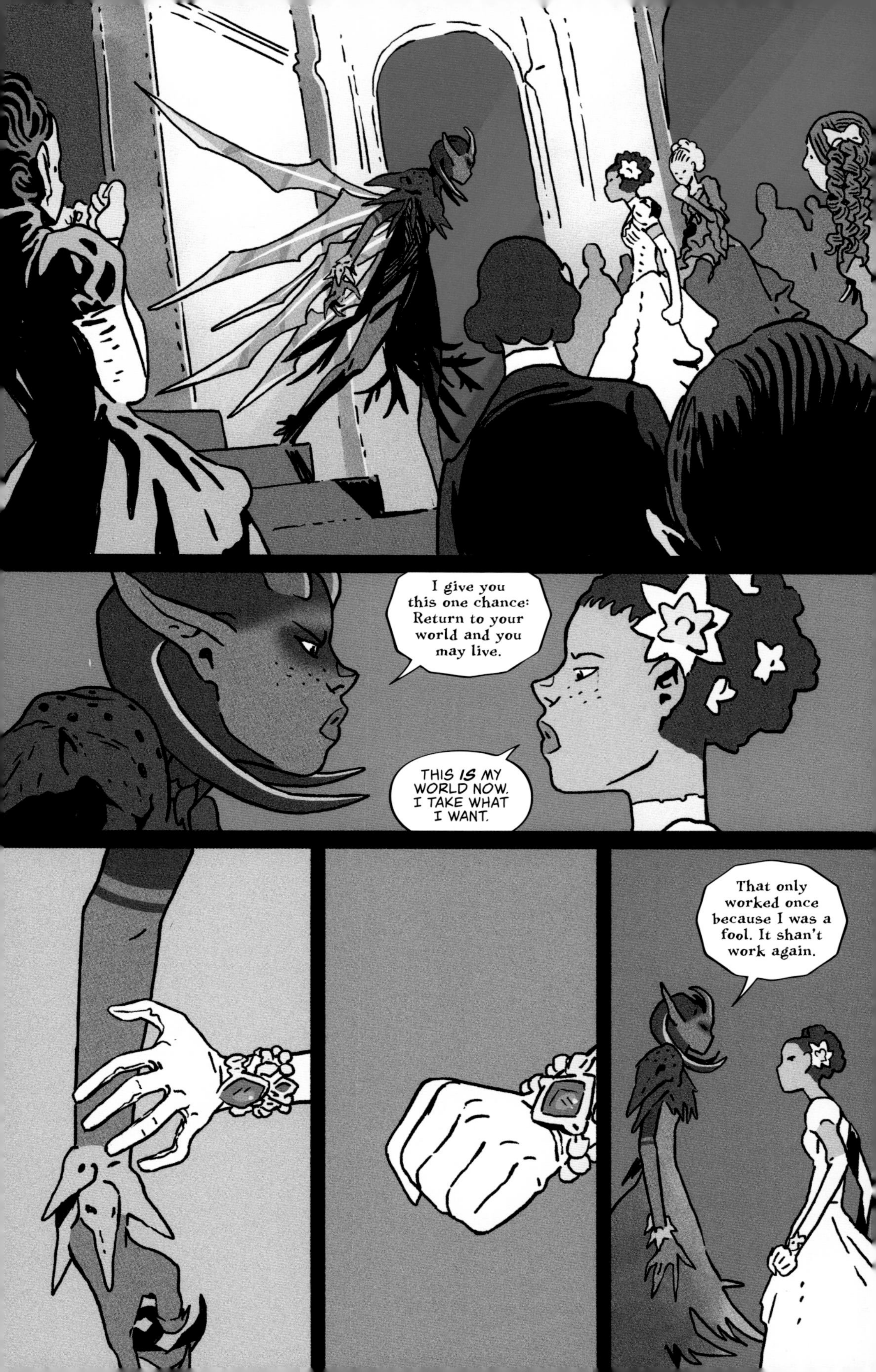
I give you this one chance: Return to your world and you may live.
THIS IS MY WORLD NOW. I TAKE WHAT I WANT.
That only worked once because I was a fool. It shan't work again.

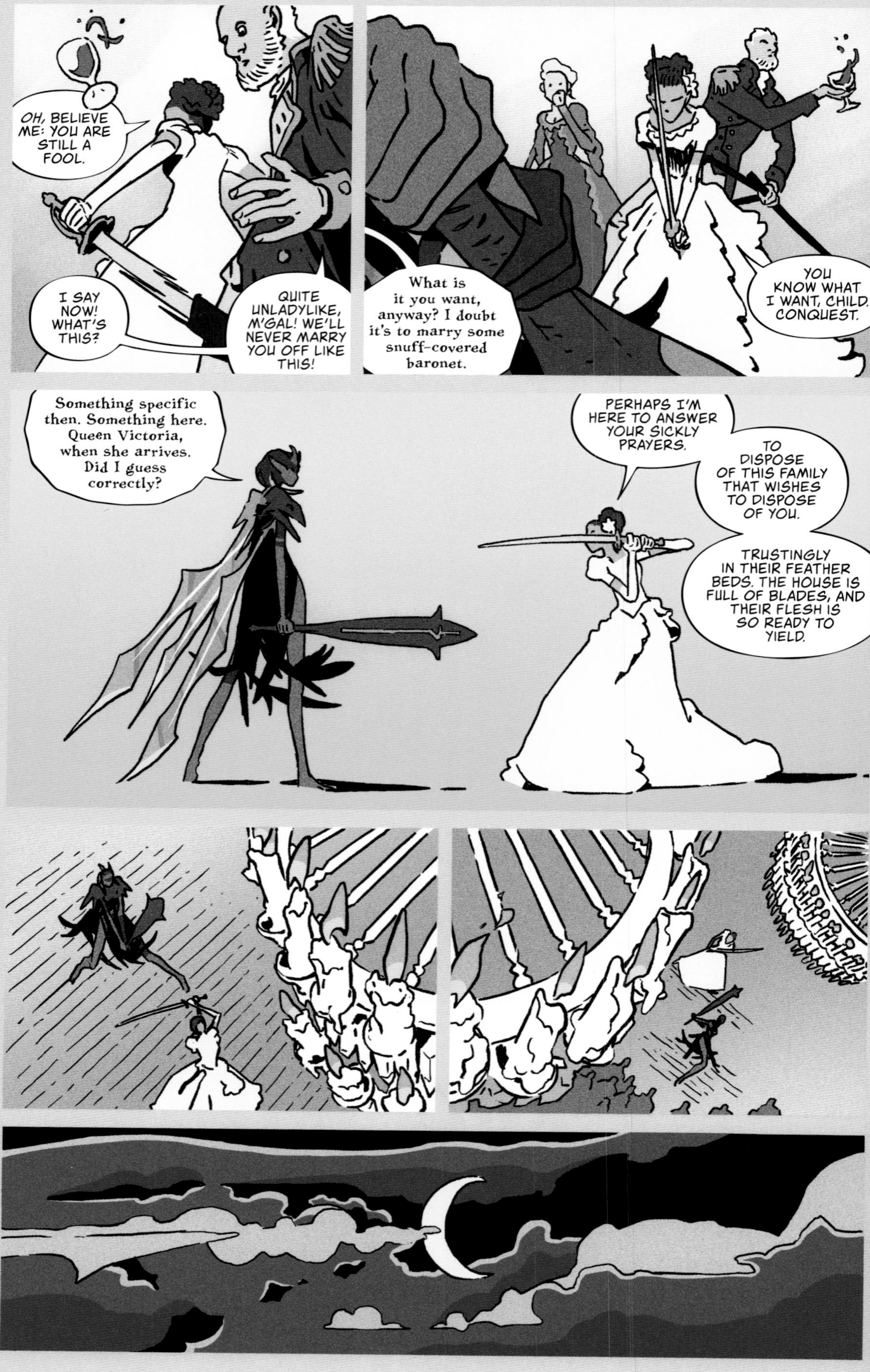
OH, BELIEVE ME: YOU ARE STILL A FOOL.
I SAY NOW! WHAT'S THIS?
QUITE UNLADYLIKE, M'GAL! WE'LL NEVER MARRY YOU OFF LIKE THIS!
What is it you want, anyway? I doubt it's to marry some snuff-covered baronet.
YOU KNOW WHAT I WANT, CHILD. CONQUEST.
Something specific then. Something here. Queen Victoria, when she arrives. Did I guess correctly?
PERHAPS I'M HERE TO ANSWER YOUR SICKLY PRAYERS.
TO DISPOSE OF THIS FAMILY THAT WISHES TO DISPOSE OF YOU.
TRUSTINGLY IN THEIR FEATHER BEDS. THE HOUSE IS FULL OF BLADES, AND THEIR FLESH IS SO READY TO YIELD.

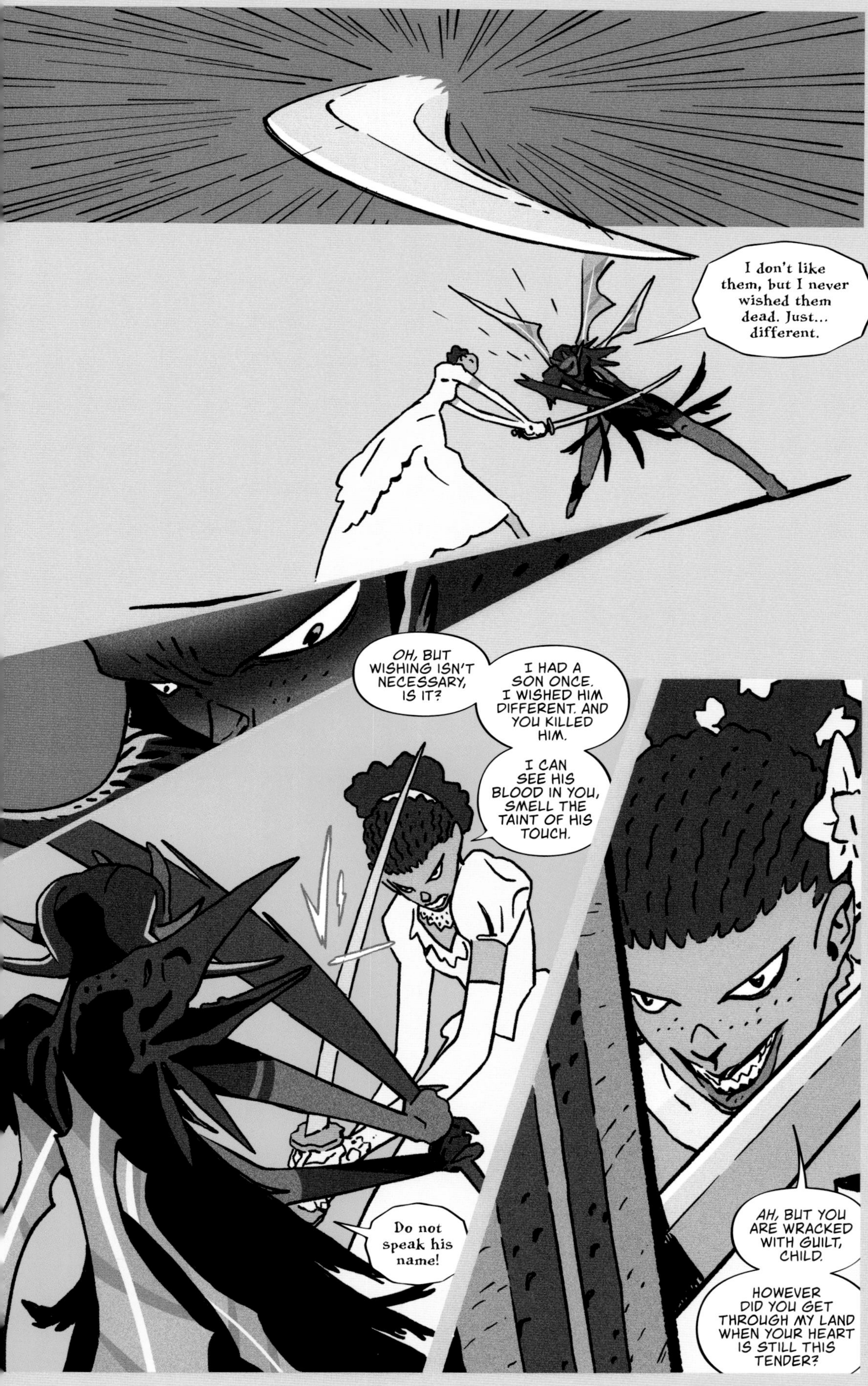
I don't like them, but I never wished them dead. Just... different.
OH, BUT WISHING ISN'T NECESSARY, IS IT?
I HAD A SON ONCE. I WISHED HIM DIFFERENT. AND YOU KILLED HIM.
I CAN SEE HIS BLOOD IN YOU, SMELL THE TAINT OF HIS TOUCH.
Do not speak his name!
AH, BUT YOU ARE WRACKED WITH GUILT, CHILD.
HOWEVER DID YOU GET THROUGH MY LAND WHEN YOUR HEART IS STILL THIS TENDER?

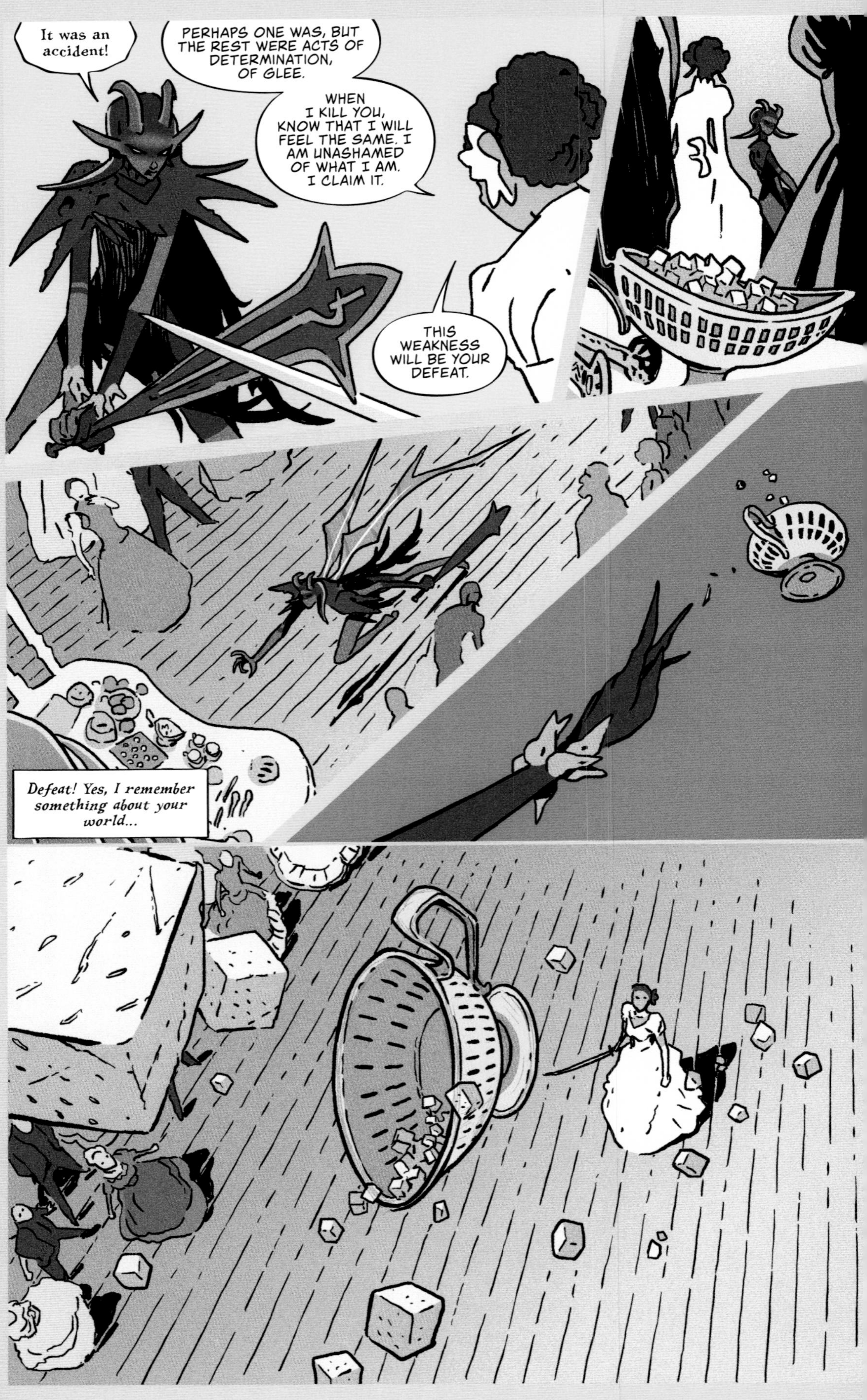
It was an accident!
PERHAPS ONE WAS, BUT THE REST WERE ACTS OF DETERMINATION, OF GLEE.
WHEN I KILL YOU, KNOW THAT I WILL FEEL THE SAME. I AM UNASHAMED OF WHAT I AM. I CLAIM IT.
THIS WEAKNESS WILL BE YOUR DEFEAT.
Defeat! Yes, I remember something about your world...

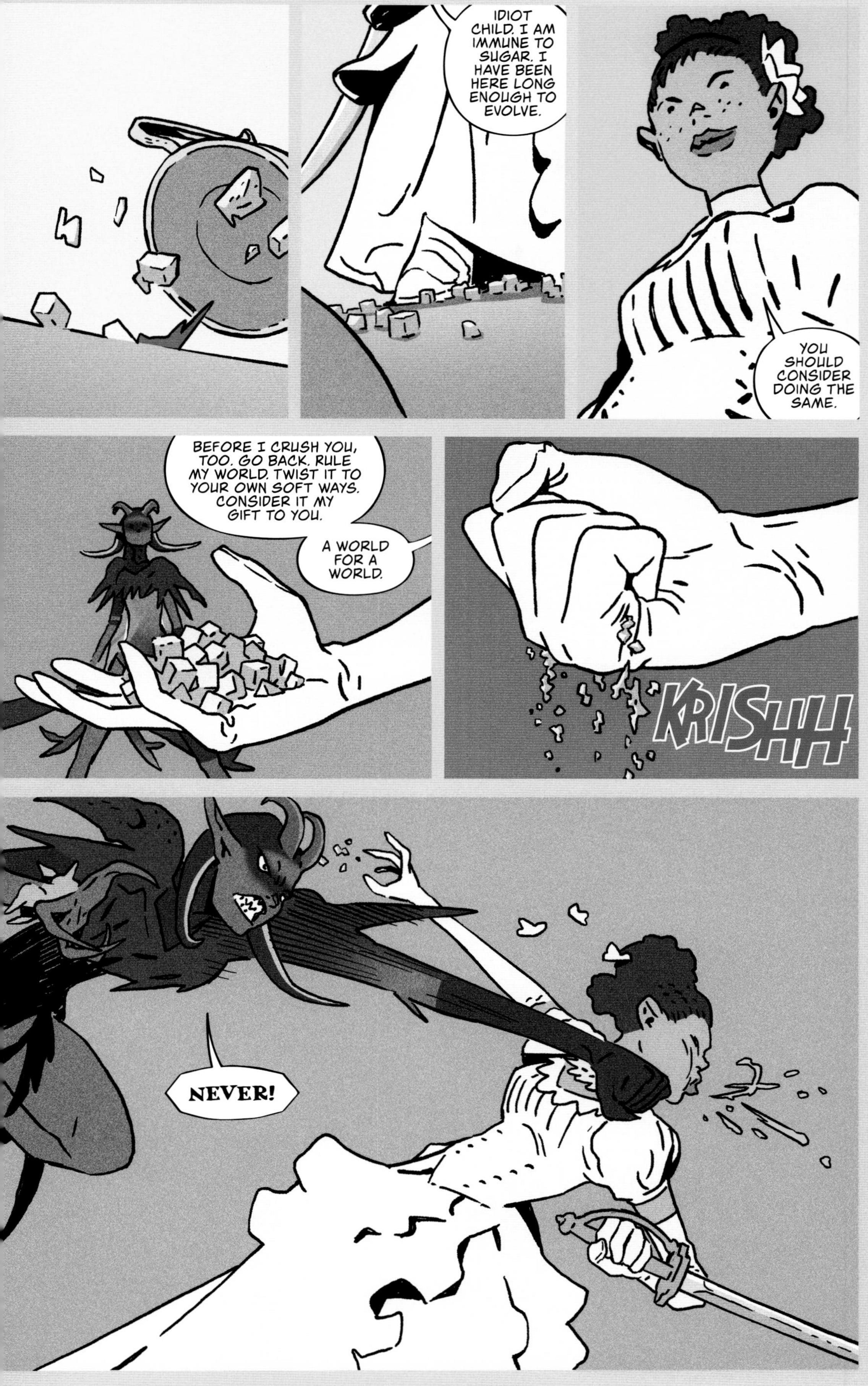
IDIOT CHILD. I AM IMMUNE TO SUGAR. I HAVE BEEN HERE LONG ENOUGH TO EVOLVE.
YOU SHOULD CONSIDER DOING THE SAME.
BEFORE I CRUSH YOU, TOO. GO BACK. RULE MY WORLD. TWIST IT TO YOUR OWN SOFT WAYS. CONSIDER IT MY GIFT TO YOU.
A WORLD FOR A WORLD.
KRISHH
NEVER!

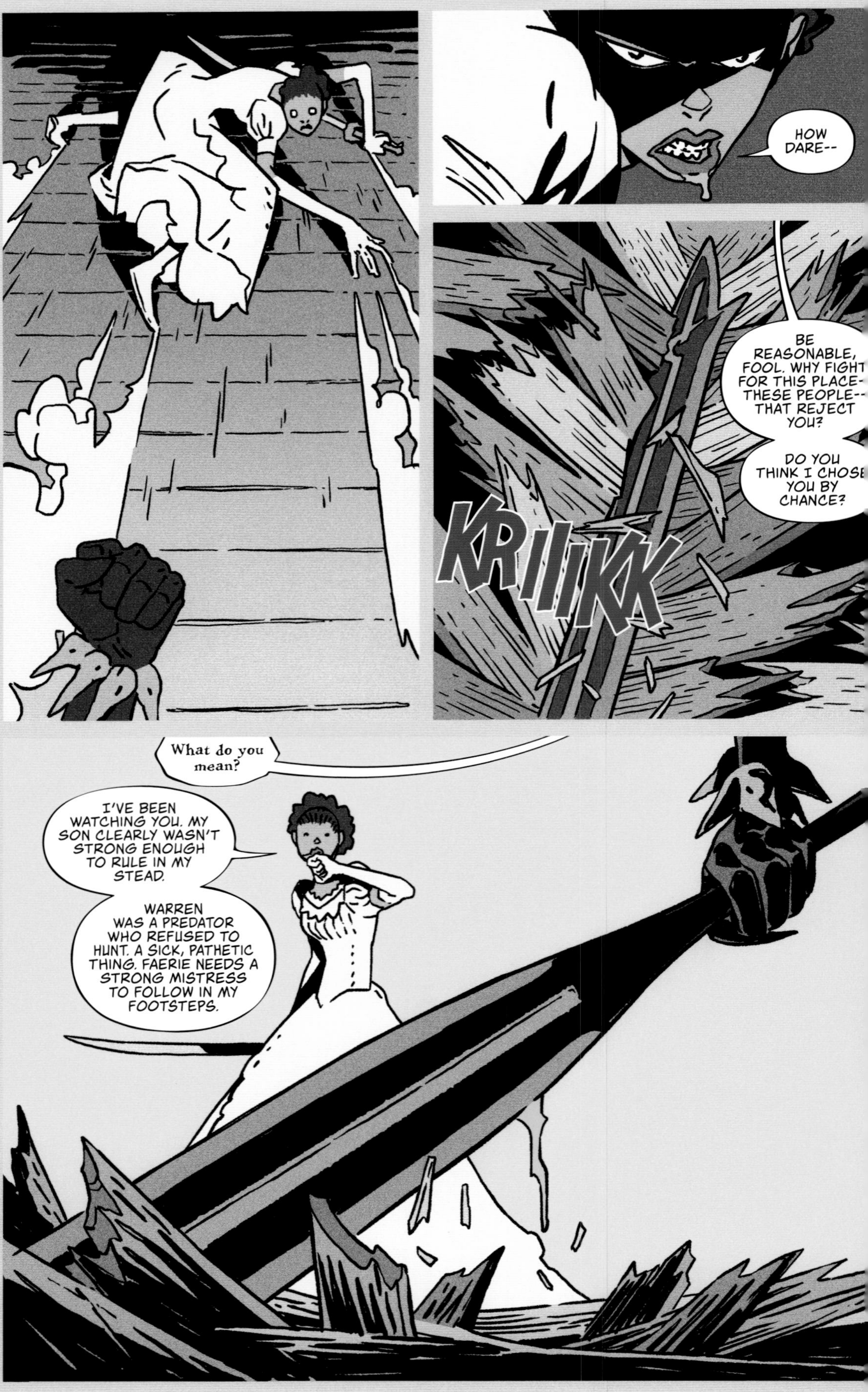
HOW DARE--
BE REASONABLE, FOOL. WHY FIGHT FOR THIS PLACE-- THESE PEOPLE-- THAT REJECT YOU?
DO YOU THINK I CHOSE YOU BY CHANCE?
KRIIIKK
What do you mean?
I'VE BEEN WATCHING YOU. MY SON CLEARLY WASN'T STRONG ENOUGH TO RULE IN MY STEAD.
WARREN WAS A PREDATOR WHO REFUSED TO HUNT. A SICK, PATHETIC THING. FAERIE NEEDS A STRONG MISTRESS TO FOLLOW IN MY FOOTSTEPS.

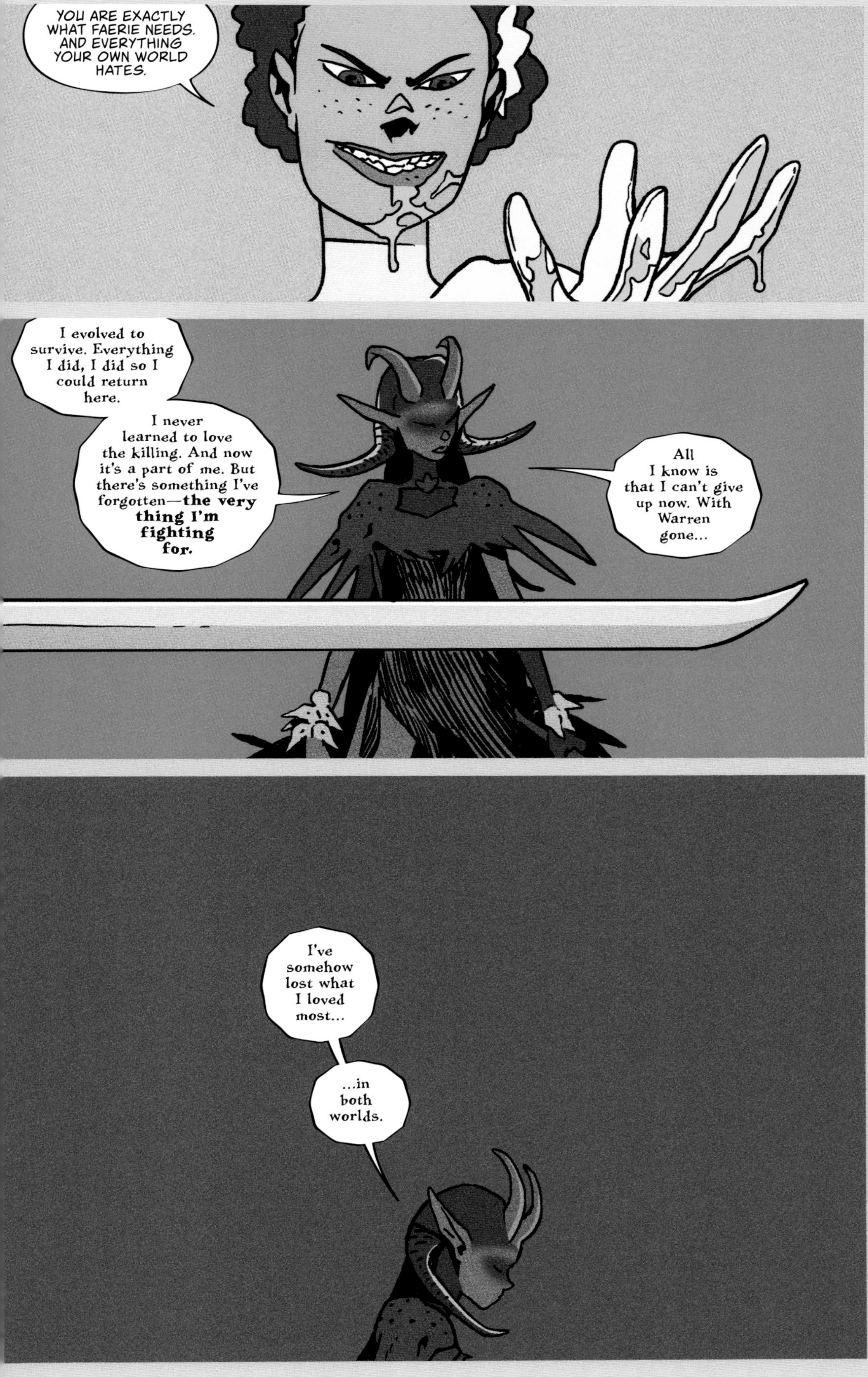
YOU ARE EXACTLY WHAT FAERIE NEEDS. AND EVERYTHING YOUR OWN WORLD HATES.
I evolved to survive. Everything I did, I did so I could return here.
I never learned to love the killing. And now it's a part of me. But there's something I've forgotten—**the very thing I'm fighting for.**
All I know is that I can't give up now. With Warren gone...
I've somehow lost what I loved most...
...in both worlds.

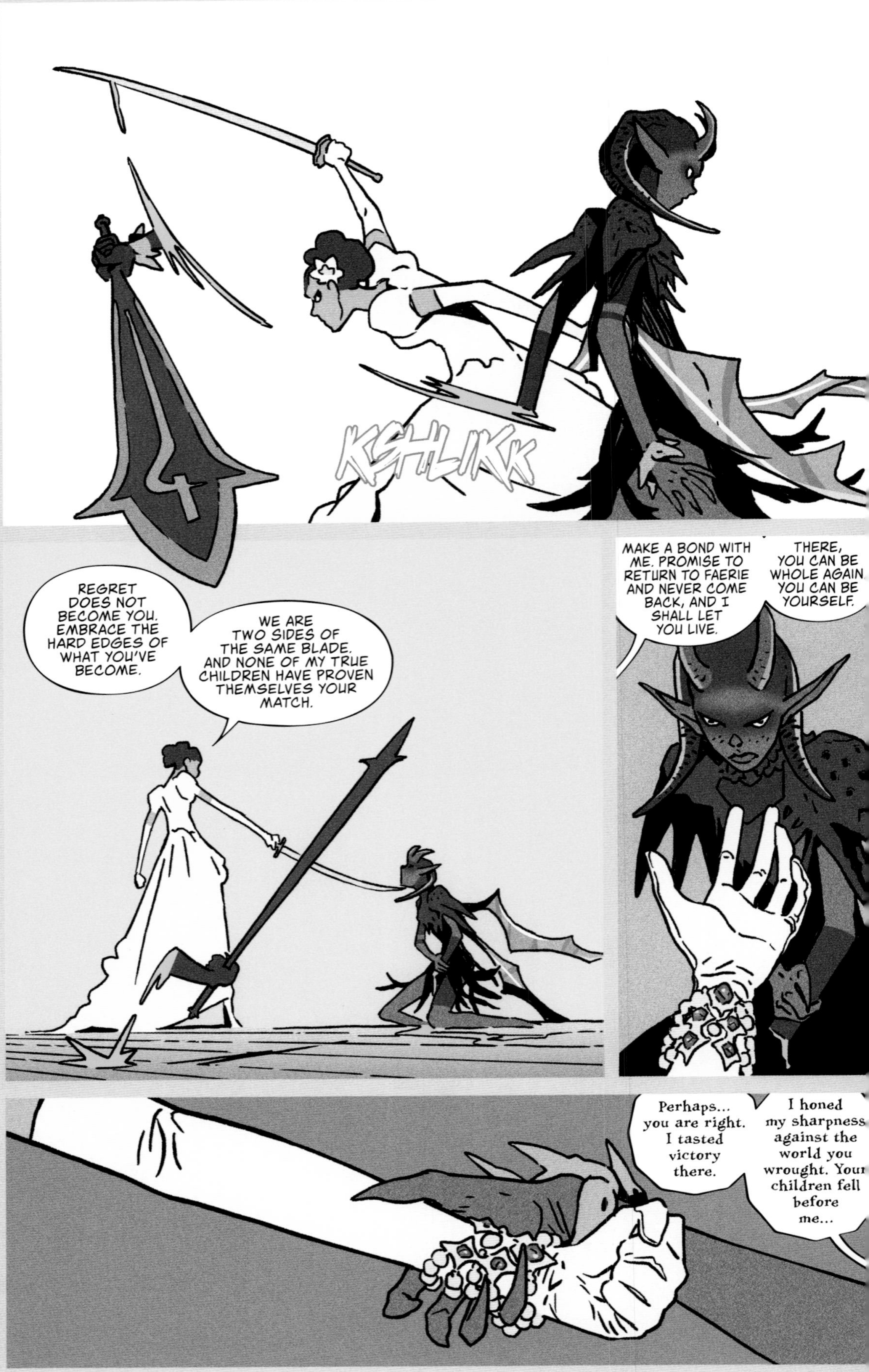
KSHLIKK
REGRET DOES NOT BECOME YOU. EMBRACE THE HARD EDGES OF WHAT YOU'VE BECOME.
WE ARE TWO SIDES OF THE SAME BLADE. AND NONE OF MY TRUE CHILDREN HAVE PROVEN THEMSELVES YOUR MATCH.
MAKE A BOND WITH ME. PROMISE TO RETURN TO FAERIE AND NEVER COME BACK, AND I SHALL LET YOU LIVE.
THERE, YOU CAN BE WHOLE AGAIN. YOU CAN BE YOURSELF.
Perhaps... you are right. I tasted victory there.
I honed my sharpness against the world you wrought. Your children fell before me...

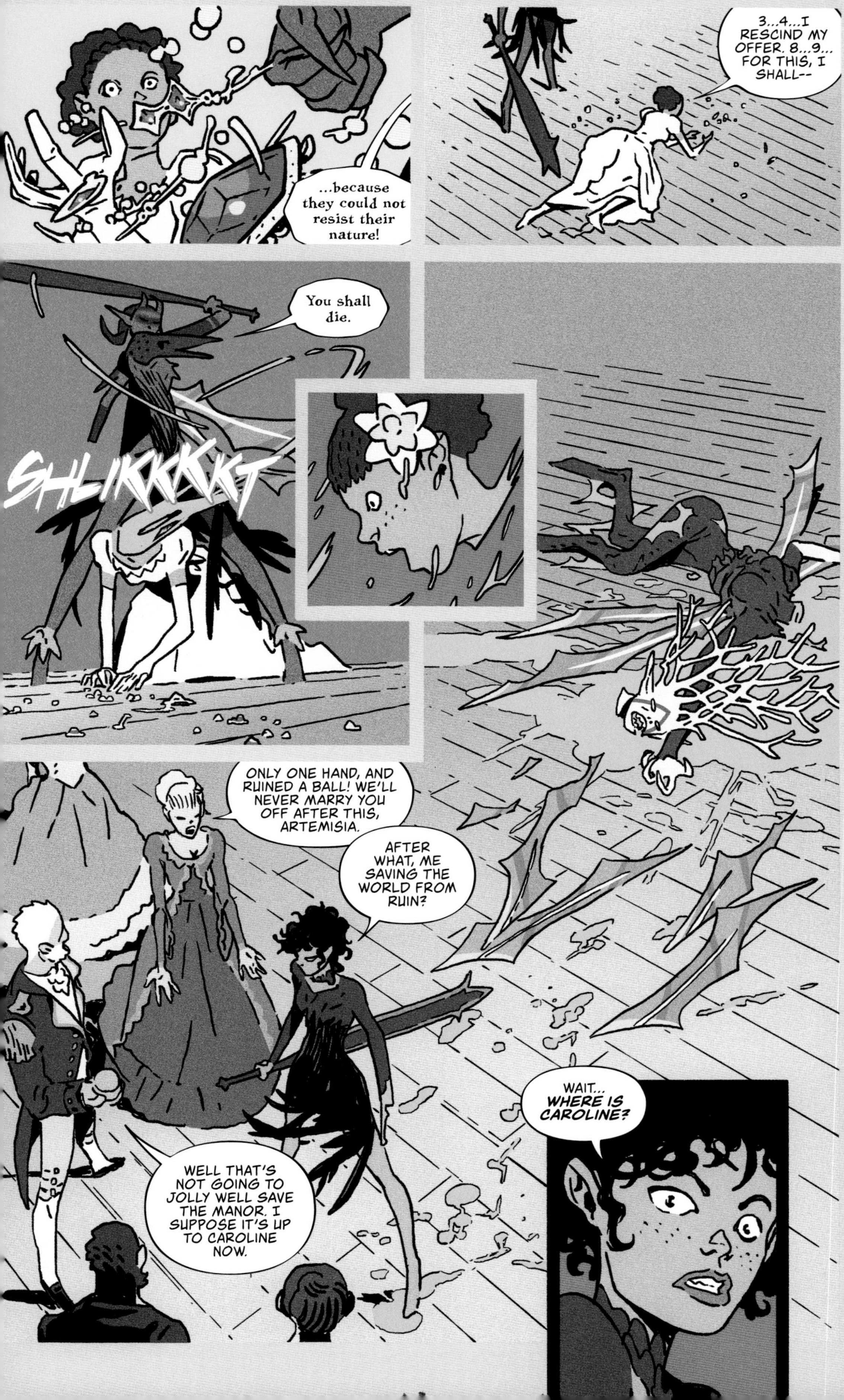
...because they could not resist their nature!
3...4...I RESCIND MY OFFER. 8...9... FOR THIS, I SHALL--
You shall die.
SHLIKKKKT
ONLY ONE HAND, AND RUINED A BALL! WE'LL NEVER MARRY YOU OFF AFTER THIS, ARTEMISIA.
AFTER WHAT, ME SAVING THE WORLD FROM RUIN?
WELL THAT'S NOT GOING TO JOLLY WELL SAVE THE MANOR. I SUPPOSE IT'S UP TO CAROLINE NOW.
WAIT... *WHERE IS CAROLINE?*

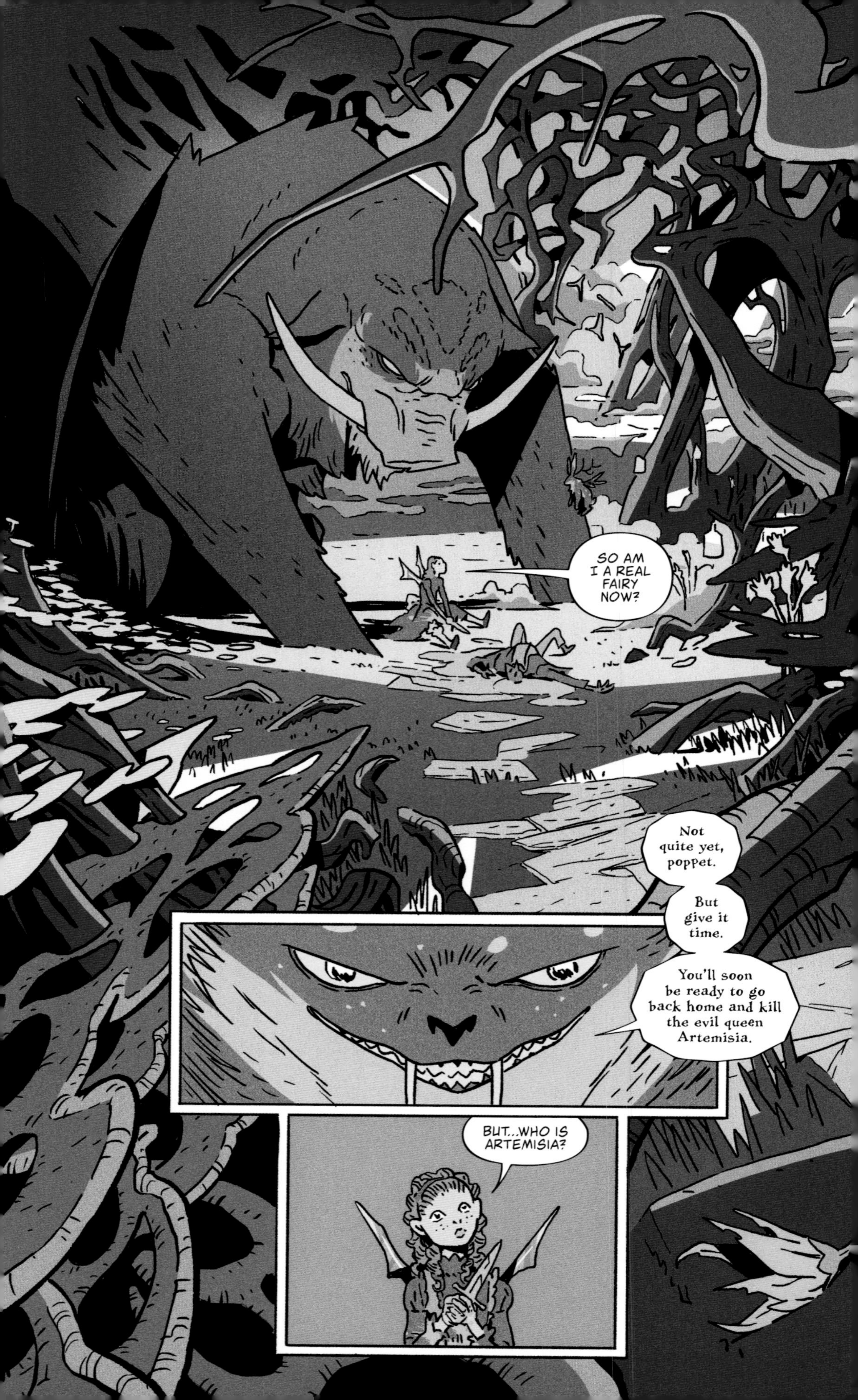
SO AM I A REAL FAIRY NOW?
Not quite yet, poppet.
But give it time.
You'll soon be ready to go back home and kill the evil queen Artemisia.
BUT...WHO IS ARTEMISIA?

SPARROWHAWK #5 COVER BY
MIGUEL MERCADO

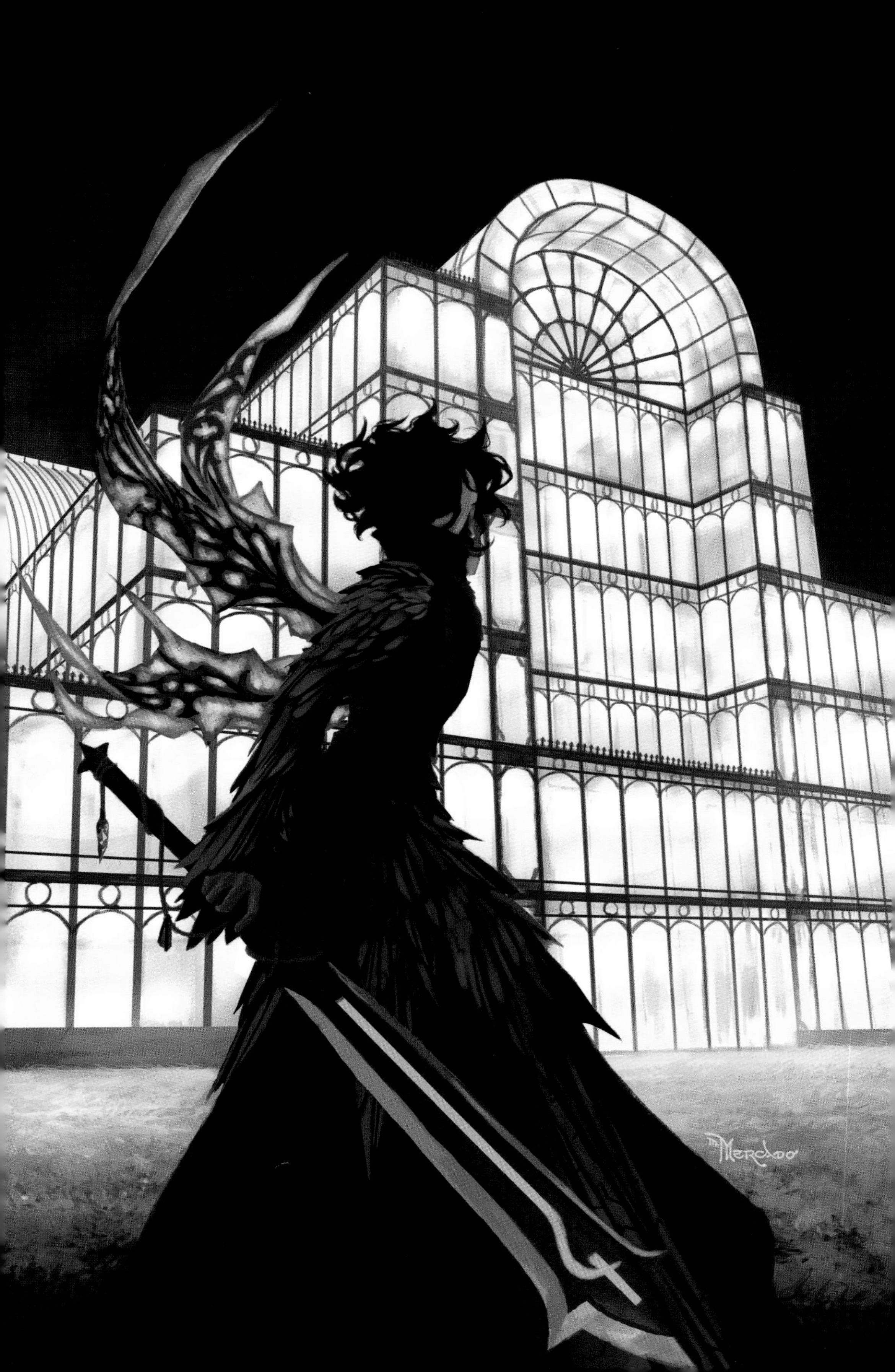
M. Mercado

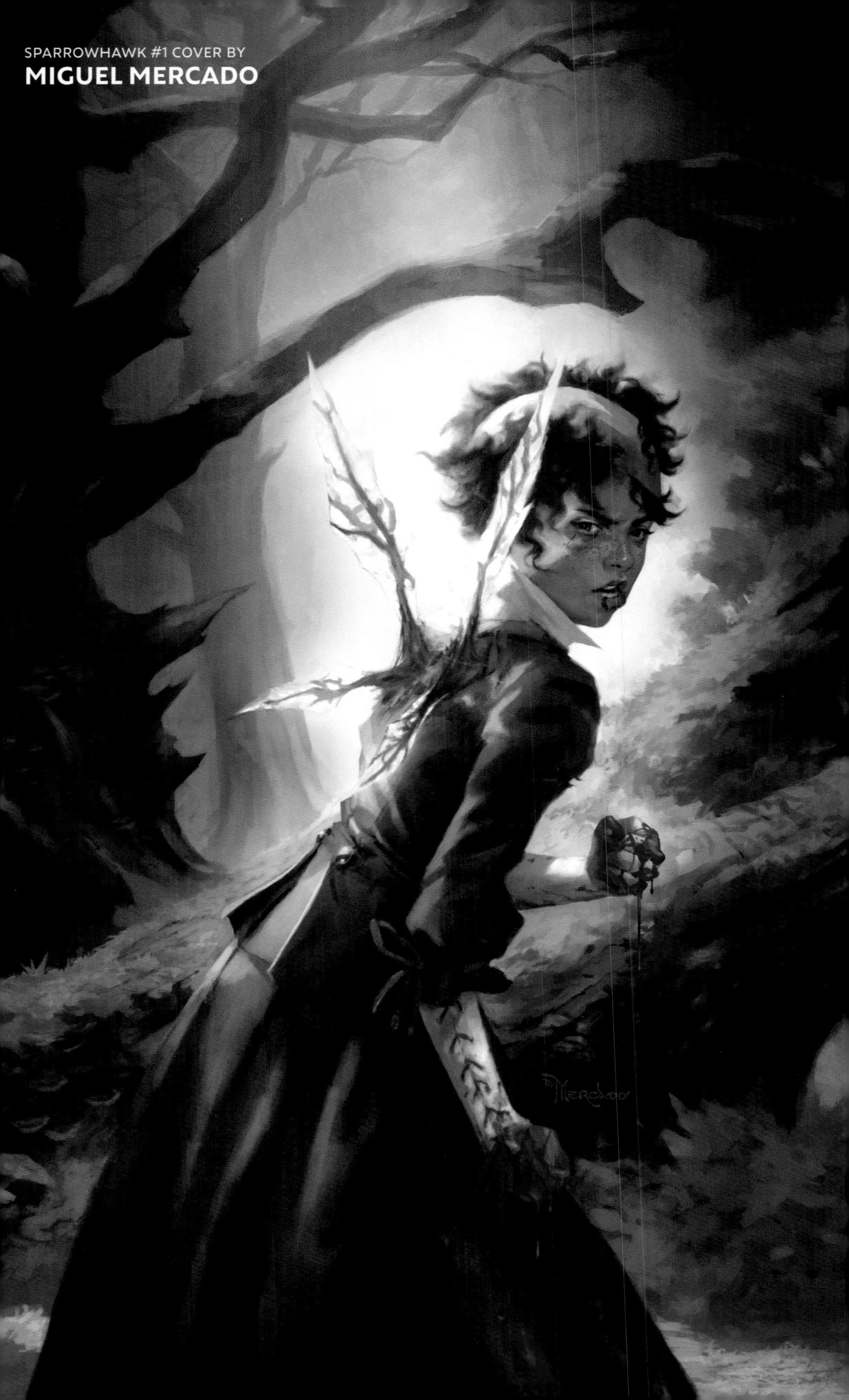

SPARROWHAWK #1 COVER BY
MIGUEL MERCADO

AFTERWORD

BY **DELILAH S. DAWSON**

My trip to Faerie began in 1996, when I was eighteen and got my first tattoo, a teal blue Cheshire Cat from *Alice in Wonderland*. I loved his wisdom, his mercurial madness, the way he acted as a guide to the philosophical rather than the physical. I hid that tattoo from my father for five years because he was the sort of man who didn't approve of what I did—or, really, deep down, who I was. He wanted a daughter who was normal and quiet and did what she was told. He got a daughter who was strange and unusual, who balked at his commands and refused to submit, even when he choked her unconscious. To this day, I don't really like doing what I'm told.

Flash forward to 2009. My second child stopped sleeping, and so did I. When the hallucinations became too troubling, I asked my husband what could be done about the rats talking in the walls? He gave me two action items. First, get some sleep—which he helped with. Second, find a hobby or creative outlet to occupy my hungry mind. He suggested writing a book. And because my brain was broken and I felt unusually fearless, I did it.

By 2010, I had a literary agent. By 2011, I had a book deal—and a mind that was greedy for stories. I saw a photoset on Tumblr of gowns from Alexander McQueen's *Savage Beauty* show, and I was struck by how he'd turned fashion into fantasy. The combination of natural shapes and textures with supernatural opulence struck a chord and reminded me of worlds I'd always loved: *Labyrinth*, *Legend*, *The Neverending Story*, *The Last Unicorn*, and, always, *Alice in Wonderland*. I bought the coffee table book and stroked the pages, marveling at how each design told a story. With that collection, McQueen gave fairyland the sharp teeth it deserved.

That's when I came up with the idea for *Sparrowhawk*: fairies in McQueen gowns fighting to the death.

At the time, I thought it was a YA book, but 16,000 words in, the story lost its magic, and I put it away. That happens with stories, sometimes: like seeds, they need a little more time to germinate somewhere dark and quiet.

In 2017, my first creator-owned comic came out with BOOM! Studios—*Ladycastle*. I was learning how to tell stories in a new medium where visuals were an integral part of the process. And when my editor asked if I had any ideas for my next comic, everything clicked.

What *Sparrowhawk* had been missing all along was artwork.

The story had come from images... and it could not be told without them.

When I considered the right heroine to leave an ocean of fairy blood in her wake, I thought back to who I was when I had that turquoise Cheshire Cat inked on my hip: a strange and unusual misfit, misunderstood by her family, who longs for something more and is willing to fight for it. And then, as if right on cue, I saw an arresting painting on Twitter of the historical figure Dido Elizabeth Belle, the daughter of a British naval officer and an enslaved African woman in the British West Indies in the late 1700s. She became the inspiration for Artemisia Grey, and putting a sword in her hands and a snarl on her face felt like justice.

Sparrowhawk is a love story to strangeness, to ferocity, to the lessons learned following an unreliable guide down a dark path, to growing beyond where you were planted. It's *Wonderland* and McQueen and Dark Lily dancing by herself. It's a collection of my favorite bits of Jane Austen books aggressively spackled with black glitter. You can fall in love with a Wolpertinger who can't lie and yet always does, or you can long for the fairy prince who looks like Tom Holland in a vampire's cape and adores you with a deliciously nontoxic masculinity.

Sparrowhawk is for those who see thestrals. For those who wish to play croquet with pixies and ride giant pigs through herds of ghost deer. For those who forever wear secret bruises that faded long ago.

I hope you'll step through the mirror and join me here.

DISCOVER
VISIONARY CREATORS

THE WOODS
JAMES TYNION IV • MICHAEL DIALYNAS
VOL. 1
THE ARROW

"The Spire is fantastic! My kind of genre free-for-all."
—BRIAN K. VAUGHAN (Saga)
THE SPIRE
SIMON SPURRIER
JEFF STOKELY
ANDRÉ MAY

MARK WAID • PETER KRAUSE
IRREDEEMABLE
AFTERWORD BY GRANT MORRISON

MARK WAID • JEAN DIAZ
INCORRUPTIBLE

MICHAEL ALAN NELSON
DAN MORA
GABRIEL CASSATA
HEXED
THE HARLOT & THE THIEF VOLUME ONE

ABNETT & CULBARD
WILD'S END
FIRST LIGHT
"IT'S REALLY GREAT!" JEFF LEMIRE

James Tynion IV

The Woods

Volume 1
ISBN: 978-1-60886-454-6 | $9.99 US
Volume 2
ISBN: 978-1-60886-495-9 | $14.99 US
Volume 3
ISBN: 978-1-60886-773-8 | $14.99 US

The Backstagers

Volume 1
ISBN: 978-1-60886-993-0 | $14.99 US

Simon Spurrier

Six-Gun Gorilla

ISBN: 978-1-60886-390-7 | $19.99 US

The Spire

ISBN: 978-1-60886-913-8 | $29.99 US

Weavers

ISBN: 978-1-60886-963-3 | $19.99 US

Mark Waid

Irredeemable

Volume 1
ISBN: 978-1-93450-690-5 | $16.99 US
Volume 2
ISBN: 978-1-60886-000-5 | $16.99 US

Incorruptible

Volume 1
ISBN: 978-1-60886-015-9 | $16.99 US
Volume 2
ISBN: 978-1-60886-028-9 | $16.99 US

Michael Alan Nelson

Hexed The Harlot & The Thief

Volume 1
ISBN: 978-1-60886-718-9 | $14.99 US
Volume 2
ISBN: 978-1-60886-816-2 | $14.99 US

Day Men

Volume 1
ISBN: 978-1-60886-393-8 | $9.99 US
Volume 2
ISBN: 978-1-60886-852-0 | $9.99 US

Dan Abnett

Wild's End

Volume 1: First Light
ISBN: 978-1-60886-735-6 | $19.99 US
Volume 2: The Enemy Within
ISBN: 978-1-60886-877-3 | $19.99 US

Hypernaturals

Volume 1
ISBN: 978-1-60886-298-6 | $16.99 US
Volume 2
ISBN: 978-1-60886-319-8 | $19.99 US

BOOM! STUDIOS

AVAILABLE AT YOUR LOCAL COMICS SHOP AND BOOKSTORE

To find a comics shop in your area, visit www.comicshoplocator.com

WWW.**BOOM-STUDIOS**.COM

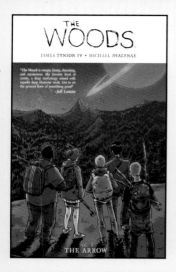

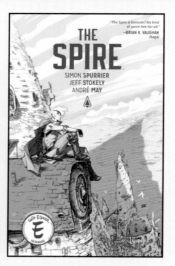

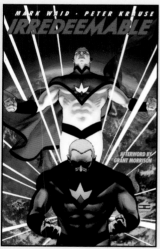

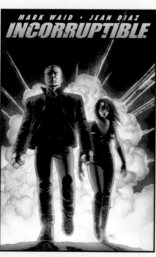

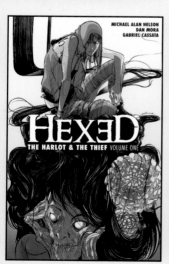

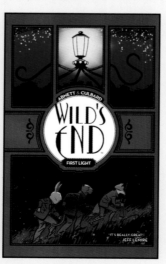

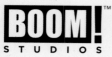